Robert Frost and the Politics of Poetry

ROBERT FROST

and the

POLITICS OF POETRY

Tyler Hoffman

MIDDLEBURY COLLEGE PRESS

Published by University Press of New England

Hanover and London

Middlebury College Press

Published by University Press of New England, Hanover, NH 03755

Text © 2001 by Tyler Hoffman

Foreword © 2001 by University Press of New England

5 4 3 2 1

Library of Congress Cataloging-in-Publication Data

Hoffman, Tyler.
   Robert Frost and the politics of poetry / Tyler Hoffman.
       p.   cm.
Includes bibliographical references (p.) and index.
   ISBN 1–58465–149–0 (cloth : alk. paper) — ISBN 1–58465–150–4
(pbk : alk. paper)
   1. Frost, Robert, 1874–1963—Political and social views. 2. Politics
and literature—United States—History—20th century. 3. Political
poetry, American—History and criticism. 4. Politics in literature.
I. Title.
PS3511.R94 Z7444 2001
811'.52—dc21   2001004170

For Lynn

Contents

Foreword

Jay Parini

Although Robert Frost is obviously one of the great American poets—
many would place him at or near the top of the heap—his work has been
oddly neglected by younger scholars in recent years. His popularity with a
mass audience and his apparent simplicity have certainly worked against
him in this regard. It is as if there can be no point in discussing a poet about
whom nothing much can be said, whose work seems to push away the kind
of scrutiny that has commonly been afforded other modern writers. Of
course, Frost himself encouraged this attitude. He consistently maintained
that his poems did not need critical exegesis, and that they meant what they
said and no more. During one public reading, he observed, "In a marriage,
it's important to know when not to take a hint. It's the same in poetry. You
don't take a hint where none was intended."

Tyler Hoffman, in this groundbreaking study, *Robert Frost and the Politics
of Poetry,* certainly knows how to take a hint. He goes to those places where
Frost seems to ward off readers, although one suspects that he enjoyed
being "found out" by the "right people," as he once suggested. Looking at
the poetry in detail, Hoffman concludes that Frost was, indeed, more sophisticated in his politics—a term he defines broadly—than many readers,
even some of the best of them (such as Richard Poirier and Reginald Cook),
have suspected. He notes how the poet worked to balance competing political interests "in the figures of his poetry and his theory of poetic form."

The story of how Frost managed to persuade many of his closest readers, such as Louis Untermeyer, that his work was apolitical is, in itself, a

fascinating story. Perhaps the most political book Frost ever published was *A Further Range,* his response to the Depression and the New Deal. In those fierce poems, he took a highly complicated political stance that defies easy categorization; nevertheless, the poems openly as well as covertly address the leading political questions of the day. In particular, Frost was weighing in on the relationship between the individual and the state: issues that were played out on the broad international scene and hotly debated by intellectuals. Still, Untermeyer flatly maintained in a review of the book that there was little politics in most of this poetry.

It is true that Frost in his poems deals mostly with "griefs" and not "grievances," as he nicely put it. But the griefs were real, and they were often political, or had a dimension that might be called political. What Hoffman argues is that Frost was, in his poetry and person, essentially progressivist in intent, and he demonstrates this in an able fashion by looking closely at the poems themselves as well as other sources, such as Frost's neglected notebooks. In 1935, for example, Frost wrote in his journal: "I heard a false progressive say that self-discipline was the only discipline, and I was tempted to say that he who has had only self-discipline knows no discipline at all." As Hoffman shows, Frost was able to take the notion of discipline into unexpected territory, connecting it to poetic form, to the disciplines enforced by rhyme and meter and other arbitrary means of shaping material in a way to enhance its value and impact. Frost believed in the affirming limits of the genre, considering free verse a kind of scandal.

Biographers and critics including Lawrance Thompson, Randall Jarrell, Richard Poirier, John Evangelist Walsh, and William H. Pritchard have spent time thinking about the impact of Frost's English experience (1912–15) on his development as a thinker and poet, but nobody until now has looked as closely at the specific politics of those poets who surrounded Frost and supported him in those crucial and formative years. Hoffman examines this aspect of Frost's education, and he ties the politics of the Georgian poets and other factions popular in England at the time to Frost's reading of William James and Henri Bergson and, finally, to Frost's contemplation of the imagist school of poetry. He uncovers, in the poet, a "complexly coded articulation of political and cultural identity in the modern world," thus enabling us to read Frost into the contemporary matrix of ideology and poetic politics in fresh and productive ways. Not surprisingly, Frost emerges as an infinitely more subtle and nuanced poet than one had previously supposed.

In his second and third chapters, Hoffman gets down to the nitty-gritty of exegesis, examining the poetry itself, stressing that Frost's emphasis on a kind of tonal ambiguity had a political dimension. I found many of his readings astonishingly fine, as when he looks at "Birches." One would have thought everything that could be said about this poem has been said, and long ago. Not so, it turns out. By concentrating on specific poetic techniques, from enjambment to the density of certain effects such as alliteration and assonance, he is able to show exactly how the poem "amounts to a redefinition of lyric in the modernist period," thus challenging easy romantic or post-romantic assumptions and calling attention to aesthetic issues that, ultimately, become political issues.

Aesthetic and political concerns have been seen, throughout the last twenty or thirty years, as opposing forces. What I like about Hoffman's book is the way he connects the two. He teases out the genuine political implications of certain artistic choices, never shying away from giving us the details as he discovers them. He will typically seize upon certain familiar literary devices or prosodic features, such as anaphora, and suggest that in allegorizing them Frost forges a relationship between the device or feature and various cultural forms and social performances. The implications of enjambment, for example, are explored in remarkable particularity in the third chapter, "The Politics of the Visual Line." There, Hoffman redefines the term "politics," as he must, and vividly argues that Frost's line enjambments constitute aesthetic choices made with a clear view to their large social resonances.

In the final chapter, he addresses a seeming dichotomy that obsessed Frost: poetry and power. He circles back to some of the lyrics discussed in the opening chapter, and he brings further pressure to bear on these readings, attending closely to the figures of the politics of form. He has previously examined the relationship between Frost's notion of "the sound of sense"—a woefully misunderstood concept—and his actual practice as a poet; not surprisingly, he suggests that major patterns in the work are not addressed or accounted for by Frost's homemade theory. In the final chapter, Hoffman reconsiders "the sound of sense" in relation to metrics, exploring the figurative force of both and suggesting the ways in which Frost's poetic practice worked to imbue aesthetic ideology with a political dimension. In effect, Hoffman attempts to account for Frost's emergence as our national poet, a poet who became widely accepted as the symbol of the national voice in poetry.

These connections are hardly arbitrary. In an address to the students of Sarah Lawrence College in 1956, Frost famously argued for what he called "measure." He said, "Measure always reassures me. Measure in love, in government, measure in selfishness, measure in unselfishness." One could hardly imagine a more moderate or "liberal" view of life. Measure becomes, for Frost, a point of civics. Since poetry was "a momentary stay against confusion," it was important for the sane poet to clear away the chaos, to take its measure, and to measure out (in the calibrations of a line of verse) the clarity of mind that one posted against the chaos of the unspoken, the wild. This rage for order becomes an act of defiance, and it is also a distinctly modernist trope.

Frost's defense of an agrarian life, of agrarian values, links nicely to his developing political stance, as Hoffman shows. Frost found unconstrained capitalism a major threat to the small farmer, and in "Build Soil"—his most explicit articulation of his political views—he articulates this point of view. He pushes toward what Hoffman calls "a dialectical progressive poetics," urging that certain boundaries—such as farm and city—remain in place. Country explains and defines city. It is part of a necessary dialectic. As ever, Frost wants a healthy balance of opposites, a measured approach. The contest, in Hoffman's exquisite reading of the poetry itself, is defined in terms that are at once aesthetic and political, with the poet treading carefully between the extremes of authority and liberty as between meter and rhythm. Which brings us back to the sound of sense, where the vernacular voice is seen to break against the formal contraints of the meter to create a living verse.

Hoffman's intense, nuanced, and sophisticated reading of the poetry itself goes a long way toward reestablishing Frost in his political time as a man and poet concerned with the issues of the day, such as the complex relationship between the individual and the state. These terms are translated, by him and others, into the politics of poetry itself. Hoffman understands these politics, and he makes them visible in ways that have not been previously accomplished.

Acknowledgments

Many people deserve thanks for helping me bring this book to form. First among them is Steve Cushman, whose guidance and support have been crucial from the start. Dell Hymes also provided invaluable assistance in clarifying for me the performative and linguistic aspects of Frost's poetry. Special thanks go as well to John Burt, Karen Kilcup, Michael Manson, Don Mull, Bill Pritchard, Mark Richardson, and Carol Singley for their insights and suggestions. I am particularly indebted to Jim Cox and Bill Cook at Dartmouth College for their early encouragement of my interest in American literature and Frost, and to Jay Parini for his generosity at an important stage later in the game.

Frost's writings are quoted by permission of Henry Holt and Co. and the Estate of Robert Frost. I am grateful both to Mimi Ross at Holt and to Peter Gilbert, the Executor of the Estate of Robert Frost, for their expedition and good will. I acknowledge with gratitude the Rutgers University Research Council Grant that helped with funding.

Parts of chapters have appeared in altered form in journals, among them *The Journal of Imagism, Modern Language Studies,* and *The Robert Frost Review.* My thanks to the editors for permission to reprint that material here. I also thank Phil Pochoda and the editorial staff at University Press of New England, who have been attentive every step of the way.

Finally, I would like to thank my family on both coasts for their rallying cries, and especially Lynn, Noah, and Sam, for their love and patience.

Robert Frost and the Politics of Poetry

Introduction

In 1919, Frost wrote a letter to his daughter Lesley, who had entered and lost a poetry contest, urging her to beware of caring about the reception of one's work: "Setting our heart when we're too young on getting our poems appreciated lands us in the politics of poetry which is death."[1] My use of the phrase "the politics of poetry" is meant to highlight not just Frost's deep involvement in literary politics—notwithstanding his advice to Lesley to forsake it—but also the liberal and nationalist ideologies and cultural politics that shape and are shaped by his poetic formalism. This book conducts a study of Frost's theory of poetic form and formal practice in full historical context. Practicing what James Breslin calls "an historically informed formalist criticism," I show how poetic form relates to other cultural forms and social performances and, specifically, how Frost politicizes form in light of British and U.S. domestic and foreign policy in his lifetime. I also reveal the ways in which Frost's prosodic theory has been read (and refigured) by postcolonial and transnational poets at the end of the twentieth century.

Although Frost's theory of form has been deemed an accurate description of his poetry, many of his most troubling statements about his method have been ignored in reaching this critical consensus. When we look at what Frost says about how his poetry works and compare it to how his poetry actually works, we find that some of his most hyperbolically charged statements do not do justice to his prosodic practice. In his 1917 essay "Reflections on *Vers Libre*" T. S. Eliot cautioned that an artist and his school "may become circumscribed by their theory and narrowed by their polemic."[2] In certain respects, this statement applies to Frost, despite the popular conception of him as a poet who resisted the trammels of theory and refused to align himself with any coteries. In fact, Frost spent a great deal of time speaking out on the formal organization of his poetry and responded in canny ways to modernist poetic rhetoric in order to capture a share of the literary marketplace for himself. At times, particularly early in his career, he courted and tweaked regnant critical positions, following with care the emergent formalism of the early modernist period. As time passed, and after his repatriation in the U.S., Frost gradually distanced himself from these same modernists, bristling at the notion of the obscure poetic text and using his theory of form as a weapon in that battle of distinction. As Vernon Shetley has shown, this hostility to modernist difficulty is not unique to Frost; other sophisticated readers of poetry saw that such difficulty spelt the demise of the "common reader"—a condition, Shetley argues, from which we have not recovered: "The last time they [general readers] were sighted in large numbers was in the 1960s, refreshing themselves in the New England landscapes of Robert Frost."[3] Although the recent rap-meets-poetry scene has done much to reenfranchise the common reader, or, more accurately, the common listener, Shetley's point is well taken, and his location of Frost as America's last widely popular poet makes it all the more important to determine the basis of that success and its bearing on his poetry and critical prose.

Although we do not run into difficult allusive texts in the manner of Pound and Eliot in Frost's work, many of his poems are not as accessible or transparent as some readers might expect in light of his popular reputation—one summed up by John F. Kennedy in these eulogistic remarks: "His [Frost's] death impoverishes us all; but he has bequeathed his nation a body of imperishable verse from which Americans will forever gain joy and understanding."[4] The "understanding" of which Kennedy speaks in fact comes at a price; it is not an easy acquisition—no "gift of idle hours"—but rather a descent into meaning without a clear bottom in many of Frost's best known (and often misunderstood or only partially understood) poems.[5] Richard Poirier's notion of Frost's "density"—a term that distinguishes him and writers like him from the difficult poetry of the high modernists—gets at this rich compounding of meaning: "By 'density' I mean to describe a kind of writing which gives, so it likes to pretend, a fairly direct access to pleasure, but which becomes, on longer acquaintance, rather strange and imponderable."[6] To be sure, Frost's poems seem on the surface fairly accessible by virtue of their colloquial sounds, and the appearance of his poetry in such mainstream magazines as *Harper's, New Republic,* and *Scribner's* attests to his success in attracting a popular audience. It was a success he actively courted. In a 1913 letter, Frost made clear his ultimate intention of getting out beyond the poetry circle in his hunt for money and fame:

[T]here is a kind of success called "of esteem" and it butters no parsnips. It means a success with the critical few who are supposed to know. But really to arrive where I can stand on my legs as a poet and nothing else I must get outside that circle to the general reader who buys books in their thousands. . . . I want to be a poet for all sorts and kinds. I could never make a merit of being caviare to the crowd the way my quasi-friend Pound does. I want to reach out, and would if it were a thing I could do by taking thought.[7]

Frost's deliberate pitch to the "general reader," though, should not confuse us as to the sophistication of his poetry and poetics, his early efforts to win over "the critical few who are supposed to know."

Of course, it is this very accessibility that has made Frost an anomalous modernist, leading many critics to exclude him from that camp. Randall Jarrell was perhaps the first to reimagine Frost in a way consistent with modernist tenets, seeing him as a figure far more "hard" and "gloomy" than the "sensible, tender, humorous poet" that the public cherished.[8] In *Modernist Quartet* (1994) Frank Lentricchia also validates Frost as a modernist poet, but his statement in his preface defending Frost's appearance as part of the quartet ("I understand how odd it must appear to include Robert Frost in modernist company") indicates the continuing critical misconception of Frost's involvement in that scene. Lentricchia follows up this statement by claiming that "One of the reasons for the oddity is that we have forgotten the heterogeneous character of modernist literature"; as I argue, though, it is not only, or even mainly, our neglect of the diversity within modernism that compels our exclusion of Frost, but rather our failure to read accurately the evolving "politics of poetry" and Frost's relationship to them—a relationship most believe he never had.[9] By examining Frost's often denied, overlooked, or at least minimized debt to modernist theory and practice, my book proposes new ways of reading Frost's writing and urges us to reconsider the categories we use to describe Anglo-American poetic modernism.

As for Frost's theory of form, Lentricchia seriously misjudges the degree to which it functions as a polemical tool in the poetry and culture wars. As he finds, if Frost shared with Pound "a target of cultural critique, then against Frost's democratic antipoetics of vernacular voice, which worked toward a novelized lyric of character in the American tradition of local-color realism, Pound worked toward the formal voice of traditional literary culture—a voice he called 'curial' with no American shame, at a time when James Whitcomb Riley may have been the most popular poet in America."[10] Lentricchia's discrimination here, which seeks to explain the different audiences to which Frost and Pound appealed in the course of their careers, does not explain the striking rhetorical coincidences in statements of their poetic practice. To say that Frost's is an "antipoetics" as a result of his emphasis on intonation in writing ignores the same emphasis in Pound and other prominent modernist writers on both sides of the Atlantic, and in effect sets him at odds with the theoretical crowd by virtue of a supposed plain dealing. In fact, Frost was not trying to escape the hyperbole and technicalities of the modernist poetic manifesto, but doing his best to keep pace with that fashionable, political mode.

Although Richard Poirier alleges that Frost's confidence in the ability of poetic form to assert order in a chaotic world and his skepticism about the "institutional power" of literature ("central to what is familiarly called modernism") necessarily set him at the edge of that movement, we cannot assert his distance from Eliot and Pound based either on his notion of formal discipline or on his conscription of aesthetic doctrine into his conservative politics beginning in mid-career.[11] Moreover, his formalist theory is no more reliable a guide to the performance of his poetry than is theirs; as Maud Ellman has shown, Eliot's and Pound's actual poetic practice diverges from their theory of poetic "impersonality" in fundamental ways.[12] While most of Frost's critics (including his most astute) have taken at face value his remarks about "the sound of sense," I seek to point out the limits of Frost's rhetoric, approaching with caution his more extravagant claims and doing so with a full comprehension of the cultures that engender them as has not been done before.

That Frost was deeply concerned about his poetic reputation (as Eliot and Pound were) has been established by several recent critics, including Lentricchia, but none explicitly links that concern to Frost's careful negotiation of literary and what Frost calls "internal" (domestic) and "external" (foreign) politics through his theory of form.[13] However, to a greater or lesser extent, these critics have begun the project of framing Frost's formalism in terms of one or more of the cultures in which it is embedded, and my study builds on (and in some cases revises) that work by providing a richer understanding of the ways in which that formalism overlaps with his social attitudes and ideological stances over the course of his career. In *The Ordeal of Robert Frost* (1997) Mark Richardson rightly encourages us to read Frost's poetics—articulated in letters, essays, and poems—as a kind of cultural criticism, and investigates Frost's poetics of conformity, that is, his view that poetic form acts as "a kind of conservation, a check against radical personal and social 'difference.'"[14] However, Richardson does not trace the evolution of his theory of form as I do, nor does he speak about intonation and its political meanings within the dialectic of Frost's poetics. On the other hand, in *Robert Frost and a Poetics of Appetite* (1994) Katherine Kearns spends a good deal of time representing Frost's notion of "the sound of sense," which she reads as a "virile" construct that works to distance Frost from his readers and from a feminized lyric voice, "with its ambivalent impulses toward confession and aggrandizement and toward guilt and rapture."[15] As I will show, though, it is not that Frost codes intonation masculine, but rather that the ability to handle speech rhythms in metrical poetry is, as he describes it, a virtue of the manly poet. For Frost, those rhythms do not symbolize "rational control," as Kearns alleges, but a liberal and liberatory politics.[16] Karen Kilcup's *Robert Frost and Feminine Literary Tradition* (1998) briefly weighs Frost's poetics, showing that "In tandem with his reliance on formal written traditions, Frost's insistence on spoken language and the vernacular redefines, wittingly or unwittingly, a binary that resonates throughout American poetry and American literature more generally: the relationship between the oral and written, their gender affiliations, and their investment in matters of popularity and canonicity."[17] As Kilcup argues, Frost's eventual distancing of himself from oral-feminine (and, thus, culturally disempowering) rhetorical and generic traditions marks his masculinity, and, as I argue, so, too, does his deepening focus on the container of metrical form. Robert Faggen in *Robert Frost and the Challenge of Darwin* (1997) remarks on this same binary as it is embodied in Frost's poetics ("Frost insists on strict meters to tame and limit the flow of speech"), and is led to downplay the influence of Henri Bergson's vitalistic philosophy on it by virtue of that insistence on meter.[18] In fact, though, Bergson is as much responsible for Frost's early formulation of tone as is Charles Darwin, and my study adds to Faggen's scientific findings and politicizes them in turn.

By reimagining the binary between form and flux in terms of Frost's evolving politics, I seek to complicate our notion of those politics and, at the same time, clarify the lines of Frost's thinking about form in poetry. Indeed, the ideological portrait of Frost that emerges from my book is radically different from the one most people know: not only do I expose his intense nationalism, a designation that has been eclipsed by Frost's reputation as a regional poet; I also illustrate the early alignment of his aesthetic with a socially concerned politics and, following his death, with an anti-imperialist global politics.[19] As I argue, Frost's shifting ideological commitments flare up in his various conceptions of the formal elements of poetry, which assume political meanings in a wide range of poems, including those whose political content often goes unregistered and others often overlooked by critics in part because of their overtly political cast and a supposed simple-minded conservatism, despite the fact that, in many of his poems from early until late in his career, Frost's declared political sympathies are quite complicated and cagey. By recognizing the importance of technique to the semantic order of poetry and the relation of poetic form to other cultural forms, my discussion moves Frost's formalism out of conservative (that is, strictly formalist literary critical) circles, and sees it for what it actually is—not a valorous resistance to flabby free verse, but a complexly coded articulation of political and cultural identity in the modern world.

In the chapters that follow I map the evolution of Frost's formalism from the social and intellectual ferment of early modernism through its intersection with an Americanism that intensifies in reaction to two world wars and an incipient cold war and, finally, to its vital postcolonial legacy. Chapter 1 establishes the close connections between Frost and the London literary avant-garde during his residency in England (1912–1915). Frost's canny cultivation of modernist artists in a position to review his work allowed him to set the terms of his own critical reception, to appear *au courant* in a milieu crowded with such claims. As important as this phase of Frost's career was, little has been done with what we now know about his life and experiences in England, with most critics sidetracked by the rather overblown story of his tangled relationship with Ezra Pound, one of his early champions. Aside from that story, Frost usually is consigned by critics to the countryside around London, where he did reside for a year, but only after full immersion in the London cultural scene; even so, critics rarely mention the political affiliations of those rural Georgian poets and the effect that those affiliations had on their response to (and instruction of) Frost's prosodic theory. As I will show, Frost's poetics takes the measure not only of the liberal thought of the Georgians and the playwright George Bernard Shaw, but also of Bloomsbury formalist aesthetic doctrine as devised by such figures as Clive Bell and Roger Fry, and, like it, reacts to fiery debates about Irish Home Rule, suffrage, and the rights of the working class in London during these years. His theory of "the sound of sense," at its inception part of a broader leftist worldview, draws attention to the individual and cuts across class lines in its recovery of the commonness of speech. Frost's formalism, then, is not immune to extra-aesthetic experience, and his revision of Fry's aesthetic anticipates Virginia Woolf's own insistence on both abstraction and representation in works of art.

In addition to these influences, the psychological and philosophical theories of William James and Henri Bergson, which were all the rage in modernist London, left a strong impression on Frost's formal theory. James's and Bergson's discussions of "the stream of consciousness"—that is, our experience of reality prior to our analytic discrimination of it—and the auditory imagination inform Frost's privileging of the ear over the eye in his aesthetic as well as his connection of speech rhythm to the human spirit. Frost's principle of "the sound of sense" responds to various discussions in James's *The Principles of Psychology,* a connection noted only partially by Richard Poirier, and incorporates James's later pragmatist and political concerns, particularly his advocacy of personal and political sovereignty. Moreover, Frost's familiarity with Bergson's *Time and Free Will, Creative Evolution,* and related speeches shapes his concept of tone of voice in writing, as do the evolutionary theories of Charles Darwin and Herbert Spencer, the latter of whom explicitly addresses the relation between those theories and literary style. Despite the importance of these cultural discourses, which Frost dwells on in his London notebooks (never discussed at length before), they have not drawn the attention that one might expect from Frost critics.

Frost's aesthetic theory is also indebted to the movement of imagism and the various modernisms of T. E. Hulme, which wielded tremendous cultural power in London during Frost's dealings there. Although critics have argued that Frost's aesthetic stands in contrast to ascendant imagist ideology, that he develops his theory "to resist" imagist doctrine, producing in self-defense a counter-theory, such a distinction obscures strong similarities between imagist ideology and the ideology of "the sound of sense"—similarities that leading imagist poets recognized in their reviews of Frost's books. In addition to tracing Pound's intellectual development as it influences Frost's unfolding of his theory, I focus on the importance of Ford Madox Ford's impressionism and the vicissitudes of early modernist doctrine as registered by Hulme, with whom Frost spoke at length about his theory just days before issuing the phrase "the sound of sense." Hulme's transit from Bergsonism through classicism to abstractionism imprints Frost's formalism—and its politics—in unmistakable ways. As I find, the phrases that meant so much to Frost and that have become the catch phrases of Frost criticism are not mere casual coinages; rather, they represent Frost's intense thought and sustained investigations, the extremely hard work that went into the making of the poet's distinctive voice.

For all its intellectual force, however, Frost's theory is not a wholly reliable description of his prosodic practice. In Chapter 2, I interrogate his contention that the only meaningful sound in poetry is speech rhythm and his concomitant denigration of the prosody of assonance and alliteration, demonstrating his careful attention to segmental sound effects in some of his most accomplished poems. Indeed, these sonic devices often attain figurative force as well, standing as a trope for poetry as culturally defined and defining—that is, for "the politics of poetry." Furthermore, some of Frost's most effective rhetorical schemes, including anaphora and chiasmus, depend at least as much upon visual apprehension as upon aural, despite his theoretical pronouncements to the contrary, and take on distinctive political faces. Finally, Frost's assertion that his poetry conveys tones of voice without the aid of graphetic cues does not make sense in light of his poetry. His professed disregard of punctuation is quite contradicted by his scrupulous practice, and his frequent use of italics, which he disparages, belies his claim that his intonation contours on the page speak for themselves.

Frost's contention that tone of voice is unambiguously embodied on the printed page also flies in the face of the prosodic performance of his poetry, where tonal indeterminacy often compounds meaning in crucial, and sometimes politically potent, ways. Insisting on the author-centered phonocentric text, Frost denies what Derrida and Foucault have shown to be the inability of authorial intention to govern the entire scene and system of writing. Derrida describes the tendency to reduce speech to a function of writing as a will to preserve the ideal of unmediated expression; Frost's emphasis on verse for the ear as opposed to the eye reduces the material identity of the text to the status of a transparent medium for the "voice" of the poet. His poetry, though, bears out the claims of poststructuralist theory. In lyrics that pivot on moments of epistemological and eschatological crisis and others that raise political points, ambiguous intonation contours encourage multiple interpretations, destabilizing Frost's authority and staking out his own ambivalence. On the silent page, we are offered opportunities not available through the spoken word; we are able to try out a range of tones that would satisfy the conditions established by a text, to turn lines in different expressive directions, without ruling out all but one. Although Frost hints that he is led to his extreme position that tone of voice on the printed page is unambiguous as a result of his growing desire to distance himself from modernist disjunctive poetics—what he regards as modernist poets' fruitless efforts to obscure meaning—the oral emphasis of his poetics is perfectly consistent with the privileging of the oral over the visual in modernist aesthetics, that is, with the promotion of the voice of the poet over the poem on the page.

In his theory of "the sound of sense" Frost also places exclusive emphasis on the unit of the sentence, which conveys tone of voice. The third chapter considers Frost's polemical disregard of the line in interaction with the sentence—the technique of line-sentence counterpointing—against the use of that procedure throughout his career. Frost's rare remarks about the technique suggest his association of it with free verse poets, against whom he begins to define himself with growing impatience after his return to America in 1915. He disparages their formal practice, particularly their breaking of lines without meter to guide them, and in doing so revives a politics of enjambment dating from the eighteenth century, at which time that prosody was linked to an ideology of license and misrule by conservative cultural critics. As a result of this identification, he is led to say almost nothing about it as it operates in his own poetry. Only when he expresses an interest in different arrangements of "sentences" in "stanzas" does he come close to suggesting its operation in his own work, but such arrangements do not necessarily involve enjambment, as his own examples show. As I argue, despite his reticence, Frost is well aware of the long history of enjambment in metrical poetry and its mimetic and expressive uses, although he evades that history in his discussions of "the sound of sense." Positing the endstopped line as normative in his theoretical discourse, Frost ignores the fact that in his poetry line boundaries often do not coincide with phrase and sentence boundaries, and that these formal events frequently relate to modes of social and political performance.

Frost's poetics of the visual line can be explained in part by Justus Lawler's theory that in metrical verse enjambment figures moments of transcendence, transformation, and (sexual) union, the superfluity of syntax representing the superfluity of psychic and bodily experience. However, that arrangement also is politically symbolic, as Frost speaks through it about contemporary culture. In some poems enjambment tropes a speaker's social disaffiliation, his or her inability or refusal to come into line with bourgeois culture and its constraints; in other poems it more generally highlights the dynamics of social hierarchy in favor of equality. Frost also repeatedly relates that pattern in the 1930s to a socialist ideology that he believes would undermine his cherished principles of self-sufficiency and self-restraint. At times, too, Frost's poems aggressively refuse enjambment, with one-sentence noncaesural lines emblematizing social isolation or political conservatism, the latter of which is seen most markedly in poems written during the Depression and the Cold War. Ironically, though, early in his career we find a pattern of endstopped lines representing the unyielding laws of industrialism that pose a threat to the individual within that system, thus conveying a liberal democratic politics. On the other hand, when syntax breaks but the line does not, Frost occasionally means to symbolize rupture, interruption, and annihilation in the world, most notably in his depictions of current events. In the "Editorials" section of *Steeple Bush* (1947) he figures the culture and politics of the Cold War and his opinion of them through well-placed caesurae that mime nuclear Armageddon. The drama of line-sentence counterpointing, then, shares the stage with the drama of tone of voice, and further testifies to the fact that Frost's verse is for the eye and the ear, despite his professed low opinion of the former: "The eye reader is a barbarian" (*CPPP* 809).

Ultimately, despite its limitations as prosodic description, Frost's theory of form attains crucial figurative significance and grows to express national political meanings as Frost grows to be a popular American poet. In his poetry and prose Frost compares the dialectical relationship between rhythm and meter in a poem to the relationship between freedom and restraint in politics and culture, much as Emerson does. In the modernist period, T. S. Eliot's articulation of the relationship between "tradition" and the "individual talent"—his (and Pound's) notion as of 1917 that poetic composition necessarily involves the discipline of meter—coincides with Frost's view. Frost's contention that modernists are concerned with "formity" (the poem in the act of finding a suitable form) but not "conformity" (convention imposed from without) is not wholly accurate, then, as many of his peers are as concerned with the values of tradition and technique. Harping on the relationship between poetic form and social performance, Frost proclaims himself "an ordinary man," a regular person in habit and temper, as symbolized by his commitment to "regular" (i.e., metrical) writing; conversely, he figures free verse writers as social eccentrics, living an abnormal life of freedom without discipline. Extending his cultural critique, Frost genders his prosody masculine, defining himself against "gushing" female lyric poets of his day, and thereby minting a machismo aesthetic that has long operated as a characteristic of the work of male modernists predicated upon an exclusion of everything associated with the feminine.

In the wake of World War I, Frost's nationalism greatly intensifies, and, in turn, his concept of "the sound of sense" turns increasingly jingoistic; fashioned in self-defense early in his career, Frost's formalism later is brandished to defend his country in the face of what he sees as threats rampant at home and abroad. The seeds of his Americanism are to be found in his early formulations of tone, particularly when he traces the genealogy of "the sound of sense" to "primitive" American Indian utterance. For Frost, and in American culture generally, intonation is increasingly read as a marker of nationality in the postwar years. Frost's friend John Erskine's

1925 *Nation* essay entitled "Do Americans Speak English?" suggests a certain anxiety about national and cultural identity at a time of heightened internationalism, as it questions the extent to which American speech rhythms conform to those of the British. The importance to Frost of Mencken's *The American Language*, which politicizes the element of tone in the preface to the 1936 edition Frost owned, further determines his linguistic chauvinism. His aesthetic reflects his fear of communism and his deepening isolationism between the two world wars and at the start of the Cold War, with the containment of rhythm by meter made to stand in his personal mythology for the healthy checks and balances of democratic government ("chartered freedom") and the balance of ideological forces in the world at large.

I end my final chapter by measuring the influence of Frost's theory of form on three Nobel Laureates—Joseph Brodsky, Seamus Heaney, and Derek Walcott—all of whom are concerned with issues of identity and nationality in their art. Reinscribing Frost's formalism in light of a new cultural politics, these three transnational poets symbolize their own intercultural inheritances through his prosodic terms, thereby revitalizing the insurgent politics of Frosts's theory. Reading closely the three poets' contributions to *Homage to Robert Frost* (1996) in light of postcolonial critical theory, I reveal the sometimes veiled discussions of their own exile and hybridity taking place within them. Showing that Frost's insistence on "the vital sentence" corresponds to the Barthesian "non-sentence," a concept that bears on the politics of postcolonial utterance, I argue that "the sound of sense" becomes for Brodsky, Heaney, and Walcott a space in which to articulate native identities—a space, that is, in which the subaltern speaks—with meter analogized as the dominant cultural tradition. I also explore the contemporary Irish poet Tom Paulin's figurings of Frost's formalist/imperialist poetry, in particular "The Vanishing Red" and "The Gift Outright," in view of Frost's ambivalence about colonialism and the project of decolonization occurring in his lifetime. As indicated by these late twentieth-century soundings, Frost fashions a poetics with sufficient depth and breadth to guide future generations of politically engaged poets.

CHAPTER ONE

The Sound of Sense and the Ethics of Early Modernism

The sound of sense, then. You get that. It is the abstract vitality of our speech. It is pure sound—pure form. One who concerns himself with it more than the subject is an artist.
— FROST TO JOHN BARTLETT, 1913

At least I am sure I can count on you to give me credit for knowing what I am about. You are not going to make the mistake that Pound makes of assuming that my simplicity is that of the untutored child. I am not undesigning.
— FROST TO THOMAS MOSHER, 1913

I

On Independence Day 1913, Frost officially kicked off his campaign on behalf of his prosodic theory, declaring in a letter to a friend: "I alone of English writers have consciously set myself to make music out of what I may call the sound of sense" (*SL* 79). In notebook entries from the same period, Frost explains that by "the sound of sense" he means "speech rhythm," which operates in conjunction with meter: "The poet is himself creative in something that is a resultant of these two."[1] It is in modernist London, not in New England, where he boldly asserts his uniqueness, having transplanted himself and his family there in 1912; in 1915, he returns to America with two books to his credit and the esteem of the literary establishment. His success has much to do not only with the poetry that he wrote, but with the theory of form that he devised to promote it. During these years, Frost speaks and writes often about "the sound of sense" to friends and reports his intention to commit his theory to a more permanent form: "I write it partly for my own benefit, to clarify my ideas for an essay or two I am going to write some fine day (not far distant)" (*SL* 113). The writer Edward Thomas, one of Frost's closest friends while in England, encouraged him to "start doing a book on speech and literature, or you will find me mistaking your ideas for mine & doing it myself" (*IMO* 184). Despite Thomas's exhortations, even his piratical designs, the "fine day" that Frost wrote about never came.

Because Frost never published his theory of poetic form, the biographer John Walsh erroneously claims that "Perhaps the most interesting aspect of this whole theoretical interlude is the fact that ultimately it played no real part at all in Frost's career" (*IMO* 123). In fact, that "theoretical interlude" played an extremely important part in his career, especially as it conditioned his early reception, which, if not handled successfully, would have made a career as a poet highly unlikely. Frost saw the value of explicating his theory to literary figures in London and to friends on the other side of the Atlantic, who would relay his ideas in reviews of his poetry or to those who might write such reviews. While his running discourse about prosody in his correspondence is partly for his own benefit, then, it primarily is meant to provide his "agents" with the terminology necessary to discredit the view of him as a parochial artist ("VURRY Amur'k'n," as Ezra Pound condescendingly put it in a letter to Harriet Monroe), and, thus, to help secure a share of the literary marketplace for himself.[2] This tactic worked to the advantage of other modernist poets, most notably Pound and Eliot, who tutored select critics—including each other—in order to lay a foundation for the proper understanding of their work.[3] In 1913, Frost even refers to Pound's ghostwriting, expressing a mixture of indignation and awe: "He had a finger in the writing of his own review, did he? Damn his eyes! An arrivist from the word go. He has something to show us there. But I'm blessed if I came all the way to London to be coached in art by the likes of him. He can't teach me anything I really care to know."[4] Frost's tortured response to Pound's example suggests his uneasiness at the epicenter of modernism, as he both desires to emulate Pound and is disgusted by the need to do so. Despite his ultimate refutation ("He can't teach me anything I really care to know"), Frost learns much from Pound, not only about the art of poetry but about the art of self-advertising. In the summer of 1913, Frost reveals his comprehension of London literary politics: "This getting reviewed for poetry over here is all sorts of a game" (*SL* 88). It was a game he intended to win.

Upon entering an English artistic scene loud with the polemics of the poetry manifesto, Frost minted one of his own and used it to leverage himself with the people who could get his books read, reviewed, and sold. As modernist doctrine changed, so did Frost's theory of form, and when he no longer needed the assistance of the critical elite to get published, he gradually withdrew and modified his stance. While it is true that his theory of "the sound of sense" begins to develop before his arrival in London, that his interest in the intellectual underpinnings of that theory predate his involvement in that scene, it is also a fact that Frost took his native interest, saw how modernism was developing, and manipulated contacts and his presentation of his theory so that he might succeed. In articulating his poetics he occasionally overstates his case with the intention of making an impression on his correspondent—trying to suggest either his closeness to his modernist peers or his distance from them. In subsequent chapters I will trace the nature and effects of such exaggeration. For now it remains to resituate Frost in the artistic avant-garde of London at the time of his residence there, to measure the unfolding of his formalist theory against the unfolding of modernism and the politics of that period.

One of Frost's first literary contacts in London was Frank Flint, whom he met at the opening of Harold Monro's Poetry Bookshop in Bloomsbury on January 8, 1913. He was also his last intended contact (by virtue of a letter that was never sent) before sailing home to America; on February 13, 1915, the day of his departure, Frost wrote Flint from Liverpool, hailing him as "the man who opened England to me" (SL 152). Looking back, Frost realized that Flint had made possible many of his most significant associations, which, in turn, helped him achieve critical acclaim. Flint was closely connected to the poet and philosopher T. E. Hulme, jointly founding a London literary circle, an offshoot of Hulme's Poets' Club, in 1909. Aware of that alliance, Frost asked Flint to arrange a meeting with Hulme, whom he knew to be a disciple of the French philosopher Henri Bergson, so that he could get "a little honest criticism" of his theory. On July 1, 1913, the three men met. It must have been a momentous occasion for Frost, since he reports to Flint a few days later, "My ideas got just the rub they needed" (IMO 118). We will consider the finer points of that meeting later in the chapter; here it is enough to point out that such a meeting took place and that, in retrospect, Frost minimized its importance. In 1961, when asked about his relationship with Hulme, he fails to mention their private exchange, instead focusing on Hulme's salon from which he says he abstained: "Yes, I knew Hulme, knew him quite well. But I never went to one of those meetings. . . . [T]hey met every week to rewrite each other's poems."5 While it may be the case that Frost requested an independent interview with Flint and Hulme to discuss his concept of "the sound of sense" rather than submit to the format of the salon, he nonetheless made contacts with Hulme and other modernist writers at such coterie gatherings.[6] His obscuring of his involvement in these circles accounts for the silence of many of Frost's critics on the matter.

Ironically, his participation in that salon culture is confirmed by Frost himself in a letter to Gertrude McQuesten (December 1913), to whom he confesses his anxiety about the need to lay claim to an aesthetic under the watchful eyes of the London avant-garde:

I shall have to run into town, as on Tuesday, for a meeting of the younger poets. We'll eat in Soho and then talk about what it is necessary not to know to be a poet. Of course the all important thing to know nothing about is metre. There are two ways out of it for the candidate: either he must never have known or he must have forgotten. Then there is a whole line of great poets he must profess not to have read or not to have read with attention. He must say he knows they are bad without having read them. I should like these fellows in or out of motley. Their worst fault is their devotion to method. They are like so many teachers freshly graduated from a normal school. I should have thought to escape such nonsense in the capital of the world. It is not a question with them of how much native poetry there is in you or how much you get down on paper, but of what method you have declared for. Your method must be their method or they won't accept you as a poet.[7]

In these remarks Frost's tone suggests his distaste for identifying himself as a member of a group, but along the way he reveals a keen insight into modernist literary politics — an insight Frost popularly is thought not to have. Although Frost says in 1961 that "I am not much interested in movements," that "I am not a person of that kind," this allegation does not square with his deliberate attempts to connect with figures in London literary circles, even if he does not align himself fully with any school.[8] Frost signals his understanding of the tendency to band together into "gangs" the previous winter to Flint: "I don't know what theory you may be committed or dedicated to as an affiliated poet of Devonshire St., but for my part give me an out-and-out metaphor" (*RFW* 85). Frost knows, though, that he cannot rely on such a straightforward formulation of his aesthetic, that his interest in metaphor alone will not satisfy the demands of *les jeunes*. He will need to be more abstruse — more technically exacting — in order to prevent being lumped together with W. H. Davies, whom Frost accuses of being an "unsophisticated nature poet of the day — absolutely uncritical untechnical untheoretical" (*SL* 123). Of course, Frost's terms of abuse are precisely those that he feels closing in on him.

When Frost met Flint, he gained access not only to Hulme, but to other prominent literary figures in London active during the early modernist period. Flint, an agent of the imagist movement, was in close contact with Pound, and Flint sent Frost a calling card with Pound's name and address on it. In the spring of 1913, Frost met through Flint and Pound many of England's best-known writers. Frost's cultivation of a relationship with the novelist and philosopher May Sinclair, to whom he was introduced by Pound, exemplifies his shrewdness, since Sinclair was a "maker and connector of modernism," a popular writer who was well known for "practicing and detecting in others' work the new formal and psychological aspects of modernism."9 Her familiarity with the writings of William James and Henri Bergson, both of whom influence Frost's formulation of "the sound of sense," as we will see, made her especially attractive; indeed, in Sinclair's review of Dorothy Richardson's novel *Pilgrimage* in the *Egoist* in April 1918, she introduces into literary criticism the Jamesian phrase "stream of consciousness," which would come to define a generation of experimental prose writing. Frost certainly knew of her interest in contemporary philosophy as well as her reputation as a poetry critic and major modernist player (it was Sinclair who introduced Pound to Ford Madox Ford and the *English Review*, thus opening England to Pound), and, in a 1913 letter delineating his London exploits, Frost observes: "And then there is May Sinclair the author of The Divine Fire etc. etc. I took tea with her yesterday and expect to go there again shortly. She professes to see something unusual in my book. I like that of course because she is known as an expert in new poetry. She is the lady who made the reputation of Vaughn Moody Torrence and Edwin Arnold [Arlington] Robinson by naming them as the principal poets in the States" (*SL* 70). Clearly, Frost saw what Sinclair could do for him, and, after his meeting with her, she arranged for *A Boy's Will* to be reviewed a second time in the *Bookman*, a popular London literary journal, since the first notice in that publication was not so flattering. She showed Frost's book and Pound's review of it (which Frost gave her) to her friend St. John Adcock, editor of the *Bookman*; later, Adcock met with Frost at his office before writing the notice himself. Shortly thereafter, Frost refers to Adcock as "my friend," an epithet that testifies to Frost's determination to keep up relationships with those in a position to advance his career (*SL* 123).

In a letter (May 1913) to his friend Susan Hayes Ward, the literary editor of the American magazine the *Independent*, Frost was able to announce proudly that "Already it [*A Boy's Will*] has attracted the attention of Yeats, Newbolt, Rhys, Pound, and Miss Sinclair over here" (*SL* 73). Although later in the year Frost tells John Bartlett, a friend and former student who was a newspaper reporter in Vancouver, British Columbia, that he is not after "success with the critical few who are supposed to know," that "really to arrive where I can stand on my legs as a poet and nothing else I must get outside that circle to the general reader who buys books in their thousands," he also knows that to become a popular success he first must attract the attention of the "critical few" who review books by the hundreds (*SL* 98). When *A Boy's Will* came out on April 1, 1913, and was going on two weeks without a review, Frost expressed his anxiety to Bartlett: "I am in mortal fear now lest the reviewers should fail to take any notice of it. Such a work isn't sold in the bookstores but through the notices in the papers entirely. It is going the rounds now and it remains to be seen whether it will fall flat or not" (*SL* 70). Frost was waiting for the returns to come in ("The boom is not started yet"), fretting that his goal of making a profession out of poetry might not be met. Pound refers to Frost's "fit of nerves" in a letter to him and dissuades Frost from appealing directly to one of his own closely held publishing contacts (*SL* 71).[10] But beyond his commercial concerns, Frost craved the approval of his fellow artists. He reveals his early interest in winning Pound's esteem in a free verse parody of that poet sent to Flint in June 1913, after his relationship to Pound had frayed:

> And here we come close to what I demanded of you
> I did not want the money that you were disbursing
> among your favorites
> for two American editors.
> Not that.
> All I asked was that you should hold to one thing
> That you considered me a poet.
>
> *(SL 86)*

These are not the words of a man unconcerned by the opinions of the "critical few," but rather those of a man intent on winning for himself the respect of a modernist literary elite committed to the task of "making it new."

Eventually, reviews began to appear, and, although critical response to *A Boy's Will* was mostly positive, Frost was disturbed by the not infrequent charge of his poetic simplicity. The review appearing in the *Times Literary Supplement* (April 10, 1913) notes: "There is an agreeable individuality about these pieces; the writer is not afraid to avoid the simplest of his thoughts and fancies, and these, springing from a capacity for complete absorption in the influences of nature and the open air, are often naively engaging."[11] Likewise, Norman Douglas in the *English Review* points out Frost's "simple woodland philosophy," and in his review in *Poetry* Pound asserts that

Frost's book is "a little raw" and "has the tang of the New Hampshire woods," using the adjectives "homely" and "simple" to describe the poetry (*CR* 3, 1–2). Frost bristled at these terms of praise, confiding in the American publisher Thomas Mosher, "At least I am sure I can count on you to give me credit for knowing what I am about. You are not going to make the mistake that Pound makes of assuming that my simplicity is that of the untutored child. I am not undesigning" (*SL* 84). Although Flint recognizes Frost's "simplicity of utterance," he also notes his "subtlety," an attribution for which Frost expresses gratitude: "Ezra Pound . . . made a mistake when he thought he knew how to praise my poetry for the right thing. What he saw in them isnt there and what is there he couldn't have seen or he wouldn't have liked them. I have to thank you for the word 'subtlety' in your review. The poems are open. I am not so sure that the best of them are simple. If they are they are subtle too" (*RFW* 88).

As a result of these charges of a lack of sophistication, Frost's interest in formulating a theory of poetic form became acute. He identified Bartlett as someone who could help in the promotional effort and proceeded to send his friend published reviews to use as fodder for his own; in his "Fourth of July" 1913 letter to him Frost unveils his revolutionary poetics, proclaiming, "I am possibly the only person going who works on any but a worn out theory (principle I had better say) of versification" (*SL* 79). Explaining the importance of the rhythm of speech to poetic composition, he instructs that "The best place to get the sound of sense is from voices behind a door that cuts off the words," as with sentences such as "You mean to tell me you can't read?" and "I said no such thing"; he ends by insisting: "If one is to be a poet he must learn to get cadences by skillfully breaking the sounds of sense with all their irregularity of accent across the regular beat of the metre" (*SL* 80). Frost informs Bartlett one month later that these principles are not taken lightly, but serve as the bedrock of his art: "I am one of the few who have a theory of their own upon which all their work down to the least accent is done" (*SL* 88). The claim is meant to show him in a new light, to disabuse critics of the idea that he is a rude regional poet and promote the view of him as a careful craftsman—a sophisticated practitioner of verse.

Despite the fact that Frost's opening salvo on "the sound of sense" is fired on America's Independence Day, his formalism is deeply indebted to the British cultural scene—both the aesthetic doctrines and the social and political revolutions that define the period leading up to his July 1913 issuance. Elie Halévy has referred to the years 1910–14 in England as one of "domestic anarchy," with the revolt of the House of Lords in 1911 sending shock waves through the capital, and uprisings by workers and suffragettes turning increasingly violent.[12] In addition to reading about such issues in the London newspapers (he says after reaching England that he "paid thrippence thruppence or six cents for my first London Times sometimes called in New York The Thunderer for the Jovian majesty of its pronouncements"), Frost encountered, even sought out, the scenes of these debates and responded to them in letters and poems (*SL* 63). In September 1912, he went to a suffragette meeting in Soho to hear George Bernard Shaw speak. John Walsh explains that the meeting was held at Caxton Hall, near Buckingham Palace, and was called by the Women's Tax Resistance League to protest against the imprisonment of Mr. Mark Wilks for his inability to pay the taxes on his wife's earned income (*IMO* 27). In a letter written after that event Frost reported that "I heard G. B. Shaw tease the Suffragettes at one of their own meetings till they didn't know whether he had come to help (as advertised) or hinder them" (*SL* 63). Surely, Shaw's ironic treatment of such sober matters would have been to Frost's liking, since he, too, was given to such playfulness (in writing and talk). It is telling that Frost should have gone to such lengths to come into contact with Shaw (in his notebook at the time he wrote down "Pursuit of G.B.S."), since Shaw was well known not only for his drama but also for his socialist politics — a politics that distinctly colors that drama (*IMO* 218). Shaw's belief in equal rights for all people led him to agitate for universal suffrage and anti-imperialist policies, but, as Sally Peters sees, Shaw's "conversion to collectivism" did not cancel out his belief in individuality (a point whose importance to Frost will become clear).[13] Joining the ranks of the socialist Fabian Society in 1884, Shaw committed himself to gradual social revolution, as opposed to utopianism, and his desire for social reform is evident in such plays as *Arms and the Man* (1894), which Frost read soon after its publication, and *Fanny's First Play* (1911), which Frost and his wife saw in London almost immediately upon their arrival.

Indeed, Shaw's conversion in the 1880s to the economics of the American socialist Henry George is reminiscent of Frost's own family history. As Jay Parini tells it, Frost's father, Will, a journalist in San Francisco, "moved from the *Bulletin* to the *Daily Evening Post* in 1875, drawn to the latter by its crusading editor, Henry George, whose ideas on Christian socialism had proved attractive to a wide range of intellectuals around the world, including George Bernard Shaw and Leo Tolstoy, both of whom corresponded with him. George developed the concept of a single tax in *Progress and Poverty* (1879), arguing that free enterprise did not mean private monopolies were morally justified. In this vein, Will's editorials called repeatedly for 'a democracy uncorrupt and sensitive to the people's needs.'"[14] His mother's interest in the socialism of George and in Edward Bellamy's *Looking Backward* (1888), a novel that takes aim at class inequities and imagines a socialist future in the year 2000, also shapes Frost's early political sympathies.

In the same January 7, 1913, letter in which he mentions Shaw's antics at the suffragist meeting, Frost dips further into political waters, expressing his awareness of the full force of British imperialism when he says that "It is well known that England owns the ocean now-a-days" (*SL* 62). Asking humorously at what point he actually arrived in England on his voyage over a few months before, he alludes to the complicated cultural identities that come with colonial rule: "[D]id I reach it when I first saw the coast of Galway which, peaceful though it looked through the haze, is where the wild and fascinating Irishman still snipes the deputies of the absentee landlord? Or did I reach it when I nearly got myself thrown overboard by a Scotchman for innocently calling the fleet I saw off the Mull of Cantire English instead of British? (I was finding out that if Ireland loves England in one way Scotland loves her in another.)" (*SL* 162–63). He would find out again as debates about Irish Home Rule roiled London during his time there.

Frost also remarked on the strict class divisions within English society upon his arrival. Referring to the success with which the upper class had subdued the working class, he drew the following analogy in December 1912: "And meanwhile the horse patiently stands through several rains the very type and image of the English lower class taught to know and accept its place" (*SL* 59). Reflecting in 1948 on the publication of his first book in England, Frost imagined himself in the position of that subservient class by virtue of his artistic method: "To be sure by 1913 I had already had it from Kipling that I was hopelessly hedged from the elder earth with alien speech. But hearing then I heard not. I was young and heedless. My vitality shed discouragement as the well-oiled feathers of a healthy duck shed wetness. And to be merely hedged off was no great matter. What was a hedge to the poacher in my blood of a shiny night in the season of the year?" (*CPPP* 802). Here Frost allies himself with those unpropertied laborers dispossessed by the enclosure of open fields and common lands beginning in the late eighteenth century in England; on the other side stands Kipling, who represents the interests of the landowners in seeking to rule Frost out of the poetic tradition on the basis of his rhythms of speech. But rather than buckling under, Frost rebels against the oppressor, poaching on the land that has been marked off by hedgerows. Like Shaw, who, born in Dublin, was attracted to certain political and aesthetic doctrines in large part because he did not feel at home in the existing English society, Frost occupies the position of the outsider ("the stray American intruder, not to say pretender") and espouses (if less conspicuously) a similar left-leaning politics (*LU* 359–60).

Frost could see, too, that the acquiescence of British laborers was not to last, a point made especially clear when he came face-to-face with striking colliers on the streets of High Wycombe, a London suburb where he was shopping for Christmas gifts for his family in 1912. He wrote a poem commemorating the event that would seem to controvert a spirit of social reform, but that in fact expresses a deep political ambivalence:

> Remember how two babes were on the street—
> And so were many fathers out on strike
> The vainest of their many strikes in vain,
> And lost already as at heart they knew.
> But the two babes had stopped alone to look
> At Christmas toys behind a window pane,
> And play at having anything they chose.
> And when I lowered level with the two
> And asked them what they saw so much to like,
> One confidentially and raptly took
> His finger from his mouth and pointed, "Those!"
> A little locomotive with a train.
> And where he wet the window pane it froze.
> What good did it do to anyone but him—
> His brother at his side, perhaps, and me?
> And think of all the world compared with three!
> But why like the poor fathers on the curb
> Must we be always partizan and grim?
> No state has found a perfect cure for grief
> In law or gospel or in root or herb.
>
> (*CPPP* 523)

This poem, entitled "Good Relief," represents Frost's staunch refusal to assert sympathy or solidarity with the proletariat when they seek to remedy their situation through collective political action, but it also registers the pathetic condition of the striking workers in sentimental tones. Again, as reactionary as such a statement may seem, it should not occlude Frost's basic working-class sympathies. In "Good Relief" he reacts against what he regards as utopianism, that is, the desire of labor activists immediately to right all the wrongs of the world—a futile (because idealistic) quest.

On the evidence of this poem, Lawrance Thompson contends that Frost "repeatedly turn[ed] his back on historical facts whenever they were not pragmatically useful to the so-called truths of his beliefs," that he scorned the poor, as "certain classes in England" did in 1913.[15] In fact, though, Frost was much closer to those in England who sympathized with and sought to relieve the conditions of the working poor, in particular two of his first friends there—the Georgian poets Wilfrid Gibson and Lascelles Abercrombie. Frost's interest in cultivating a relationship with Gibson may have had to do with Gibson's popularity—a popularity Frost desired—but it no doubt also had to do with Gibson's political sympathies as embodied by his dramatic and lyric verse about English miners and other oppressed laborers. In *Daily Bread* (1910), Gibson's poem "The Furnace" stages a sentimental dialogue in a tenement dwelling over the body of a stoker dying as a result of an accident at the mine. His wife confronts the horror of the situation in talk with a neighbor woman:

> Bessie. How did it happen?
> Eleanor. None can tell.
> They found him on his face
> Before the furnace-door,
> The life well-nigh burnt out of him;
> His head, and breast, and hands . . .
> Oh, it's too terrible to think of, neighbour![16]

Although perhaps not as proficient as Frost's blank verse is at representing realistic tones of voice in an unstilted diction, Gibson's poem unmistakably points toward the dramatic dialogues of Frost's second volume of poetry, *North of Boston* (1914).

Gibson's book *Fires* (1912) also radiates his liberal politics, and one poem entitled "The Slag," which is in the sentimental mode, figures the dehumanizing effects of labor in mill and mine—effects that were on Frost's mind at the time as well:

> Among bleak hills of mounded slag they walked,
> 'Neath sullen evening skies that seemed to sag
> O'er-burdened by the belching smoke, and lie
> Upon their aching foreheads, dense and dank,
> Till both felt youth within them fail and flag—
> Even as the flame which shot a fiery rag
> A fluttering moment through the murky sky
> Above the black blast-furnaces, then sank
> Again beneath the iron bell close-bound—
> And it was all that they could do to drag
> Themselves along, 'neath that dead-weight of smoke,
> Over the cinder-blasted, barren ground.[17]

In this wasteland a girl, who has been "close stitching at her dull machine" all day, looks for some sign of life—some romantic aspiration—in her lover, who has been reduced to the status of a "lout" by his labor. With "The daylong chattering whirr of her machine / Humm[ing] in her ears again—the straining thread / And stabbing needle starting through her head," she nearly gives up hope, when suddenly a crisis awakens her lover's humanity, filling her with "joy"; as he rushes to rescue a boy on the brink of "a fiery, gaping pit" at the mill,

> She saw him reel and fall . . .
> And thought him done for . . . then
> Her lover, brave and tall,
> Against the glare and heat,
> A very fire-bright god of men!
> . . . .
> She saw him bend with tender care
> Over the sobbing child who lay
> Safe in his arms, and hug him tight
> Against his breast—his brow alight
> With eager, loving eyes that burned
> In his transfigured face aflame . . .

The book in which this poem appears came out in the midst of strikes by miners and, in the year of its publication, the British government passed a bill guaranteeing a minimum wage to those men—a goal for which Gibson's melodramatic poem aims. Thus, while Karen Kilcup has shown the influence of the sentimental strain in American poetry by women on Frost's early work, the sentimental realist tradition in English verse was as powerful an agent, as these poems by Gibson reveal.[18]

Gibson's review of *North of Boston* entitled "Simplicity and Sophistication" set out to correct the critical balance—all on the side of "simplicity" in reviews of *A Boy's Will*—by pointing out the skill behind Frost's art, which he finds infused with democratic feeling. Although Walsh has noted the review's ambivalence—an ambivalence perhaps motivated by jealousy—Gibson in effect establishes Frost as a political ally when he suggests that the speech contours in Frost's poems are a sign of his capacity for sympathy: "He has become so absorbed in the characters he delineates that he has neither time nor inclination to put on frills, or in any way to attract attention to his originality" (*IMO* 176). Hailing his "native veracity and truth to local character," Gibson sees Frost as intensely focused on the unique individual, on the crowning importance of character. Lascelles Abercrombie's politically inflected notice of *North of Boston* in the *Nation* also reflects his close personal association with Frost, and Frost acknowledged his approval of Abercrombie's review to John Haines:

I liked it very well. The discussion of my technique wouldn't have been what it was if Abercrombie had had nothing to go on but the book. He took advantage of certain conversations in which I gave him the key to my method and most of his catchwords. "Method" is the wrong way to call it: I simply use certain principles on which I accept or reject my own work. It was a generous review to consider me in all ways so seriously and as I say I like it. (*SL* 127)

Frost's admission that Abercrombie could not have described the poems as he does with the book alone in front of him testifies to the fact that Frost had foisted onto his friends the theoretically exacting terms that he hoped would gain him the favor of the poetic establishment and, eventually, through the strength of their reviews, a public following. Abercrombie, who, along with Gibson, was sympathetic toward the Fabian attempts to have the Poor Law repealed, and, thus, to secure a more adequate welfare for the poor, frames his praise of *North of Boston* in such a way as to conjure up those political ideals: "Poetry, in the book, seems determined . . . to invigorate itself by utilizing the traits and necessities of common life, the habits of common speech, the minds and hearts of common folk" (*CR* 14). Gibson's and Abercrombie's friend Edward Thomas wrote a like-minded review of *North of Boston* in which he observes that Frost "sympathises where [William] Wordsworth contemplates," and states that in his poetry Frost is more like Dorothy Wordsworth in his sensibilities: his "tenderness" arises from his politics, which are seen as at odds with William Wordsworth's detached conservatism (*CR* 15). As Eleanor Farjeon reports, one day on a walk Frost demonstrated to her and Thomas what he meant by "the sound of sense" by calling to a farmer in a distant field: "Whatever the words, the man on the cart could not have heard them," but the farmer understood and "shouted some answer that rang through the air"; although "it was impossible for us to distinguish what was said," she remarks that "the cadence of the answer was as clear as that of the question."[19] Through this demonstration, Frost brings home the point that his theory of form is rooted in—and proved by—colloquy in the field, not the genteel parlor.

Frost's sympathetic depiction of mill workers in poems he wrote in America a few years before moving to England (and later suppressed) attests to his belief in personal sovereignty and expresses his solidarity with workers. Notably, too, these poems are untouched by strikes. In a sonnet from 1906 or 1907 that went unpublished, he represents the desperation of New England mill workers, who are physically and spiritually exhausted and alienated from their labor:

> When the speed comes a-creeping overhead
> And belts begin to snap and shafts to creak,
> And the sound dies away of them that speak,
> And on the glassy floor the tapping tread;
> When dusty globes on all a pallor shed,

And breaths of many wheels are on the cheek;
Unwilling is the flesh, the spirit weak,
All effort like arising from the dead.

But the task ne'er could wait the mood to come,
The music of the iron is a law:
And as upon the heavy spools that pay
Their slow white thread, so ruthlessly the hum
Of countless whirling spindles seems to draw
Upon the soul, still sore from yesterday.

(CPPP 511)

This poem strikes the same chord as the first part of Frost's 1933 poem "A Lone Striker," where the mill, a "many-many-eyed" monster that sees without being seen (reminiscent of a panopticon), is imagined as most workers actually experienced it; however, this early sonnet does not succumb to the fictions of that later poem, where the following aestheticized image of a female mill worker appears: "Her deft hand showed with finger rings / Among the harp-like spread of strings." Perhaps this difference is not so surprising, since Frost's own stint as a worker in the mills—and the oppressive conditions of that space—would have been fresher on his mind in 1906 or 1907, but it is also true that political conditions in the country are not what they will be in the 1930s, allowing Frost to display his sympathies openly and unapologetically at this early point in the century. (I will consider his political shift later in this study.) In "When the speed comes a-creeping overhead" the "homicidal roar" of industrial machinery wrecks the workers, whom we see going through the paces as their lives ("Their slow white thread") wind down (*CPPP* 279). That Frost originally sent this sonnet to the New York magazine the *Independent,* a liberal periodical that advocated labor, social, and government reforms, suggests his awareness that there was a market for such "protest" poetry in the first decade of the twentieth century and his readiness to identify himself publicly with the cause of the mill worker at that time.[20] However, when the poem was not accepted, it did not resurface in Frost's lifetime.

Another early sonnet, this one written in 1905, also represents Frost's sharp sense of the oppression of the working class. In "The Mill City" he takes account of his own relatively privileged position and expresses his sympathy for laborers trapped in deplorable conditions:

It was in a drear city by a stream,
And all its denizens were sad to me,—
I could not fathom what their life could be—
Their passage in the morning like a dream
In the arc-light's unnatural bluish beam,

Then back at night, like drowned men from the sea,
Up from the mills and river hurriedly,
In weeds of labor, to the shriek of steam.

Yet I supposed that they had all one hope
With me (there is but one). I would go out,
When happier ones drew in for fear of doubt,
Breasting their current, resolute to cope
With what thoughts they compelled who throng the street,
Less to the sound of voices than of feet.

(*CPPP* 509)

The octet of this sonnet imagines the working men as drowning victims; the water that powers the mill rushes over them and, at the whistle, they are dredged up from the stream bed ("In weeds of labor") to drift home as ghosts. The speaker is different from them ("I could not fathom what their life could be"), but sympathetic to their plight; he extends himself to them when other, "happier" people refuse to look for fear that their faith in industrial "progress" will be shaken. At the end of the sestet, Frost expresses his willingness to grapple with the problem of industrialized labor, to listen to the concerns of these oppressed workers. Indeed, he recently had heard from one such worker, his friend Carl Burrell, who was seriously injured while working in a box factory in 1896. Frost's poem "The Self-Seeker," written in England in 1913, portrays the insensitivity of the mill owners, whose lawyer offers token compensation to the victim, and the disgust of the victim's friend at such tactics.

In light of Frost's early antagonism to industrial capitalism and the injustices of that economic system, it is appropriate that his early appreciation of the liberatory potential of tone in writing comes while working in the mills of Lawrence, Massachusetts, just after leaving his job as a booking agent for an elocutionist whose specialty was reciting Shakespeare. Lawrance Thompson describes the scene as follows:

For his reading in this lofty wheelhouse Rob carried a small pocket-sized book, usually a volume from a complete set of Shakespeare which he had purchased in Boston during his recent flurry there. Never before had he read any of the plays carefully. Now, with the intonations of the elocutionist still in mind, he began to study certain passages in Hamlet, Macbeth, and The Tempest, pencil in hand for making marginal notes on how the passages should be spoken if the lines were to convey, dramatically, the essential meanings. . . . For the first time he realized that in Shakespeare's poetry—and, he supposed, in any good poetry—there was an interplay between the basic rhythm of the metrical line and the natural intonations of the spoken sentence. In his own writing, he decided, he would try to achieve these qualities. Day after day, as he continued to study Shakespeare's dialogues, while the slight breeze of the turning belt wheel fanned the pages of his book, he kept searching for hints and clues that might help him to understand and master these technical aspects of poetry.[21]

Thompson's romanticized depiction of life in the mills ("while the slight breeze of the turning belt wheel fanned the pages of his book") does not square with Frost's own experience of it, as human tones of voice in poetry allow Frost to escape (for a time) the dehumanizing effects of industrialism, to recover the integrity of the individual in the face of the machine. Although Thompson claims that Frost read with interest the muckraking journalism of such writers as Ida Tarbell, Lincoln Steffens, and Richard Stannard Baker in *McClure's* in the early years of the twentieth century but stopped reading such exposés when he concluded that their way was not his, the fact is that his poetry of that period and the theory behind it express a deep concern for the effects of social and economic injustice.[22]

Indeed, Frost's concept of "the sound of sense" ought to be read as an element of opposition culture at a time when, as Christopher Reed argues with respect to the Bloomsbury group, "a rhetoric of individualism could be conceived as a radical act."[23] We must understand Frost's prosodic commitment as deeply moral and, therefore, as part of a revolution to restore human subjectivity to the center of aesthetic experience—a theory and practice that are explicitly inscribed as part of a broader leftist worldview in their inception. As Reed explains, the Bloomsbury artist's "reliance on subjective aesthetic response was not just a vague utopian impulse, but a considered attempt to wrest art from the imperatives of capitalist consumerism and the control of the dominant classes served by conventional aesthetic judgment."[24] Frost's statements of his aesthetic show that he cared deeply about the remodeling of literature on a democratic basis as well. He tells Sidney Cox in a letter on "the sound of sense" of his interest in language as actually spoken: "No if I want to deal with the word I must sink back to its common usage at Castle Garden" (*SL* 141). The "alien speech" of Castle Garden, New York, an immigration station where one does not hear the language "that everybody exclaims Poetry! at" is, Frost asserts, a resource of the modern poet: "We write of things we see and we write in accents we hear. Thus we gather both our material and technique with the imagination from life, and our technique becomes as much material as material itself" (*SL* 141). Frost's negative reaction to Pound's attempt in 1913 to place "The Death of the Hired Man," a poem that eventually appeared in *North of Boston,* with the New York magazine *The Smart Set* indicates a coincident desire to speak to common people—the very same people who speak in Frost's verse.[25]

The Bloomsbury formalist subculture included such figures as Clive Bell, Roger Fry, Maynard Keynes, and Virginia Woolf, and had a very wide influence, one that Frost could not have escaped while in London. Fry, an early exponent of postimpressionism, published in 1909 "An Essay in Aesthetics," where he describes the existence of emotional elements of design in art, independent of the depicted subject matter, and in 1914 Clive Bell's *Art* summarized these formalist principles, placing emphasis on the value of abstract form as opposed to mimesis. Later, second-generation formalism (beginning roughly at the end of World War I) in Bloomsbury would attempt to reintegrate representation into the formalist paradigm without sacrificing an ideal of purely aesthetic experience, but Virginia Woolf makes this correction early on. In Woolf's 1915 novel *The Voyage Out* she satirizes Fry's formalism through the character of Terence, who reads Milton aloud "because he said the words of Milton had substance and shape, so that it was not necessary to understand what he was saying."[26] Woolf goes on to observe that "The words, in spite of what Terence had said, seemed to be laden with meaning, and perhaps it was for this reason that it was painful to listen to them," thereby poking fun at the notion that pure aesthetic experience cannot contain any signification. At first glance Frost's position might seem akin to Terence's and, thus, to Fry's, particularly in light of his view of Milton's acoustics: "Tones, . . . pauses and rushes and intensities of sound are more revealing than the definition value of the words. 'Lycidas' . . . sympathetically read aloud would be stirring and charming if heard through a wall that muffled all the words."[27] In fact, though, Frost here is in step with Woolf's critique of Fry, since "the sound of sense" stands against a Victorian poetics of what Frost called "harmonised vowels and consonants"—that is, the "substance and shape" of words (*SL* 79). In Frost's statement about "Lycidas" he does express his interest in what Milton is saying but as registered not through words but through evocative intonation contours.

Woolf's rejection of Fry's formalism—her attention to the rhythms of the inner life in her writing exemplified by her use of interior monologue—is consistent with Frost's view that tone of voice in writing depicts individual character. Indeed, Frost's theory of "the sound of sense" anticipates Woolf's call for a new aesthetics of psychological realism in her essay "Modern Fiction," which was not published until 1919. If Woolf, in reaction to the formalist insistence on the separation of aesthetics from other realms of experience, feels that novelists should look for formal significance in the traditionally feminine realm of the everyday, what she calls "the life of Monday or Tuesday," Frost also returns us to the mundane and emphasizes its social value.[28] When Woolf says she despairs of finding an arbiter of literary pattern who can "take a stick and point to that tone, the relation in the vanishing pages, as Mr. Roger Fry points with his wand at a line or a color in the picture displayed before him," she reveals the importance of the prosodic feature of speech rhythm to her literary project.[29] (As we will see, Frost sets himself up as just such an arbiter, and in doing so denies the ambiguity of tone in writing.) In rejecting the materialism of realist fiction of her day, Woolf explicitly comments on the anti-imperialist politics of her art, noting that it is the novelist's concern "to express character—not to preach doctrines, sing songs, or celebrate the glories of the British Empire."[30] Frost's interest in the vocalics of character—and here we might recall Frank Lentricchia's description of the theory of "the sound of sense" as itself "work[ing] toward a novelized lyric of character"—similarly serves as an antidote to personal and political impingement, and is shaped not only, or even mainly, by a tradition of American local-color realism, as Lentricchia alleges, but by an emergent British formalism and the political welter of Edwardian England in the light of which it grew.

II

If Frost's personal egalitarian politics left its impress on his theory of form, so, too, did the politically inflected psychological and philosophical theories swirling around London at the time of his residence there. In November 1911, the year before Frost's entrance onto the London scene, T. E. Hulme noted the vogue of the French philosopher Henri Bergson: "In the course of its varied history philosophy has been many things, but never before has it attained the dignity of being 'news,' and news which was so pressing that it had to be got out before a certain edition."[31] Hulme also suggests the currency of the American philosopher William James in his first published article, "The New Philosophy" (July 1909), an essay-review of James's *A Pluralistic Universe* (London, 1909), a book he judges "in one way the most important that has yet appeared in the much-advertised English pragmatic movement."[32] Saturating literary debates of the day, this new science of mind shaped Frost's concept of "the sound of sense" in significant ways, although that fact is not well known. Usually when critics discuss Frost's debt to Bergson and James, it is Frost's poetic figures that are read in their light, not his poetic formalism.[33] Richard Poirier is one of the few critics to draw a relationship between Frost's theory of tone and Jamesian pragmatism, but then only to a single passage in James's *The Principles of Psychology* (1890) and without a consideration of its ethical and political implications.[34] In addition, Robert Faggen has noted the Darwinian empiricist underpinnings of Frost's formalism, but in his illuminating discussion he does not address squarely the impact of James and Bergson (heirs of Darwin) on it. As I argue, Frost's decision to engage so fully these two thinkers in crafting his poetics is motivated by his desire to keep in step with other modernist artists drinking in the new philosophy (that is, by his sense of literary politics) as well as by his awareness of the democratic politics implicated in their writings. Once we read more widely in and look more closely at Frost's discourses on "the sound of sense," including those in his London notebooks, we can measure the extent and depth of his borrowings and their precise bearing on his early ideology of form.

By the time Frost arrived in London, he had read James's *The Will to Believe* (1897) and, as a student at Harvard, James's *Psychology: Briefer Course* (1892), a condensed version of *The Principles of Psychology* published two years earlier. Although he had no personal contact with James, who was on a leave of absence from Harvard when he was enrolled in classes there (1897–99), Frost credits James for the impact he had on his thinking: "My greatest inspiration when I was a student, was a man whose classes I never attended."[35] He taught James's *Briefer Course* and *Talks to Teachers on Psychology* (1899) in a psychology course at the Plymouth Normal School (1911–12) just before moving to England, and read James's *Pragmatism* (1907) while he was an instructor at that school. At the same time, Frost pursued his interest in Henri Bergson, reading and annotating his copy of Arthur Mitchell's translation of *Creative Evolution* (1907; trans. 1911). He also owned a copy of *Mind-Energy,* a collection of Bergson's lectures and essays written between 1901 and 1913.[36] Although this book was not published until 1920, some of the lectures appeared in print (in English) prior to Frost's theorizing of "the sound of sense," as did *Time and Free Will* (1889; trans. 1910) and *Matter and Memory* (1896; trans. 1911), which inquire into related issues of mind and body and with which he surely was familiar.

Frost found much in common between the philosophical positions of Bergson and James, and no doubt was led to read Bergson as a result of James's own ebullient response to *Creative Evolution*. The first sign of that acclaim, which later would become public (in *A Pluralistic Universe*), appears in a letter that James wrote to the author in 1907: "O my Bergson, you are a magician, and your book is a marvel, a real wonder in the history of philosophy, making, if I mistake not, an entirely new era in respect of matter, but unlike the works of genius of the 'transcendentalist' movement (which are so obscurely and abominably and inaccessibly written), a pure classic in point of form."[37] James goes on to say that the "vital achievement" of the book is "that it inflicts an irrecoverable death-wound upon Intellectualism," and he sees in it strong similarities to his own work, but couches that recognition in all modesty: "You will be receiving my own little 'pragmatism' book simultaneously with this letter. How jejune and incomparable it seems in comparison with your great system! But it is so congruent with parts of your system, fits so well into interstices thereof, that you will easily see why I am so enthusiastic. I feel that at bottom we are fighting the same fight, you a commander, I in the ranks." The congruence between Bergson and James is evident in earlier works, as we will see, although in many ways *Pragmatism* and *Creative Evolution* represent the full flowering of their anti-intellectualist philosophies. Frost was attracted to the styles of both James and Bergson, and by their assault on those who would reduce the whole of reality, including human nature, to a system of determinate laws. He shared their view that the intellect and its operations lead us away from our own presence, and Frost's concept of "the sound of sense" is meant to restore that presence to us—an act that is in keeping with Bergson's sense of the role of the artist ("Encouraged by him, we have put aside for an instant the veil which we interposed between our consciousness and ourselves. He has brought us back into our own presence") and the politics of radical individualism at the heart of that poetic project.[38]

In his chapter "The Stream of Consciousness" in *Briefer Course,* James expresses his understanding of the nature of human consciousness, asserting that the sensations we get from the same object are not identical, because our states of mind are constantly in flux: "We feel things differently accordingly as we are sleepy or awake, hungry or full, fresh or tired; differently at night and in the morning, differently in summer and in winter; and above all, differently in childhood, manhood, and old age."[39] When we give our thought a name, however, we fix that thought and become blind to the fact that our feelings toward it shift in time. James also points out that our thought is sensibly continuous, that we feel as if a present moment of consciousness bears some relation to moments that precede it: "it would be difficult to find in the actual concrete consciousness of man a feeling so limited to the present as not to have an inkling of anything that went before."[40] This "actual concrete consciousness" James terms our "stream of consciousness," and he finds within it two different types of mental state:

When we take a general view of the wonderful stream of our consciousness, what strikes us first is the different pace of its parts. Like a bird's life, it seems to be an alternation of flights and perchings. The rhythm of language expresses this, where every thought is expressed in a sentence, and every sentence closed by a period. The resting places are usually occupied by sensorial imaginations of some sort, whose peculiarity is that they can be held before the mind for an indefinite time, and contemplated without changing; the places of flight are filled with thoughts of relations, static or dynamic, that for the most part obtain between the matters contemplated in the periods of comparative rest. . . . *Let us call the resting-places the "substantive parts," and the places of flight the "transitive parts," of the stream of thought.*[41]

James reports the failure of traditional philosophies of mind to register the existence of these "transitive parts" of consciousness:

If there be such things as feelings at all, *then so surely as relations between objects exist* in rerum natura, *so surely, and more surely, do feelings exist to which these relations are known.* There is not a conjunction or a preposition, and hardly an adverbial phrase, syntactic form, or inflection of voice, in human speech, that does not express some shade or other of relation which we at some moment actually feel to exist between the larger objects of our thought. . . . [T]he relations are numberless, and no existing language is capable of doing justice to all their shades."[42]

James's linguistic skepticism—a skepticism that lies at the center of his pragmatist philosophy—is keen, as he believes that language is incapable of expressing immediacy of feeling, of justly representing our true self.[43]

In his poetics Frost makes known his abiding interest in the "transitive parts" of human thought and speech, with "the sound of sense" corresponding to James's "inflection of voice," and accordingly detracts from the signifying capacity of discrete lexical units: "The best place to get the abstract sound of sense is from voices behind a door that cuts off the words." In 1915, his polemic intensifies: "Words are only valuable in writing as they serve to indicate particular sentence sounds" (*SL* 152). That same year, Frost again overstates his case: "What we do get in life and miss so often in literature is the sentence sounds that underlie the words. Words in themselves do not convey meaning, . . . which may seem entirely unreasonable to any one who does not understand the psychology of sound."[44] Here he reveals his debt to contemporary scientific discourse: one cannot appreciate the relative unimportance of substantive parts of speech, he suggests, if one does not know psychology, which uncovers for us the transitive parts of human consciousness. In a 1935 letter to his daughter Lesley,

Frost again connects his auditory aesthetic to the field of psychology, with reference to the poetics of imagism—a poetics I will measure more fully in relation to Frost's theory a bit later: "An Imagist is simply one who insists on clearer sharper less muddled half realized images (chiefly eye images) than the common run of small poets. Thats certainly good as far as it goes. Strange with all their modernity and psychology they didnt have more to say about ear images and other images—even kinesthetic" (*CPPP* 735).[45] In light of these remarks, Robert Kern's claim that "To see what he was up against, and to appreciate the loneliness of Frost's position, one need only recall the virtual hegemony of visualist thinking, both in philosophy and poetics, during this period" must be reconsidered, since modernist philosophy (my concern for the moment) is not as visually biased as Kern alleges.[46]

Indeed, when Frost tells Bartlett in 1913 that "Those sounds [of sense] are summoned by the audile (audial) imagination," his diction points us in the direction of James's research on sound and its bearing on the human imagination in *Briefer Course* (*SL* 80).[47] Frost's supplementing of the technical term "audile" with the parenthetical "audial" suggests his tentative approach to the science; probably he forgets exactly what word James uses in his discussion. In the chapter entitled "Imagination" in *Briefer Course*, James cites the different forms of imagination of which people are capable, including the "visual," "auditory," and "motor." Under the chapter subheading "Images of Sounds," he quotes from Alfred Binet's *Psychologie du Raisonnement* (1886) to explain the "auditory" form: "*This type . . . appears to be rarer than the visual*. Persons of this type imagine what they think of in the language of sound. In order to remember a lesson they impress upon their mind, not the look of the page, but the sound of the words. They reason, as well as remember, by ear."[48] Binet refers to the person with such an "'auditory type'" of imagination as "'the *pure audile*,'" a phrase that he takes from the Victorian polymath Sir Francis Galton, who refers to individuals "'who think by preference in auditory images'" as "'*audiles*.'"[49] Although "audile" is a noun referring to the person who depends mainly on his hearing or whose imagery is chiefly in terms of sound, Frost turns it into an adjective, preferring it to the less clinical "auditory" because it calls attention to his scientific knowledge and, thus, promotes his cause in the high-stakes game of literary politics, where scientific formulations of poetic principles carried clout.

In the extended chapter of "Imagination" in *The Principles of Psychology*, James quotes Galton at greater length, reporting in full his argument against the notion of there being a single "Imagination" with universal validity and in favor of the notion of plural imaginations. Illustrating the variations in imagination among people, Galton reports that he asked participants in an experiment to describe their breakfast table that morning, to consider the mental image of the table as it presented itself to them in terms of a set of objective criteria, including illumination, definition, and coloring: "To my astonishment, I found *that the great majority of the men of science to whom I first applied protested that mental imagery was unknown to them. . . .* On the other hand, when I spoke to persons whom I met *in general society,* I found an entirely different disposition to prevail. *Many men and a yet larger number of women, and many boys and girls, declared that they habitually saw mental imagery, and that it was perfectly distinct to them and full of color.*"50 Ultimately, Galton concludes that scientists are intellectually more advanced than the average person and that "an over-ready perception of sharp mental images is antagonistic to the acquirement of habits of highly-generalized and abstract thought," and James corroborates Galton's findings in light of his personal experience in a footnote: "(I am myself a good draughtsman, and have a very lively interest in pictures, statues, architecture and decoration, and a keen sensibility to artistic effects. But I am an extremely poor visualizer, and find myself often unable to reproduce in my mind's eye pictures which I have most carefully examined.)"51 This personal testimony was probably all the encouragement Frost needed to elevate the auditory imagination over the visual imagination in his theory of "the sound of sense," to focus not on the mind's eye, but on "the minds ear" (*PJ* 133).

Beginning with his first major work, *Time and Free Will,* Bergson expresses views nearly identical to James's, highlighting the flow of our thought and demonstrating that the intellectual concepts that order our practical existence do not reflect our actual perception of external objects, which we register differently every time we encounter them according to our particular mood and context. Arguing that our consciousness, or "duration," is constantly changing, Bergson challenges the determinist assumption that "the same cause can appear a second time on the stage of consciousness."52 When we pass a house in our daily walk, we notice it slightly differently each time in our "real duration," even though our intellect does away with these alterations and practically represents it to us as an already known sign, one that we can count on as consistently the same. Like James, Bergson is compelled to take a bleak view of language: "Not only does language make us believe in the unchangeableness of our sensations, but it will sometimes deceive us as to the nature of the sensation felt. . . . In short, the word with well-defined outlines, the rough and ready word, which stores up the stable, common, and consequently impersonal element in the impressions of mankind, overwhelms or at least covers over the delicate and fugitive impressions of our individual consciousness."[53] By giving a fixed form to fleeting sensations, we distort those sensations and lose their immediacy. When Bergson goes on to say that "This overwhelming of the immediate consciousness is nowhere so striking as in the case of our feelings," he anticipates Frost's view of the affective and progressive politics of "the sound of sense."[54]

Not only do James's and Bergson's concepts ground Frost's; their rhetorical formulations bear directly on his descriptions of "the sound of sense." For instance, his use of the adjective "concrete" stems from his readings in both philosophers. In a lecture on Bergson, James uses the word in articulating the view that the welter of sensory data residing in our stream of consciousness is not practically useful, that it only would confuse if not masked from us in our daily existence: "Sensible reality is too concrete to be entirely manageable."[55] As we have seen, in *Briefer Course* James refers to our directly apprehended reality as our "concrete consciousness"; Bergson likewise labels duration "concrete."[56] The "concrete" stands in opposition to intellectual abstraction, which James praises Bergson for rejecting: "He alone denies that mere conceptual logic can tell us what is impossible or possible in the world of being or fact."[57] James also employs a form of the word to define a pragmatist's orientation toward reality, that is, "the world of being or fact": "A pragmatist turns his back resolutely and once and for all upon a lot of inveterate habits dear to professional philosophers. He turns away from abstraction and insufficiency, from verbal solutions, from bad *a priori* reasoning, from fixed principles, closed systems, and pretended absolutes and origins. He turns toward concreteness and adequacy, toward facts, toward action and toward power."[58] Following their lead, Frost enjoins the reader: "Seek first in poetry concrete images of sound—concrete tone images" (*PJ* 119). In a later interview Frost again stresses the importance of the "concrete" to poetic composition: "One critic says that I make my imagination too concrete. As if imagination could be made too concrete" (*I* 25). He even invokes the related Jamesian term "fact" to name "the sound of sense": "Poetry is a dwelling on the fact, a gloating over the fact, a luxuriating in the fact. It's first pleasure is in the facts of the voice" (*PJ* 119).

Frost's sonnet "Mowing," which he identified as one of his earliest attempts to incorporate speech rhythm into poetry (in it, he said, "I come so near what I long to get that I almost despair of coming nearer"), is in part about "the sound of sense," and, strikingly, in its penultimate line we encounter the pragmatist term "fact": "The fact is the sweetest dream that labor knows" (*CPPP* 26).[59] Frost once admitted that the poem "has a defi-nition of poetry in it," singling out that one-sentence line: "['Mowing'] was one of my earliest ones [poems]. That is one of my earliest convictions about poetry: the fact is the sweetest dream that labor knows, that poetry is gloating on facts. I found that for myself when I said that."[60] The "sounds of sense" in "Mowing" constitute aural "facts" that respond to "the sum-mons of the imaginative ear," and it is appropriate in light of the demo-cratic ethos of Frost's aesthetic that here a common laborer is the one reap-ing tones of voice from nature (*PJ* 119). That Frost discovers his belief in the act of saying that sentence in the poem points to the epistemological power of articulated sound, as he imagines it.

Frost also admires a figure of speech with roots in the natural world that plays a prominent role in Bergson's and James's descriptions of the work-ings of the human mind. James proposes the metaphor in (and places it as title of) Chapter 11 of *Briefer Course*, "The Stream of Consciousness": "Consciousness, then, does not appear to itself chopped up in bits. Such words as 'chain' or 'train' do not describe it fitly as it presents itself in the first instance. It is nothing jointed; it flows. A 'river' or 'stream' are the met-aphors by which it is most naturally described. *In talking of it hereafter, let us call it the stream of thought, of consciousness, or of subjective life.*"[61] For his part, Bergson adopts the same image to illustrate his point that duration is sen-sibly continuous, arguing in *Creative Evolution* that "if a mental state ceased to vary, its duration would cease to flow" and that such psychic states "con-tinue each other in an endless flow."[62] In the same book he calls "duration" "a stream against which we cannot go," since "It is the foundation of our being, and, as we feel, the very substance of the world in which we live."[63] Frost's marginal notations in his copy of *Creative Evolution* suggest his fas-cination with Bergson's tropes; next to a description of the opposite move-ments of "descent" and "ascent" at work in the world, he exclaims, "Meta-phor again!"[64] His own figuration of "the sound of sense" points back unambiguously to the metaphors of river and stream in Bergson's and James's writings, as seen in the following entry in a notebook that he kept in England: "Fool psychologists treat the five sense elements as of equal weight. One of them is nearly the whole thing. The tone-of-voice element is the unbroken flow on which the others are carried along like sticks and leaves and flowers" (*PJ* 132). The phrase "the unbroken flow" (resembling James's "unbroken stream") is meant to delineate personal consciousness as continuous.[65] In another notebook entry, Frost relies on a similar image to portray the relationship between tone of voice and human consciousness: "The flow of talk goes forward. Words or no words, we must make a sound of voices to each other and we will; but it will be better if we can launch a thought now and then on the stream of words."[66] As Frost finds, any meaningful communication between people must issue from the stream of experience, and it is just such communication that is essential to life ("we must . . . and we will"). Despite such metaphorical richness, Frost is quick to point out that he is not just dealing in trope, that "the sound of sense" is "no mere figure of speech," but has basis in fact (*SL* 140). Bergson similarly heads off his critics in the opening chapter of *Creative Evolution*, where he lays out his conception of time in duration: "This, it will be said, is only a metaphor."[67] Not only in the substance of his figures, then, but in his defensiveness about them, Frost is in step with Bergson.

Frost's ambivalent phrase "Words or no words" in his description of the "flow of talk" reemphasizes his indifference to language as a signifying system, as he prefers to dwell on the felt structure of the sentence apart from the words that comprise it and, by tying that structure to the contours of human consciousness, brings it in line with his politics of individualism. In a letter of December 1914, he writes, "It may take some time to make people see—they are so accustomed to look at the sentence as a grammatical cluster of words. The question is where to begin the assault on their prejudice"; his intention is to "establish the distinction between the grammatical sentence and the vital sentence" (*SL* 140). In making that distinction, Frost associates "the grammatical sentence" with rational thought as opposed to the perceptual flux: "Such a sentence serves for much necessary workaday writing and also for certain overintellectual writing that most of us find dull—for two extremes[:] hasty journalism and heavy philosophy" (*PJ* 115). To John Bartlett in February 1914, he unveils his "new definition of the sentence": "A sentence is a sound in itself on which other sounds called words may be strung" (*SL* 110–11). He follows up this statement with a homely analogy: "You may string words together without a sentence-sound to string them on just as you may tie clothes together by the sleeves and stretch them without a clothes line between two trees, but—it is bad for the clothes." Frost's understanding of the sentence is informed by James's notion that that structure stands for "the sensible continuity and unity of our thought as contrasted with the apparent discreteness of the words, images, and other means by which it seems to be carried on"; it expresses the flux of our immediate experience as intellectualist abstractions are incapable of doing.[68] However, the figure of strung words comes from Hulme, who, in turn, takes his cue from Bergson: "Words," Hulme insists, "are nothing more than 'beads on a chain,' and meaning is conveyed by the 'chain,' the relation between the words, more than by the 'beads,' the words in themselves."[69]

In his psychological discourses Bergson focuses relentlessly on the sentence of sound, or, as James puts it, "the blank verbal scheme," as opposed to the "rational sentence."[70] In *Matter and Memory* Bergson cites evidence from the study of the pathology of aphasia, specifically the loss of the ability to recognize the sounds of words, that supports his cognitive view: "To hear some theorists discourse on sensory aphasia, we might imagine that they had never considered with any care the structure of a sentence. They argue as if a sentence were composed of nouns which call up the images of things. What becomes of those parts of speech, of which the precise function is to establish, between images, relations and shades of meaning of every kind?"[71] Like James, Bergson directs attention away from "the images of things," believing that such images alone fail to communicate "the movement of thought."[72] In the same chapter of *Matter and Memory* Bergson dismisses the idea that memory is an inert and passive thing on the evidence that a word in a phrase or sentence takes on different pronunciations and so requires us to search out similitude between the sound and its image: "[A] word has an individuality for us only from the moment that we have been taught to abstract it. What we first hear are short phrases, not words. A word is always continuous with the other words which accompany it and takes different aspects according to the cadence and movement of the sentences in which it is set: just as each note of a melody vaguely reflects the whole musical phrase."[73] Similarly, Frost asserts that the rhythm of an utterance—its particular pronunciation—takes precedence over the static word, that the sound of the sentence (or "sentence-sound") conveys our continuous thought, with its full emotional register, not some abstracted slice of it.

In "The Soul and the Body," a lecture that he delivered in Paris in 1912, Bergson further establishes the unit of the sentence as that which most faithfully represents our subjective stream ("the thought translated by the sentence is an indivisible moment, and . . . the ideas corresponding to each of the words are simply the images or concepts which would arise in the mind *if* the thinking halted; but it does not halt"), and points up the politics involved in it.[74] Stressing sound communication as against logical sequence-making, he argues:

The words may then have been well chosen, they will not convey the whole of what we wish to make them say if we do not succeed by the rhythm, by the punctuation, by the relative lengths of the sentences and parts of the sentences, by a particular dancing of the sentence, in making the reader's mind, continually guided by a series of nascent movements, describe a curve of thought and feeling analogous to that we ourselves describe. . . . The truth is that the writer's art consists above everything in making us forget that he is using words. The harmony he seeks is a certain correspondence between the comings and goings of his mind and the phrasing of his speech, a correspondence so perfect that the waves of his thought, borne by the sentence, stir us sympathetically, and the words taken individually no longer count: there is nothing left but the flow of meaning which runs through the words, nothing but two minds which, without intermediary, seem to vibrate directly in unison with one another.[75]

In this passage Bergson alleges that diction (the "well chosen" word) is unimportant and that the artist must be intent on the vital sentence, what he refers to in *Matter and Memory* as "the living reality of the word."[76] An epigrammatic statement in one of Frost's early notebooks suggests his debt to Bergson (and James) on this matter: "Something in the sentence that is more effective than any chosen word" (*IMO* 220). Frost's contention that "we must make a sound of voices to each other and we will" sounds much like Bergson's expression of the need to communicate "into the soul of another." The ability to identify with someone else through the rhythms of speech (they "stir us sympathetically") becomes, then, the test of a writer's effectiveness and proof of his or her ethical nature, as those rhythms relate to "moral feelings," which show us "the need of helping our fellow-men and of alleviating their suffering."[77]

Frost explicitly attributes his sense of the structure of the sentence in writing to Bergson in one of his English notebooks: "Bergson's is a literary philosophy because it uses for everything the idea of every sentence being a fresh start not a sure logical derivation from the last sentence" (*IMO* 219). By this he means that every sentence that bears a striking "sound of sense" stands separate and apart from the rational intellect ("logical derivation"), that the finest sentences do not build on each other in exposition, but "spring away from each other and talk to each other like repartee": "I sometimes doubt if I value meaning except as it th[r]ows the sentences into group relations[,] like the characters in a play, and makes them act up with spirit" (*PJ* 14–15). Throughout his early notebook writings on "the sound of sense" Frost harps on the connection between his aesthetic and the human spirit: "The sentence form almost seems the soul of a certain set of words"; "The mind or spirit is not really active unless it is finding constantly new tones of voice"; "The imagination of the ear flags first[,] as the spirit dies down in writing. It is the part of expression nearest the spirit" (*IMO* 220, 222; *PJ* 132). Yet another entry refers to "the sound of sense" as the "essential sentence," a phrase signaling his belief that intonation contours communicate our deepest thoughts and feelings, our essential (inalienable) self (*IMO* 223).

As Frost finds, when the artist attends to "the sound of sense," he or she is able to get back in touch with what Bergson terms the "fundamental self," and, therefore, is free, as we are not in our daily lives, since our thought is determined by the abstract concepts through which we represent our reality.[78] In *Time and Free Will* Bergson attests: "As a result of our habitual neglect of real duration, we become less 'vital' beings who are free and constantly developing, and more like mechanical entities that are determined and remain perpetually the same."[79] In *Creative Evolution* he extends these remarks, locating our "personality," or "character," which is always changing and growing, in duration, and arguing that "the act which bears the mark of our personality is truly free":

> What are we, in fact, what is our *character*, if not the condensation of the history that we have lived from our birth—nay, even before our birth, since we bring with us prenatal dispositions? Doubtless we think with only a small part of our past, but it is with our entire past, including the original bent of our soul, that we desire, will and act. Our past, then, is made manifest to us in its impulse; it is felt in the form of tendency, although a small part of it only is known in the form of idea.[80]

In *The Principles of Psychology* James makes a similar point: "It could only be a blunder if the notion of personality meant something essentially different from anything to be found in the mental procession. . . . There are no marks of personality to be gathered *aliunde*, and then found lacking in the train of thought."[81] Under the influence of these remarks, Frost calls the sentence without a striking "sound of sense" "characterless" (*IMO* 222). Indeed, he goes so far as to call "sentence-sounds" "marks of personality"—the same phrase we find in Bergson and James.[82] Further linking speech rhythm to the concept of free will, Frost contends: "There is something in the living sentence (in the shape of it) that is more important than any chosen word. And it's something you can only achieve when going free" (*SL* 217). In his essay "The Figure a Poem Makes" (1939) Frost expresses more generally his interest in keeping "the freedom of my material—the condition of body and mind now and then to summons aptly from the vast chaos of all I have lived through" (*CPPP* 778). That "vast chaos" stands for what James calls "the free water of consciousness," and the ability to gain access to it signifies the degree of our personal freedom, "the measure of [our] liberty."[83]

Frost also looks to another of James's philosophical inquiries to help stamp his theory of "the sound of sense" as avowedly anti-deterministic. In

The Will to Believe James states that there are "cases where a fact cannot come at all unless a preliminary faith exists in its coming," that *"faith in a fact can help create the fact."*[84] Frost draws on this notion when he discusses belief both in religion and in literary composition: "Believing in God you believe the future in[,] believe it into existence. Belief is the end of the sentence more felt than seen—the end of the paragraph[,] the end of the chapter[.] There is no end so final[,] no form so closed that it hasn't an unclosed place that opens into further form" (*PJ* 80). In "Education by Poetry" (1930) he again mentions literary belief—"that believing the thing into existence, saying as you go more than you even hoped you were going to be able to say, and coming with surprise to an end that you foreknew only with some sort of emotion"—in conjunction with religious belief ("the relationship we enter into with God to believe the future in—to believe the hereafter in") (*CPPP* 727–28). As Frost concludes, tone of voice permits you to say more than you could say through language alone, and allows the reader to anticipate the conclusion of the sentence (and other, larger segments of prose composition) through a feeling of tendency. Frost's claim that "There is no end so final[,] no form so closed that it hasn't an unclosed place that opens into further form" contests a deterministic view of the universe, insisting as it does that there is no such thing as a fully closed form, that we operate according to the belief that the world is open and, therefore, allows for freedom of human action within it. The pragmatist, James says, turns away from "closed systems" and toward "action" and "power," convinced that "The actual universe is a thing wide open, but rationalism makes systems, and systems must be closed."[85] Frost's aesthetic is pragmatist, then, insofar as human speech rhythm (what Frost calls "the ACTION of the voice") repudiates the rational intellect and its system-building and promotes the ethics of individual agency (*RFW* 143).

Frost's view that the writer is not an originator but an imitator of these "sounds of sense" further adheres to the politics of pragmatism in its embrace of a radical empiricism. In statements of his poetics Frost proclaims the supremacy of the "reproductive imagination," asserting that a writer's "sounds of sense" must have "root in experience" (*IMO* 225; *RFPP* 262–63). In a letter to John Bartlett (February 1914), Frost claims that "A man is all a writer if *all* his words are strung on definite recognizable sentence sounds," and a few lines later he expounds, "A word about recognition: In literature it is our business to give people the thing that will make them say, 'Oh yes I know what you mean.' It is never to tell them something they dont know, but something they know and hadnt thought of saying. It must be something they recognize" (*SL* 111). In "The Stream of

Thought" James describes the pleasure that accompanies such a sensation: "Again, what is the strange difference between an experience tasted for the first time and the same experience recognized as familiar, as having been enjoyed before, though we cannot name it or say where and when? A tune, an odor, a flavor sometimes carry this inarticulate feeling of their familiarity so deep into our consciousness that we are fairly shaken by its mysterious emotional power."[86] When we "recognize" something, we call up a "fringe of felt familiarity" rather than a particular instance from our past sensible experience, entering into what Frost calls "the stream of time" in his epithalamium "The Master Speed" (*CPPP* 273).[87] In the second chapter of *Matter and Memory* ("Of the Recognition of Images. Memory and the Brain"), Bergson likewise insists that man's ability to "call up the past in the form of an image" constitutes immediate experience or conscious existence, as through memory we prolong the past into the present.[88] Like Bergson (or, more accurately, Bergson's translator), Frost uses the verb "call up" to describe the activity of retrieving these images from our sensory stream, explaining that the poet's job consists of "calling up with the imagination, and recognizing, the images of sound" (*RFPP* 263).

Behind Bergson and James stand the evolutionists Charles Darwin and Herbert Spencer, both of whom demonstrate for Frost the reproductive imagination as it relates to the arts of music and poetry. In *The Expression of the Emotions in Man and Animals* (1872) Darwin argues that music has its source in emotional speech, in particular the courtship utterances of "the early progenitors of man."[89] Although largely in agreement with Darwin on the matter of the primitive standing of tone, Spencer asserts that "music has its germs in the sounds which the voice emits under excitement," not exclusively amatory sounds: "That certain tones of voice and cadences having some likeness of nature are spontaneously used to express grief, others to express joy, others to express affection, and others to express triumph or martial ardour, is undeniable. . . . The whole body of these vocal manifestations of emotion form the root of music."[90] In "The Philosophy of Style" (1852) Spencer discusses the importance of tones of voice ("the natural utterances of excitement") to poetic composition in a way that Frost would have admired: "As the musical composer catches the cadences in which our feelings of joy and sympathy, grief and despair, vent themselves, and out of these germs evolves melodies suggesting higher phases of these feelings; so the poet develops from the typical expressions in which men utter passion and sentiment, those choice forms of verbal combination in which concentrated passion and sentiment may be fitly presented."[91] Indeed, Spencer's articulation of the nature and effect of intonation predicts Frost's:

All speech is compounded of two elements: the words and the tones in which they are uttered—the signs of ideas and the signs of feelings. While certain articulations express the thought, certain modulations express the more or less of pain or pleasure which the thought gives. Using the word *cadence* in an unusually extended sense, as comprehending all variations of voice, we may say that *cadence is the commentary of the emotions upon the propositions of the intellect*. This duality of spoken language, though not formally recognized, is recognized in practice by every one; and every one knows that very often more weight attaches to the tones than to the words. Daily experience supplies cases in which the same sentence of disapproval will be understood as meaning little or meaning much, according to the vocal inflections which accompany it; and daily experience supplies still more striking cases in which words and tones are in direct contradiction—the first expressing consent, while the last expresses reluctance; and the last being believed rather than the first.[92]

Considering those "forms of speech" that arise from "mental excitement," Spencer sets down the following examples of what Frost later will call "sentence sounds": "'Out with him!' 'Away with him!' are the cries of angry citizens at a disturbed meeting. A voyager, describing a terrible storm he had witnessed, would rise to some such climax as: 'Crack, went the ropes, and down came the mast.' Astonishment may be heard expressed in the phrase, 'Never was there such a sight!'"[93] Spencer's view that such speech rhythms also "excit[e] our sympathy" locates their political value as well, with our ability to partake of the emotional state of another through tone leading us "to behave justly and kindly to one another."[94] As Robert Faggen has shown, Frost's belief in "the primacy of voice" reflects the Darwinian empiricist notion that "poetry is the recovery of primordial 'sound'" and that poetry constitutes "a 'reproductive' act of biological inheritance," and I would add that that empiricist notion—and its literary significance—also is indebted to Frost's political readings of Spencer, Bergson, and James.[95]

The empiricist core of Frost's poetics is, then, not politically neutral; rather, it rises both out of Frost's liberalism and out of his class and gender politics—a politics consistent with that of other male modernists. As Patricia Rae has observed, both T. E. Hulme and Wallace Stevens "share a need to represent poetry-making as good, honest, hard work: a laborious, painstaking activity and something of genuine use in the world."[96] Distressed by feminizing conceptions of poetry, each insists that it is the engagement with real experience as a poet that makes him a man. Like Hulme, Stevens sees that James shared his anxiety about preserving his virility: in *Pragmatism*

James counterposes the "tender-minded" intellectualist to the empirically minded "Rocky-mountain tough," and in *The Will to Believe* he contrasts the "feminine-mystical" mind with a tougher kind of mind that resists metaphysical thinking.[97] Frost similarly seeks to assert his working-class manliness in his focus on his engagement with "actuality," and insists in "Mowing" that the cultivation of "the sound of sense" is hard work ("No easy gold at the hand of fay or elf") (*SL* 159). The poet who would try to harness tones of voice, Frost maintains, is in a virile "fight" to the finish "against the people who want him to write in a special language that has gradually separated from spoken language" (*SL* 141).[98]

Frost's theory of tone in poetry reflects not only a culturally coded empiricism but also an ethics of personal and political sovereignty. Frank Lentricchia has said that James "began to know his philosophy as pragmatism only after he found the political terminus of his thought in his anti-imperialist activism at the turn of the century," and we might say that Frost, though not the activist that James becomes, began to know his theory of form as pragmatist only after his immersion in the progressive politics of the early modernist period.[99] Frost would have been keenly aware of the resonance of pragmatism in contemporaneous political debates, too, not least through his dealings with Hulme, who reflected on Bergson's relation to political theory in his article entitled "Mr. Balfour, Bergson, and Politics" published in *New Age* on November 9, 1911, the day after Arthur Balfour, British prime minister from 1902–05, resigned as leader of the Tories in the House of Commons. There Hulme takes exception with Balfour's co-optation of Bergson in an article that appeared the previous month in the *Hibbert Journal* as well as with a *Nation* article that criticized Balfour's analysis from a liberal democratic point of view, and he is prompted to speak out against any political reading of that philosopher: "Bergson no more stands for Democracy than he stands for paper-bag cookery. . . . The fact is, of course, that while Bergson has in reality no connection with politics, the various sects can restate their positions in terms of his vocabulary."[100] Notwithstanding Hulme's dismissal of the link between Bergson and politics, Frost, along with others of his day, sought to state his aesthetic in terms of Bergson's (and James's) vocabulary with the intent of promoting the democratic ideology behind it. In this way, Frost is able to propound his political belief in the dignity and value of the individual that flows from an appreciation of the "rhythms of life at the centre of our minds" and, at the same time, secure the scientific backing that will help him achieve literary success.[101]

All the while that Frost had his ear to these philosophical currents, he followed closely the ideological evolution of imagism—what he called "the new Movement" in poetry—and plotted his theory with it in mind (*CPPP* 734). Critics have noted a relation, arguing that his aesthetic stands in contradistinction to ascendant imagist ideology, that, as John Sears states, Frost develops his theory of "the sound of sense" "to resist the Imagist definition of his work."[102] Robert Kern also finds that Frost's is a "counter-theory"—one that "evolved as a deliberate, even defensive, reaction against imagism."[103] Both base their claims on the fact that, whereas Pound stresses the visual imagination, Frost dwells on the "audile (audial) imagination" (*SL* 80). More recently, Katherine Kearns insists that Frost was engaged in a "repudiation of imagism, with its attention to and valorization of the visual," a statement that is correct to a point, but, ultimately, fails to account for the central tenets of imagism and the political value inherent in them.[104] Distinctions between Frost and the imagists, which Frost himself tends to emphasize later in his career, obscure similarities that he strives to accentuate in London, fully aware of the advantages to be obtained by doing so. In his essay Kern ultimately hints at the possibility of a correlation between Frost's theory of form and imagist creed, retreating from his earlier claim when he surmises that "we may be justified in saying that Frost is not opposing imagism so much as attempting to redefine it, to extend its limits," that he "seems to be insisting, in spite of himself, on his own involvement in modernism."[105] However, if we trace the unfolding of the concept of "the sound of sense" over time, we find that Frost is not so much attempting to redefine imagism as he is embracing the critical positions that define that movement—positions that reflect his political inclinations. Moreover, Frost does not try to link his theory to modernism "in spite of himself," as Kern suggests; instead, his is a canny attempt to credential his formalism as avant-garde in a quest to gain critical favor, no matter his later disparagement of that experimentalism.

The three figures Ford Madox Ford, T. E. Hulme, and Ezra Pound—all of them central to the history of imagism in the light of which Frost's theory of "the sound of sense" takes shape—loom large through these years. In mid-1912, Pound announced the formation of the imagist movement, and Ford (who at this time went by the surname Hueffer) began theorizing impressionism. Pound introduced Frost to Ford, who was able to state in his 1914 review of *North of Boston* that "I have the privilege of knowing Mr. Frost quite well."[106] Although in a late interview Frost, having fallen out with Pound, gave Frank Flint primary credit for imagism, in a 1934 letter to his daughter Lesley he confided that "Ezra Pound was the Prime Mover in the Movement and must always have the credit for whats in it" (*CPPP* 734).[107] As a result of his recognition of Pound's position in the vanguard, Frost watches with care his polemics, responding to them as to a bellwether. While debate has raged over whether Ford or Hulme deserves more credit for the ideas that shape imagism, Michael Levenson has shown the impact of both figures on Pound. By untangling the complex history of that movement, he allows us to see that "English modernism divided between Fordian and Hulmean principles," that it consists of two phases: "The first, up to the compilation of the anthology [*Des Imagistes* in the summer of 1913] and before Pound's swerving to the plastic arts, was characterized by the predominant influence of Ford. The second [Hulmean] phase . . . dates roughly from the beginning of 1914 and involved the *rewriting* of Imagism in line with new aesthetic commitments."[108] Frost's theorizing of "the sound of sense" spans these two phases, and his evolving rhetoric reflects the aesthetic commitments (and politics) of both.

We will begin with the first—the Fordian (or impressionist) phase of imagism—as it imprints Frost's aesthetic. Of Ford, Pound wrote in 1914: "I find him significant and revolutionary because of his insistence upon clarity and precision, upon the prose tradition; in brief, upon efficient writing—even in verse."[109] Pound acknowledges his debt often, claiming that Ford defends "direct speech and vivid impression," believes that "poetry should be written at least as well as prose," and pronounces "the importance of good writing as opposed to the opalescent word, the rhetorical tradition" (*EPPP* 1:209, 245, 244). Literature is to be cleansed of superfluous language and made to represent in clear outline the object of study. The first and second tenets of imagism, broadcast by Pound in March 1913, are informed by these principles: "Direct treatment of the 'thing,' whether subjective or objective"; "To use absolutely no word that does not contribute to the presentation" (*EPPP* 1:119). Pound states later in the most succinct of terms: "The 'image' is the furthest possible remove from rhetoric" (*EPPP* 1:276). Frost reveals an identical point of view, and in a letter (November 1913) to Sidney Cox, thunders, "You do right to damn grammar: you might be excused if you damned rhetoric and in fact everything else in and out of books but the spirit, which is good because it is the only good that we can't talk or write or even think about" (*SL* 99). To students at the Browne and Nichols School in 1915, he presses the attack: "Get the stuff of life into the technique of your writing. That's the only escape from dry rhetoric" (*CPPP* 688). By "the stuff of life" Frost means those tones of voice that are not ensconced already in literature.

Frost made clear his anti-rhetorical critical perspective to Pound, who in a letter of reply affirmed Frost's negative judgment of a contemporary imagist poet: "As for your remarks about J. G. F. [John Gould Fletcher], I agree. Free verse is of use to 'cut out the slush', to get rid of rhetoric etc. etc. If it dont, it is of no more value than ten quarts of the poluphloisbios element, or anglice, than a fahrt in a gale of wind."[110] In 1934, Frost refers to this exchange with Pound and the issues at stake: "One of the first things Pound thought of was that rhyme and meter made you use too many words and even subsidiary ideas for the sake of coming out even. He and his friends Flint H. D. and Aldington used to play a game of rewriting each others poems to see if they couldnt reduce the number of words. Pound once wrote to me that John Gould Fletcher failed as a free verse writer because he failed to understand the purpose of free verse, which was, namely, to be less free, not more free, with the verbiage" (*CPPP* 734). Frost writes in meter and often uses rhyme, but he agrees with Pound that the artist must forswear "decorative vocabulary" in favor of clear and direct speech (*EPPP* 1:120): "Suppose we write poetry as we make a dynamo without ornament well only the great poetry can be written that way" (*IMO* 224). Although Kern contends that Frost does not subscribe to "the imagist avoidance of 'rhetoric,'" instead evincing "a conscious indulgence in rhetoric, understood as the careful fashioning (or capturing and preserving) of speech-sounds," nothing could be further from the truth.[111]

Both Ford and Pound associate clarity and precision with the prose tradition, and Ford is led to link *North of Boston* to that tradition by virtue of those qualities: "Mr. Frost's verse is so queer, so harsh, so unmusical, that the most prosaic of readers need not . . . be frightened away."[112] In an essay on the new poetry Ford states that poets "should have insisted on capturing prose for themselves at the start," and he clearly sees Frost as a poet who does.[113] Ford's high opinion of the poetry of Christina Rossetti, Walter de la Mare, and Robert Browning is based on "the prose qualities" of their work. It is telling that Frost praises the work of all three poets. In 1913, he names de la Mare's "The Listeners" "the best poem since the century came in" and the following year hails him as "greatest of living poets" (*SL* 104, 132). He also commends "the sentence sounds" in Rossetti's poem "Uphill" and in Browning's dramatic monologues (*PJ* 116).[114] Like Ford, Edward Thomas relates Frost's poetry to the prose tradition, stating in one of his reviews of *North of Boston* that "Decoration has been forgotten" and in another that "There are moments when the plain language and lack of violence make the unaffected verse look like prose, except that the sentences, if spoken aloud, are most felicitously true in rhythm to the emotion" (*IMO* 191; *CR* 15). Frost shares the sense that prose presents a model of limpidity, believing that "A poem ought *at least* be as good as the prose it might have been."[115] His position is indistinguishable from that of Pound, who says under Ford's influence: "Don't think any intelligent person is going to be deceived when you try to shirk all the difficulties of the unspeakably difficult art of good prose by chopping your composition into line lengths."[116]

Ford's insistence on the prose tradition—his view that the poet should use "such language as he ordinarily uses," that literary jargon and inversions of phrase should be abolished—profoundly affects Pound's and, in turn, Frost's democratic poetics.[117] Pound vents his displeasure with the convoluted syntax of Victorian verse, exhorting in a letter to Harriet Monroe: "Objectivity and again objectivity . . . no hind-side-beforeness, no straddled adjectives . . . no Tennysonianness of speech; nothing—nothing, that you couldn't, in some circumstance, in the stress of some emotion actually say."[118] In "The Serious Artist" (1913) he notes the virtue of "clarity" in writing attainable through "syntactical simplicity" (*EPPP* 1:199). This interest in the rhythms of natural speech is precisely what Frost seeks to promote through his artistic method. Not only should poetic diction be "unliterary"; "the sounds of sense" should be as well, as Frost tells a friend to be on the watch for tones that are "not bookish," but "caught fresh from the mouths of people" (*SL* 113). Here we find Frost taking to heart Ford's caution: "LITERARY! LITERARY! Now that is the last thing that verse should ever be, for the moment a medium becomes literary it is remote from the life of the people, it is dulled, languishing, moribund, and at last dead."[119] Unmistakable here is the rigorous insistence on poetry as a vital democratic enterprise, a critical perspective far different from the cultural elitism associated with high modernism.

Although Frost claims to focus on "ear images," as opposed to visual images, he further aligns his aesthetic with the anti-rhetorical bias of imagist doctrine by co-opting the ideology of precision. As we have seen, in his notebook Frost directs: "Seek first in poetry concrete images of sound—concrete tone images" (*PJ* 119). Pound uses the same adjective "concrete" (a word with meaning to Bergson and James as well) to warn in "A Few Don'ts by an Imagiste" (March 1913) that the image in poetry must be precise, not vague: "Don't use such an expression as 'dim lands *of peace.*' It dulls the image. It mixes an abstraction with the concrete" (*EPPP* 1:120). In a letter to Bartlett (February 1914) Frost harps on the precise aspect of well-imagined "sentence sounds," using the tag "definite" four times: they are, he charges, "as definite as words." Because they are precisely rendered, Frost argues, they are not susceptible to misinterpretation: "There are tones of voice that mean more than words. Sentences may be so shaped as definitely to indicate these tones. Only when we are making sentences so shaped are we really writing" (*SL* 204). Similarly, Pound praises "the definiteness of Dante's presentation" in his imagist guidelines (*EPPP* 1:122). He also calls attention to the imagist desire to locate "the exact word," noting that "Since March 1913, Ford Madox Hueffer [Ford] has pointed out that Wordsworth was so intent on the ordinary or plain word that he never thought of hunting for *le mot juste.*"[120] Frost takes exception with this notion, complaining that he lives in "an age of mere diction and word-hunting," and insists that in *North of Boston* he was intent on the ordinary or plain word: "I kept to an everyday level of diction even Wordsworth kept above" (*SL* 192, 83–84). However, while Frost expresses disinterest in *le mot juste,* he *is* interested in tonal exactitude, and, as Amy Lowell puts it in her exposition of imagism, in "produc[ing] poetry that is hard and clear, never blurred nor indefinite."[121] In a letter at the end of 1914, Frost uses yet another term that flows in part from Fordian precisionism: "We value the seeing eye already. Time we said something about the hearing ear—the ear that calls up *vivid* sentence forms" (my emphasis; *SL* 140). Once again we find Frost using the descriptive vocabulary of the imagists at the same time as he distances himself from their alleged fixation on visual criteria.

Because they place such emphasis on "the rendering of the material facts of life, without comment and in exact language," Ford praises Pound and the imagists as belonging to the "category of realists," a category in which Frost, on the strength of his theory of form, can be located.[122] Pound's essay "The Serious Artist," which Michael Levenson aptly describes as "a catechetical rendering of Ford's literary principles," defends a representational and realist position: "Good art is art that 'bears true witness,' 'art that is most precise.' And bad art is 'inaccurate art. It is art that makes false reports.'"[123] Frost implicitly agrees, claiming in 1914 that "We write of things we see and we write in accents we hear" (*SL* 141). When Frost says that a tone of voice in writing is "only there for those who have heard it previously in conversation," he insists on the realistic rendering of the "facts of the voice" (*SL* 107; *PJ* 119). He even uses the terms "reality" and "realism" in his descriptions of this prosodic feature, writing in his notebooks of his concern for "Vocal reality. . . . observation of the voice" and "Realism of the voice" (*RFW* 81; "Notebook" 148). Ford, who in 1913 states that "the business of poetry is not sentimentalism so much as the putting of certain realities in certain aspects," alludes to Frost's realism in his review of *North of Boston:* "He is not in fact a sentimentalist. Not to be a sentimentalist is to be already half-way towards being a poet."[124] Edward Garnett also lauds Frost's "fearless realism" and refers to Ford's literary program when he points out Frost's "cunning impressionism" at work in the same book.[125]

But whereas impressionism is a realism, it is also, Ford insists, a "frank expression of personality."[126] Although these two positions might seem contradictory, Levenson explains that they are compatible because for Ford realism and private perception are inextricably linked: "[T]he Impressionist, in Ford's view, is entitled, even obliged, to be personal in the presentation of reality, since there must be no pretense of a neutral body of knowledge. To render reality then *is* to manifest individuality. Since they are necessarily personal, perceptions of the real are expressions of the self."[127] Until 1914, Pound is willing to accept not only Ford's realism but also his egoism. In 1912, he observes that the poet is "the advance guard of the psychologist on the watch for new emotions"; what "the analytical geometer does for space and form, the poet does for the states of consciousness" (*EPPP* 1:75). In 1913, Pound keeps up this psychological emphasis, defining the image as "that which presents an intellectual and emotional complex in an instant of time," and explaining that he uses the term "complex" in the "technical sense employed by the newer psychologists, such as Hart" (*EPPP* 1:120). Later the same year, in "The Serious Artist," Pound states: "The arts give us our data of psychology, of man as to his interiors, as to the ration of his thought to his emotions" (*EPPP* 1:188).

Frost's belief that "the psychology of sound" underpins his aesthetic is in keeping with Pound's understanding that the visual image is produced by the thoughts and feelings of the creating artist. Although Edward Thomas states that in *North of Boston* Frost "shows us directly less of his own feelings, and more of other people's than Wordsworth did," confirming Frost's own sense that the book is more "objective" than *A Boy's Will,* it is no less "personal," if by "personal" we mean representative of a single egoistic perspective (*IMO* 191; *SL* 85). That the poet must "call up" emotive tones of voice from his stream of consciousness—that subjective, sensory stream that harbors our impressions before they are formulated into language—firmly establishes them as psychic constituents: "We summon them from Heaven knows where under excitement with the audile [audial] imagination. And unless we are in an imaginative mood it is no use trying to make them, they will not rise" (*SL* 140). While Frost does not advocate that the poet adopt a crude confessionalism—turning literature into a repository for "the last scrapings of the brain-pan"—he does embrace the artistic effects of "intimacy" and "sincerity"—the notion of the work of art as an expression of individual consciousness—and in doing so underscores the liberal political contours of his poetic theory (*CPPP* 714, *SL* 159).

In an effort to distinguish between his imagism and Pound's, Frost twists a phrase in "A Few Don'ts by an Imagiste" that speaks to the relationship between the image and the mind of the artist, but in doing so he also suggests the extent to which their aesthetic is a shared one. In his manifesto Pound observes: "The part of your poetry which strikes upon the imaginative *eye* of the reader will lose nothing by translation into a foreign tongue; that which appeals to the ear can reach only those who take it in the original" (*EPPP* 1:122). Frost assents to this view, expressing in a statement on "the sound of sense" that adequate translation is impossible when dealing with suprasegmentals: "Really to understand all that is embodied in a foreign masterpiece it must be read in the original, because while the words may be brought over, the tone cannot be" (*RFPP* 262). More to the point, though, Pound's phrase "the imaginative *eye*" generates Frost's phrase "the imaginative ear," which, while it focuses on another faculty, points in the same direction, that is, toward the consciousness of the poet. Nevertheless, in the notebook where the expression "the imaginative ear" appears, Frost takes pains to distinguish his method from that of the imagists, invoking Pound's phrase in the process: "It is the imagination of the eye we think oftenest of in connection with poetry. We remember the poet's injunction to poets to write with the eye on the object. We value poetry too much as it makes pictures. The imagination of the ear is more peculiarly poetical than the imaginative eye, since it deals with sound[,] which is what poetry is before it is sight. Write with the ear to the speaking voice" (*PJ* 119). The poet who enjoined other poets to write with their eye on the object is identified by Frost at a later date: "When Wordsworth said, 'Write with your eye on the object,' or (in another sense) it was important to visualize, he really meant something more. That something carries out what I mean by writing with your ear to the voice" (*RFPP* 262). Frost's erasure of any trace of the visual from the list of Wordsworth's aesthetic concerns proceeds from his desire to resist what he takes to be the crux of imagism—what Pound will go on to label "phanopoeia," "a casting of images upon the visual imagination."[128] For Frost, Wordsworth's charge, "Write with your eye on the object," simply smacks too much of Poundian doctrine, a point not lost on Pound, who refers to that romantic poet as a "silly old sheep with a genius, an unquestionable genius, for imagisme, for a presentation of natural detail."[129] But even as Frost tries to separate his work from Pound's poetic priorities, he reveals their striking similarity through his strict insistence on the radical subjectivism of his aesthetic.

Frost's construction of Pound's imagism as exclusively of the eye led him to remark in a lecture at Harvard in 1932 that "The imagists made the mistake of insisting on visual images only. Ezra Pound called himself an imagist on being concerned with pictorial images only."[130] Frost's charge irritated Pound, who, having been told of the remark, sent an angry letter to Frost condemning as "a deliberate damned lie" his contention that he "believed only in visual images and denied tone" and accusing him of "filling up the young on misinformation to relieve your inferiority complex"; after alluding to the assistance that he provided Frost in London twenty years earlier, Pound consigns him to "the swine class."[131] There would seem to be reason behind Pound's testiness, since he and other imagists spent much time discussing the need to attend to the sound of poetry. The third plank of the imagist credo testifies to this concern: "Compose in the sequence of the musical phrase, not in sequence of the metronome" (*EPPP* 1:119). Indeed, Pound's view that poetic cadence must be self-expressive foreshadows Frost's. Here is Pound: "I believe in an 'absolute rhythm,' a rhythm, that is, in poetry which corresponds exactly to the emotion or shade of emotion to be expressed. A man's rhythm must be interpretative, it will be, therefore, in the end, his own, uncounterfeiting, uncounterfeitable" (*EPPP* 1:60). Here is Frost: "There is the sense the words convey, and there is also an emotional quality, an interpretative quality, in the tone in which the words are uttered. To gather these, because they are significant and vital and carry through the ear an appeal of sincerity, is a main effort in poetry" (*I* 25). Indeed, Frost explicitly agrees with Pound's remark in conversation with Reginald Cook: "Ezra Pound once said that everyone has a rhythm of his own and that's what he expresses. Once you get it going you can adventure very far with it."[132]

Pound, though, did not find meter appropriate, at least not in 1913, agreeing with Ford that free verse "allows a freer play for self-expression than even narrative prose; at the same time it calls for an even greater precision in that self-expression . . . the unit of vers libre is really the conversational sentence of the author. As such it is the most intimate of means of expression"; on the other hand, "Verse which is cut to a pattern [i.e., metrical verse] must sacrifice a certain amount . . . of the personality of the writer."[133] For these reasons, Ford states in his review of *North of Boston*, "I am not suggesting that Mr. Frost should write *vers libre*; I am only saying that it seems queer that he does not."[134] Frost admitted to a friend that

"Hueffer's [Ford's] three columns in The Outlook rather bungled the technical question but on the whole I could not quarrel with it" (*SL* 129). He could not quarrel with it, because Ford's suggestion amounts to high praise: it "seems queer" that Frost writes in meter since Ford associates meter with rhetoric and free verse with self-expression. While Ford refuses to prescribe the appropriate form ("I am not suggesting that Mr. Frost should write *vers libre*"), Pound is less accepting, as Frost notes in a letter to a friend: "You will be amused to hear that Pound has taken to bullying me . . . He says I must write something much more like *vers libre* or he will let me perish of neglect. He really threatens" (*SL* 84). Only later, in 1917, does Pound relax his view (a shift that I document in my final chapter): "I think one should write vers libre only when one 'must,' that is to say, only when the 'thing' build up a rhythm more beautiful than that of set metres, or more real, or more a part of the emotion of the 'thing,' more germane, intimate, interpretative than the measure of regular accentual verse; a rhythm which discontents one with set iambic or set anapestic."[135] Frost disturbs "set iambic" with tones of voice sufficiently for Amy Lowell to feel that his "variety of blank verse was merely a step away from cadence and free verse," and, thus, more intimate a form of expression than meter without such rhythms would be.[136]

In light of these qualities, reviewers in the imagist camp were quick to point out, at least implicitly, the imagist principles underlying Frost's poetic technique. In his notice of *A Boy's Will* Flint finds that "Each poem is the complete expression of one mood, one emotion, one idea. I have tried to find in these poems what is most characteristic of Mr. Frost's poetry, and I think it is this: direct observation of the object and immediate correlation with the emotion—spontaneity, subtlety in the evocation of moods, an ear for silence" (*CR* 4). Not only does he praise Frost's "direct" treatment, that is, his refusal of rhetoric, but also his ability to produce a rhythm that is (as Pound said it should be) "more a part of the emotion of the 'thing.'" Flint's only fault-finding comes in the midst of praise: the "intrinsic merits [of the poems] are great," he states, "despite faults of diction here and there, occasional inversions, and lapses, where he has not been strong enough to bear his own simplicity of utterance. It is this simplicity which is the great charm of the book; and it is a simplicity that proceeds from a candid heart" (*CR* 3). In his review of *North of Boston* the imagist poet Richard Aldington also commends Frost's "directness of treatment," as well as his "[s]implicity of speech," although he is bothered by Frost's rhythm (what he calls "rather stumbling blank verse"), presumably because he has not taken the next step and written free verse (*IMO* 174–75).

Pound's notice of *A Boy's Will* in the *New Freewoman* (September 1913) similarly hails Frost's achievement in imagist terms: "The man has the good sense to speak naturally and to paint the thing, the thing as he sees it. And to do this is a very different matter from gunning about for the circumplectious polysyllable" (*EPPP* 1:138). His review of *North of Boston* (December 1914) points up Frost's egoistic perspective: He is "an honest writer, writing from himself, from his own knowledge and emotion." Yet, as Pound declares, he is no less a realist for his subjectivism: Frost "holds up a mirror to nature"; his "people are distinctly real. Their speech is real; he has known them. I don't want much to meet them, but I know that they exist, and what is more, that they exist as he has portrayed them." Pound also asserts that Frost's poetry stands outside the rhetorical tradition; it is a case of "sheer presentation," and the diction is "natural spoken speech" (*EPPP* 1:318–19). Like Pound, Lowell focuses on Frost's photographic realism in her appraisal of *North of Boston:* "His imagination is bounded by what he has seen, he is confined within the limits of his experience"; "The pictures, the characters, are reproduced directly from life, they are burnt into his mind as though it were a sensitive plate" (*CR* 18, 20). She also remarks on Frost's clarity of presentation: he "tells you what he has seen *exactly* as he has seen it. And in the word *exactly* lies half of his talent. The other half is a great simplicity of phrase" (*CR* 20). Her emphasis on the seen and not the heard conflicts with Frost's emphasis on "the sound of sense" and prompts him to say that in her review she "pervert[s] me a little to her theory, but never mind" (*SL* 156). He does not mind because he knows the political value of such identification and encourages it through his rhetorical posturing, even as he seeks to make certain fine distinctions.

We have proceeded as far as the advent of the second phase of imagism—what Levenson calls the "Hulmean" phase, based on the impact of Hulme's critical position as of 1913–14 on the evolution of that poetic movement. Before taking account of its effect on Frost, though, we would do well to recall Hulme's ideological development up to the time of his meeting with Frost in 1913 about his theory of form. One major reason behind Frost's attraction to Hulme was Hulme's attraction to Bergson, who significantly shapes Hulme's ideas about poetry. Under Bergson's sway, Hulme adopts a radically subjectivist aesthetic that resembles Ford's, arguing in a lecture on modern poetry (1909) that free verse allows the poet to communicate "some vague mood," that the arrangement of images enables him "to suggest and to evoke the state he feels."[137] Like Frost, Hulme is indebted to Bergson for his linguistic skepticism, which, as Herbert Schneidau notes, sets Hulme apart from Pound; as Hulme believes,

"Language only expresses the lowest common denominator of the emotions of one kind. It leaves out all the individuality of an emotion as it really exists and substitutes for it a kind of stock or type of emotion."138 In "Notes on Language and Style" (1925) Hulme expresses his "Contempt for Language" (the title of one of its sections) and his faith in the ability of the artist to conjure what Frost calls "the vital sentence": "A sentence and a worm are the most stupid animals and the most difficult to teach tricks. Tendency to crawl along; requires genius, music, to make them stand up (snake charmer)."139 In his notebook Frost sets down an analogy in his musings on "the sound of sense" that bespeaks his closeness to Hulme: "the sin I have loathed in verse free or regular[:] the rolling sonorousness of straighth[-]on sentences logey with descriptions of nature and the weather. They have the structure and charm of earthworms placed end for end" (*PJ* 16).

But by the time Frost met with Hulme, Hulme had passed beyond Bergson under the pressure of the classicism of the French conservatives Pierre Lassere and Charles Maurras and, ultimately, to the theory of aesthetic abstraction promulgated by the German philosopher Wilhelm Worringer. In January 1914, Hulme celebrates the new constructive geometric art for its refusal of the humanist bias that classicism evinces; Michael Levenson puts the distinction nicely: the classical sensibility is "representational, vital, and human-centred," while the geometric sensibility is "anti-representational, anti-vital, and anti-human."140 In his revision of imagism, Pound similarly swerves away from realism and toward abstraction. In his essay "The New Sculpture" (February 1914) he retreats from his praise of the mimetic in art of only a few months before, flatly declaring that "Realism in literature has had its run" (*EPPP* 1:222). However, this redirection does not lead Pound to abandon self-expression as a literary priority. In "As for Imagisme" (January 1915) he continues to insist that "emotion is an organiser of forms" and that "emotional force gives the image" (*EPPP* 2:9). Levenson plots the parameters of this ideological reorientation: "from 1912 onward . . . this emphasis [on egoism] was overlaid with a renewed attention to the internal structure of art, and in the nine months before the war [fall 1913–summer 1914], the outlines of an extreme formalist aesthetic were drawn."141

While Levenson argues that "when egoism converged with abstraction, when Ford converged with Hulme, they converged upon" Pound, it would be as true to say that they converged upon Frost.142 In a letter to Flint in June 1913, Frost makes plain his understanding of the new formalist imperatives: "Do you suppose you could get Hulme to listen with you some night to my theory of what would be *pure form* in poetry?" (my emphasis;

IMO 118). He uses the phrase again in his "Fourth of July" 1913 letter to Bartlett about "the sound of sense": "It is the abstract vitality of our speech. It is pure sound—pure form. One who concerns himself with it more than the subject is an artist" (*SL* 80). Frost's politically minded investment in "pure form" coincides with its explosion onto the modernist scene, including within the precincts of Bloomsbury. David Bomberg, one of the first of the new abstract artists to be given a one-man show, announces in the foreword to his exhibition catalogue (July 1914): "My object is the *construction of Pure Form*. I reject everything in painting that is not Pure Form."[143] In his essay "Modern Art III" in *New Age* (March 1914) Hulme labels Bomberg one of the "real fanatics of form," someone who "want[s] to exclude even the general emotions conveyed by abstract form, and to confine us to the appreciation of form in itself *tout pur*."[144] Pound also wields the phrase in his art criticism of the period. His essay "Edward Wadsworth, Vorticist" (August 1914) applauds that painter's "arrangements in pure form" (*EPPP* 1:273). He argues a month later in "Vorticism" that Kandinsky's notion of "pure form" in painting can be applied profitably to the writing of poetry (*EPPP* 1:279).

In January 1915, the phrase again appears—this time in another of Pound's essays on vorticism—along with the phrase "pure sound," which also marks Frost's description of "the sound of sense" ("It is pure sound— pure form"):

Energy, or emotion, expresses itself in form. Energy, whose primary manifestation is in pure form, i.e., form as distinct from likeness or association can only be expressed in painting or sculpture. . . . Energy expressing itself in pure sound, i.e., sound as distinct from articulate speech, can only be expressed in music. When an energy or emotion "presents an image," this may find adequate expression in words. . . . The verbal expression of the image may be reinforced by a suitable or cognate rhythm-form and by timbre-form. (*EPPP* 2:9)

Pound's insistence that "pure form" is only possible in painting or sculpture and "pure sound" in music is at odds with Frost's application of both phrases to his poetry.[145] Frost's calculated use of the phrase "pure form" is meant to call attention to the "abstract" quality of "the sound of sense"— that is, "form as distinct from likeness or association"; his use of the phrase "pure sound" is meant to detract from words ("verbal expression") and emphasize timbre, or the wordless rhythm of speech. In an earlier article "On Music" in *New Age* (February 15, 1912) Pound elaborates on the meaning of that phrase: "Song demands now and again passages of pure sound, of notes free from the bond of speech, and good lyric masters have given the

musicians this holiday with 'Hallelujah' and 'Alba' and 'Hey-nonny-nonny'"
(*EPPP* 1:68). Frost is interested in "notes free from the bond of speech"—
tones of voice that do not rely on the semantic meaning of words for their
emotive effect—yet insists that these notes are not a holiday from sense, but
rather are charged with sense. Gertrude Stein's writing also was labeled
"pure sound" by her critics, but "the sound of sense" is far from the "sensu-
ous music" that Stein's poetry makes when read aloud, and Frost's appropriation of that phrase represents his continuing effort to critique modernist
formalism at the same time as he aligns himself with it.[146]

Frost's linkage of "the sound of sense" to the musical arts prefigures the
importance that the fine arts begin to assume in discussions of art generally
as of about 1914, and his remark about one composer of his day further
betrays his rhetorical alignment with leading imagists. In a letter to Flint
dated December 10, 1913, he observes: "I almost overtook something about
rhythm that I am after when Liebich played Debuyssy [*sic*]" (*IMO* 154).
Pound also cites Debussy in his discussion of experimental poetic technique in "Prologomena [*sic*]" (February 1912): "I think that only after a
long struggle will poetry attain such a degree of development, of, if you
will, modernity, that it will vitally concern people who are accustomed, in
prose, to Henry James and Anatole France, in music to De Bussy [*sic*]"
(*EPPP* 1:60). In the preface to her anthology *Some Imagist Poets* (1916)
Lowell asserts that the music of Debussy serves as an "immediate proto-
type" of the modern arts, of which imagist poetry is one.[147] By suggesting
a connection between Debussy and his theory of "pure sound" in poetry,
Frost seeks to demonstrate that his method of versification also is to be
identified with "modernity," with the insurgent poetics of abstract form.

However, this was not the end of Frost's, or imagism's, evolution. Inspired largely by the nonmimetic painting and sculpture that he admired,
particularly that of Wyndham Lewis, who was determined to correct the
"passivity" of Picasso's cubism, Pound reformulates imagism in 1914: "the
new emphasis fell on energy and movement; in place of the static implications of an 'intellectual and emotional complex,' the image now appears as
a confluence of powers, 'a radiant node or cluster . . . a VORTEX, from
which, and through which, and into which, ideas are constantly rush-
ing.'"[148] Frost's rhetoric reflects this ideological reorientation as early as
April 1915, when he writes a letter to Edward Thomas praising a poem entitled "Lob" that Thomas had sent him: "I like the first half of Lob best: it offers something more like action with the different people coming in and
giving the tones of speech" (*SL* 164). The next month he advises students
that "The vital thing, then, to consider in all composition is the ACTION of

the voice,—sound-posturing gesture" (*RFW* 143). The word "ACTION"—
capitalized in the transcript of Frost's remarks to register his oral emphasis
of it—does not appear in any prior statements of "the sound of sense," despite what Richard Poirier sees as "the enormous investment in the word
everywhere in Emerson and in pragmatism generally."[149] In June 1915,
Frost uses the word again, this time in a letter to Edwin Arlington Robinson about his play, *The Porcupine*, which Frost cites as an example of "good
speaking caught alive. . . . And the action is in the speech where it should
be" (*SL* 180). In a letter to the realist writer Hamlin Garland in February
1921 about William Dean Howells's "beautiful blank verse" in *The Mother
and the Father* (1909), the term persists: "No one ever brought them [tones
of voice] more freshly to book. He recorded them equally with actions, indeed as if they were actions (and I think they are)" (*SL* 265).

Coupled with this new concentration on energy and movement, the
value of tradition assumes prominence during Pound's vorticist phase, and
that value further affects the development of Frost's aesthetic. Although
Michael Levenson argues that "Both Imagists and Vorticists shared the
hostility to an established and constraining tradition and its entrenched
dogmas, in particular the notion that certain forms have a validity sanctioned by long use," he excepts Pound, who "always remained attracted to
specific literary accomplishment of the past."[150] While Levenson is correct
to note that Pound values the tradition throughout his career, Pound's
statements of the vorticist position focus more sharply on it than ever before; as Herbert Schneidau observes: "Pound had made 'tradition' an open
campaign by helping to found the Vorticist movement. The name
'Vorticism' itself represented the fruit of his effort to conceptualize a dynamic tradition: it is an emblem of pure form created and maintained by
powerful force, and the force that Pound had most in mind was one of 'racial process,' or culture and tradition."[151] Pound announces that, as against
the futurist, "The vorticist has not this curious tic for destroying past glories. . . . We do not desire to evade comparison with the past. We prefer that
the comparison be made by some intelligent person whose idea of 'the
tradition' is not limited by the conventional taste of four or five centuries
and one continent" (*EPPP* 1:282). In the same essay ("Vorticism") he states
that the imagist tradition "is as old as the lyric, and as honourable, but until
recently, no one had named it" (*EPPP* 1:276). He reaffirms his negative assessment of futurism's categorical repudiation of the past in another article
published less than a month later: "Vorticism refuses to discard any part of
the tradition" (*EPPP* 2:14). Frost presumably draws the same distinction
between himself and the futurists to the *Atlantic Monthly*'s Ellery Sedgwick,

who reports of Frost after a conversation with him: "He does not, like the futurists, with whom he is little in sympathy, attack the parent stock of poetry, but holds with justice that the piping modern voices we have so long heard about us are simply thin echoes of sounds once great" (*SL* 176). Pound's intensified interest in the historicity of his aesthetic sets the stage, then, for Frost's promotion of the literary historical roots of his concept of "the sound of sense."

Frost's first recorded mention of the literary past as it pertains to his theory of form outside of notebooks occurs in February 1915, when he cites in a letter "the beautiful sentences in a thing like Wordsworth's To Sleep or Herrick's To Daffodils" (*SL* 151). In a May 1915 interview published in the Boston *Evening Transcript,* Frost is more expansive, charting the full diachronic dimension of his theory. He begins with a rather remarkable assertion: "do not let your readers be deceived that this is anything new"; of course, if readers had been deceived, it was Frost who had deceived them, since he implies publicly for two years that his theory is without precedent. But he now corrects that impression, naming Shakespeare, Shelley, Wordsworth, and Emerson as poets committed to representing speech rhythms in their poetry. Referring to a passage of Emerson's poem "Monadnoc," Frost claims that "in almost a particular manner, he sets forth unmistakably what I mean. . . . Understand these lines perfectly and you will understand what I mean when I call this principle 'sound-posturing' or, more literally, getting the sound of sense" (*RFPP* 260–61). As Albert Gelpi has observed, he finds "in Emerson not the precursor of free verse, as Whitman had, but the writer of sound (in both senses of the word) sentences."[152] Frost quotes from Emerson's discussion of Montaigne's sentences ("Cut these words and they would bleed; they are vascular and alive") in articulating the esteemed history of his theory: "I run into people who say: Of course you don't mean, the great Emerson you speak of, you don't mean him as a poet? And that's just what I do mean. . . . Cut these sentences and they bleed. . . . There's a way of saying every sentence that's different, though the sentences all look short and about the same. You see, they're alive to the ear, and that had something to do with my career.[153] Although Frost takes license in his rendering of Emerson, changing "words" to "sentences" ("Cut these sentences and they bleed") to reflect his own prosodic priorities, he remains true to the essence of Emerson's remark, enlarging the linguistic unit for which the poet is responsible.

In a February 1916 lecture Frost traces the genealogy of "the sound of sense" back further, rating poets relative to his theory as he goes: "Wordsworth . . . caught the sound images. And Milton, especially in 'Lycidas.'

But Shakespeare is supreme."[154] His positive view of Milton distinguishes him from Pound, who considered Milton to be a mere rhetorician, but his interest in "the tradition" is in line with Pound's. In his zeal to ground his aesthetic in the Western cultural tradition, Frost contradicts his earlier claim (January 1914) that "the sound of sense" "is not for us in any Greek or Latin poem because our ears have not been filled with the tones of Greek and Roman talk" by remarking on the importance to him of one classical and one Renaissance text: "I first heard the voice from a printed page in a Virgilian eclogue and from Hamlet" (*SL* 107).[155] By 1915, Frost is willing to credit the achievements of precursor poets, even though he insists that these poets "did not formulate the principles by which they obtained these subtle artistic effects, but accomplished it wholly unconscious of its exact importance" (*SL* 259). His readiness to grant his principle of form a literary ancestry does not mean that he is willing to give up his claim to being its principal theoretician.

But Frost passes beyond even the frame of literary history to establish his credentials in an altered modernist milieu, relating in May 1915 that "If we go back far enough we will discover that the sound of sense existed before words, that something in the voice or vocal gesture made primitive man convey a meaning to his fellow before the race developed a more elaborate and concrete symbol of communication in language" (*RFPP* 261–62). Later in the same interview Frost elaborates on the psychological dynamic of this mode of self-expression: "In primitive conditions man has not at his aid reactions by which he can quickly and easily convey ideas and emotions. Consequently, he has to think more deeply to call up the image for the communication of his meaning. It was the actuality he sought; and thinking more deeply, not in the speculative sense of science or scholarship, he carried out Carlyle's assertion that if you 'think deeply enough you think musically'" (*RFPP* 262–63). Quoting from Thomas Carlyle's chapter entitled "The Hero as Poet" in *On Heroes, Hero-Worship, and the Heroic in History* (1841), Frost echoes Victorian thought on the relation between art and primitive sentiment:

Nay all speech, even the commonest speech, has something of song in it. . . . Observe too how all passionate language does of itself become musical,—with a finer music than the mere accent; the speech of a man even in zealous anger becomes a chant, a Song. All deep things are Song. It seems somehow the very central essence of us, Song; as if all the rest were but wrappages and hulls! The primal element of us; of us, and of all things. . . . Poetry, therefore, we will call *musical Thought*. The Poet is he who *thinks* in that manner. At bottom, it turns still on power of intellect;

it is a man's sincerity and depth of vision that makes him a Poet. See deep enough, and you see musically; the heart of Nature *being* everywhere music, if you can only reach it.[156]

"The speech of a man . . . in zealous anger" taken as song matches Darwin's and Spencer's notion of the music of tone of voice, and Frost's rewriting of Carlyle ("if you 'think deeply enough you think musically'") is in accord with his rewriting of Wordsworth, with the visual faculty ("See") expunged from the record. In a letter to Walter Eaton from this same period (September 1915), Frost reasserts the primitive dimension of "the sound of sense," at the same time as he waves off all claims to originality: "I am really not so very novel—take it from me. . . . They [tones of voice] are always there—living in the cave of the mouth. They are real cave things: they were before words were. And they are as definitely things as any image of sight" (*SL* 191). When Frost says that "the sounds of sense" "are real cave things," he means both that they emanate from "the cave of the mouth" and, anthropologically speaking, that long ago they served as a mode of communication among ancestral cave dwellers, who depended on "groans and murmurs" ("um-hnm," "unh-unh," "mmm") to express their thoughts and feelings (*I* 201).

Given what we have noted already of Frost's canny responses to shifts in modernist polemic, it should come as no surprise that in 1914 an interest in the primitive assumed primary importance in English literary doctrine. Wilhelm Worringer justifies the use of primitive models in the company of abstract form and passes that idea along to his protégé, Hulme, who aligns the primitive attitude with the new geometrical art in his essay "Modern Art and Its Philosophy" (1914). However, as William Wees finds, "The Vorticists outdid Hulme in invoking the creative energies of a great, primitive, barbaric will that could produce a 'barrenness and hardness' satisfying to a primitive 'Art-instinct' and appropriate to a modern world of machine forms."[157] Pound even likens the vorticist to primitive man, noting that his capacity for "subtle and instantaneous perception" is akin to the perception that "savages and wild animals have of the necessities and dangers of the forest" (*EPPP* 2:5). In "The New Sculpture," where Pound turns away from realism and toward abstraction, he first stresses the primitivism of the vorticist: "The artist recognizes his life in the terms of the Tahiytian [*sic*] savage. His chance for existence is equal to that of the bushman. His dangers are as subtle and sudden." In the same essay he refers to these contemporary abstract artists as "heirs of the witch-doctor and the voodoo" (*EPPP* 1:222).

In part, Pound's appreciation of the primitive stems from the American Orientalist Ernest Fenollosa's notion that primitive languages are close to nature: "Poetry only does consciously what the primitive races did unconsciously."[158] Fenollosa defines the unit of the sentence, which, he believes, has been wrongly characterized by professional grammarians, in terms of the primitive: "The sentence form was forced upon primitive men by nature itself. It was not we who made it; it was a reflection of the temporal order in causation. All truth has to be expressed in sentences because all truth is the *transference of power*."[159] Contesting the notion that the sentence can be defined as the expression of a complete thought, he demonstrates that "practical completeness may be expressed by a mere interjection, as 'Hi! there!,' or 'Scat!,' or even by shaking one's fist. No sentence is needed to make one's meaning more clear."[160] In essence, he makes the same distinction between the "grammatical" sentence and the "vital" sentence that Frost makes in theorizing "the sound of sense" (*SL* 140). Of course, behind Fenollosa stands Emerson, who in his essay "The Poet" (1844) observes:

For poetry was all written before time was, and whenever we are so finely organized that we can penetrate into that region where the air is music, we hear those primal warblings and attempt to write them down, but we lose ever and anon a word or a verse and substitute something of our own, and thus miswrite the poem. The men of more delicate ear write down these cadences more faithfully, and these transcripts, though imperfect, become the songs of the nations. For nature is as truly beautiful as it is good, or as it is reasonable, and must as much appear as it must be done, or be known. Words and deeds are quite indifferent modes of the divine energy. Words are also actions, and actions are a kind of words.[161]

In Emerson's evocation of the primitive order, we note the emphasis on "action" and can trace back to it Frost's definition of poetry as "words that have become deeds" (*CPPP* 701). By virtue of intonation the sentence, too, assumes dynamic form, according to Frost: "It is the common way to think of a sentence as saying something. It must do something as well" (*IMO* 224). But as important as Emerson's thinking may have been to Frost, Frost's discussion of the primitive dimension of "the sound of sense" does not come until after the vorticist fascination with it, a change in tack that suggests his close monitoring of modernist aesthetic debates and careful navigation of those political waters.

Although Frost will go on to emphasize his estrangement from these debates (in 1931, he reports, "I started calling myself a Synecdochist when others called themselves Imagists or Vorticists"), the rhetoric of his theory of "the sound of sense" reveals that he participated vigorously in them.[162]

Even as early as 1915, he insists that "I have nothing in common with the free-verse people. There is no more distressing mistake than to assume that I have," despite the fact that many of his critical positions are inseparable from theirs, as he recognized the prestige identification with that movement could confer (*SL* 191). As Frank Lentricchia has argued, the doctrine of the image as developed by Pound and Hulme grows out of their understanding of perception as radically individualistic, and Frost is as committed to that idea.[163] Mark Richardson implicitly sets Frost's formalism against imagist creed by virtue of that subjectivism, claiming that while the doctrine of the image is "essentially anticommunitarian," Frost's aesthetic is communitarian, expressing as it does his antipathy to radical individualism, his belief that the artist should reconcile "personal 'difference' to larger social constraints and 'correspondence.'"[164] Richardson is right if we take into account the political direction in which Frost's theory of form moves; however, during his days in London, Frost is much less interested in extolling the virtues of social and metrical constraints than he is in celebrating the sanctity of the self through the formalist ethics of "the sound of sense." From the start, then, Frost's aesthetic is fully entangled in "the politics of poetry," and that fact requires that we undertake a more rigorous analysis of his poetry and the ideologies of its forms.

CHAPTER TWO

The Sense of Sound and the Silent Text

Take care of the sound and the sense will take care of itself.
—FROST TO LOUIS UNTERMEYER, 1915

Take care of the sense and the sounds will take care of themselves.
—THE DUCHESS TO ALICE IN LEWIS CARROLL'S
Alice's Adventures in Wonderland (1865)

In a letter to Frost dated July 3, 1913, Frank Flint followed up on the meeting he had had with Frost and Hulme on the subject of poetics a few days before: "I told Hulme that you had still more to say. He said he was sorry he stopped you on a point of logic, as he did, which he did because he thought you were at the end" (*IMO* 119). Although Flint does not elaborate on the nature of Hulme's objection in this letter, it is quite possible that Hulme had moved to correct, or at least dilute, one of Frost's more hyperbolic claims about "the sound of sense." Despite his tendency to exaggerate, many of Frost's critics have been only too willing to take his statements at face value, and then to read his poetry in light of his explanations of it. But what Hulme says of explicators of Bergson should sound as a warning: "Every critic explained Bergson in precisely the same phrases and the same metaphors, which were at the same time Bergson's own. No one ventured to go outside even the most trivial illustrations that Bergson himself used to elucidate his thesis."[1] As a result, Hulme finds that the pat phrases of Bergson's critics "began to have quite a hypnotic effect on me," standing in the way of a true understanding of the philosophy. Assessments of Frost's practice have had a similar "hypnotic effect," bristling as they do with the terms that Frost used to expound his theory.

Such critical accommodation means that many of Frost's aesthetic biases have gone unexamined. For instance, does his fixation on the prosodic feature of intonation account for the range of schematic design in his poetry? How do we square his denigration of graphetic cues in his critical prose with his use of them in his poetry? Is it possible—or, for that matter, desirable—to disambiguate completely poetic utterance, as Frost alleges he does? This chapter seeks answers to these questions, probing Frank Lentricchia's skeptical claim about the value of Frost's theory:

[W]e ought to reject the position because it illuminates such a very narrow range of poetic possibilities. What Frost meant when he told Sidney Cox that he was interested in the meaning that is caught from behind the door, when the words themselves are indistinguishable, is clear. But how much has he thereby opened up for poetry? Not much more, I think, than a few very broad effects. Meaning of any subtlety and depth is not available; the position is ultimately as limiting as the one that Frost censured in Tennyson.[2]

As we will see, Frost's poetry conveys meaning of both subtlety and depth, often by virtue of his imagination of "the sound of sense," despite Lentricchia's claim to the contrary, but a new approach to that poetry—and the theory on which it is founded—is necessary in order to take a full accounting of it. To begin to open up possibilities, we must explore the significance of formal patterns that he dismisses or disparages in the course of his theorizing—patterns unrelated to the mimetic reproduction of human tones of voice—and read them in the context of the literary and cultural politics to which Frost was attuned.

Like some other modernist poets' pronunciamentos, Frost's statements of his theory of "the sound of sense" do not always describe his prosody very accurately, as his revision of a chiastic sentence in Lewis Carroll's *Alice's Adventures in Wonderland* (1865) indicates.[3] In a letter to Louis Untermeyer, he sets down the axiom, "Take care of the sound and the sense will take care of itself," inverting the terms of the Duchess's charge to Alice: "Take care of the sense and the sounds will take care of themselves" (*LU* 16).[4] The Duchess's remark includes the allusive echo of the common apothegm about pence and pounds, so that pence : pounds = sense : sounds, and in a way her words are self-descriptive. The fundamental poetic trope by which if "a" sounds like "b," then "a" and "b" are metaphorically identified, depends upon lexical phonology, if not syntactic suprasegmentals (those speech rhythms that Frost's theory promotes).[5] Frost's "Take care of the sound and the sense will take care of itself" also makes a kind of sense, since if one pays attention to speech rhythm in poetic composition, one can convey emotional meaning (irony, acquiescence, doubt, etc.). But Frost's restriction of "sound" to tone of voice neglects the semantic weight of other sounds of language (those, say, on which the Duchess insists). To Sidney Cox his hyperbole reaches crescendo: "Words are only valuable in writing as they serve to indicate particular sentence sounds. I must say some things over and over. I must be a little extravagant too" (*SL* 152). Here, of course, Frost is in manifesto mode, but such exaggerated claims have real consequences: Frost's sustained detraction from meaning apart from "meaning by tone of voice" has led critics deaf to his trumped-up dicta down the rabbit hole (*SL* 204).

A sampling of critical uptakes will serve to illustrate the danger of Frost's extremism. In his review of *A Boy's Will* Lascelles Abercrombie notes that "Language *qua* language does very little here; the selection and arrangement of the substance do practically everything" (*CR* 13). While it is true that Frost often opts for an unflashy diction, it is wrong to say that language—either the meanings of words or their phonemic properties—does not amount to much in his writing; in some poems, as we will see, verbal performance is the heart of the matter. In the only book-length study of "the sound of sense," Mohan Singh Karki says of Frost's poem "The Generations of Men": "[I]t is not important what the Stark boy and girl talk about, nor there is [*sic*] much importance of the meaning of words *per se*. It is the talk as a medium in itself that reflects the sense."[6] Karki's too-literal interpretation encourages him to dismiss the semantic importance of all patterned sound except, as Frost puts it, "tones with a meaning" (*PJ* 134). Even better critics who do not take Frost literally or repeat reverentially his most biased statements rarely discuss at length prosodic features other than speech rhythm (and the counterpoint of speech rhythm and meter) in his poetry, despite in some cases recognizing that there are "vulnerable elements in the theory."[7] It is not, then, as Joseph Garrison claims, that "We do not let his theory inform our [critical] practice," but rather that it informs it too much, or at least with too little sense of its excesses and shortcomings, as Garrison's extreme notion that Frost "is a poet of the spoken word," that his "theory of poetry is a corrective, a way out of the linear bondage of typography," attests.[8]

If we examine in detail Frost's poetics of "the sentence-sound" against the prosodic performance of his poetry, it becomes clear that serious discrepancies exist. Marie Borroff has demonstrated that many of Frost's poems are shaped to a significant degree by both assonance and alliteration (what Frost dismisses as "harmonised vowels and consonants"), and, to her credit, she is one of the only critics to have remarked on the "disparity between the pronouncements of Frost the theorist and the voices of Frost the poet."9 As she finds, his slighting of these phonological patterns in his theorizing does not make sense in light of his formal practice, since "some of his most important and memorable poems are couched, in part or throughout, in a language whose conspicuous sound systems may legitimately be described, if not as Swinburnian, at least as Tennysonian."10 Borroff distinguishes between two branches of sound symbolism—"mimetic" and "systematic"—in poetic language, the former concerned "with relations between the sounds of words and the nonverbal 'realities' of experience and utterance," and the latter "with relations between or among word sounds themselves." Frost, she claims, "was as skilled at mimetic sound symbolism as he was at every other aspect of the poet's craft," and she calls attention to the device of onomatopoeia at work in his "references to the buzz saw that 'snarled and rattled' in 'Out, Out—' and the passage describing the sound of thawing ice falling to the ground, 'shattering and avalanching on the snow crust,' in 'Birches.'"11

Too much could be made, though, of such mimetic sound symbolism in Frost's poetry, since it occurs so rarely. Indeed, Frost cautions against the notion, and, in this instance, his verse for the most part bears him out:

Onamatapeia [*sic*]: God said to Adam[, "]You wait here till I drive up some of these new animals for you to name.["] So God went over into the woods[,] and pretty soon he came back driving a bear ahead of him[.] And he shouted to Adam to have a name ready to give the bear as he went by. And Adam made his mind just as blank as he could[,] so that when the bear came into his head there wouldnt be anything else there and he should get a snap result from his first impression. Well[,] the minute he got a full view of him he got it. He made the first sound that came into his mouth, "Bear." "Bear," God said, "what do you call him that for?" "Because it sound[s] the way he looks[.] Don't you think so?" And God said[, "]It doesnt yet[,] but it will when I've heard it in connection with him often enough[.] We'll let it go at that. Men will be children. Stay where you are and I'll go drive you up another." Thus was started one of the most dangerous and foolish theories in poetry. (*PJ* 122–23)

In this fable Frost dismisses the "foolish" notion that there is a constitutive relationship between a linguistic sign and an entity in the world to which it refers. Believing that "words can only 'sound like' other words, and it is thereby that they sound like nature if at all," Frost finds that the systematic aspect of sound symbolism is far more important than its mimetic aspect, even if he says so only through his poems.12

In her illustration of systematic sound symbolism, Borroff points to a passage from Frost's poem "A Leaf Treader," highlighting its phonemic patter through capitalization:

All SuMMer Long THey [the leaves] were overhead, More Lifted up Than I.
To CoMe to their final PlaCE in earTH THey had to PaSS Me by.
All SuMMer Long I THought I heard THeM THreatening under THeir breaTH.
And WHen THey CaMe it SeeMed WiTH a Will to Carry Me WiTH TheM to
   DeaTH.

Borroff classifies this passage as exhibiting the "chanting" voice, in contrast to the "speaking" voice, which is less given to segmental sound effects and which she finds exemplified in the following lines of "On a Tree Fallen Across the Road":

> The tree the tempest with a crash of wood
> Throws down in front of us is not to bar
> Our passage to our journey's end for good,
> But just to ask us who we think we are
> Insisting always on our own way so.

While it may be true that assonance and alliteration are more abundant in this passage of "A Leaf Treader," her classification by voice follows from Frost's rather reductive distinction between "intoned" (chanting) and "intonational" (speaking) poetry (*RFW* 80). The problem with subsuming all poetic effects under the rubric of tone is that many rhetorical forms that help shape meaning in Frost's verse are passed over as a result. Moreover, Borroff's compelling conclusion that poems featuring the "chanting" voice represent a "threat faced by the speaker," which "is always in some sense the threat of death, death being defined as the removal from the world, the blotting or blanking out, of a self that has left no lasting trace of its labors," while perhaps true of "A Leaf Treader" and the other lyrics she cites, is not true of all of Frost's poems with such dense verbal texturing.[13]

It would be easy enough to show that Frost's poetry features alliteration and assonance, as nearly all poetry does, but the fact that they achieve figurative force in poetry written throughout his career is remarkable in light of his theory of "the sound of sense," which so thoroughly deemphasizes that function of language. In some of Frost's poems these sound patterns come to symbolize not some mortal threat, but rather poetry as culturally defined and defining. For example, in "Bond and Free," a poem published in *Mountain Interval* (1916), Frost traces the dialectic between the two conditions of his title—conditions that bear on poetic making—in a rustling of language:

Love has earth to which she clings
With hills and circling arms about—
Wall within Wall to shut fear out.
But Thought has need of no such things,
For Thought has a pair of dauntless wings.

On snow and sand and turf, I see
Where Love has left a print trace
With straining in the world's embrace.
And such is Love and glad to be.
But Thought has shaken his ankles free.

Thought cleaves the interstellar gloom
And sits in Sirius' disc all night,
Till day makes him retrace his flight,
With smell of burning on every plume,
Back past the sun to an earthly room.

His gains in heaven are what they are.
Yet some say Love by being thrall
And simply staying possesses all
In several beauty that Thought fares far
To find fused in another star.

(*CPPP* 116–17)

Love is earth-bound; Thought is heaven-ward. Love is subject to all of the pressures of this world—clinging to it for comfort, conforming to its limits; Thought throws off the bridle, darting back and forth across those limits in his license, unafraid of the unknown. Through what Roman Jakobson calls the "poetic function" of language—the dominant, determining function of verbal art that promotes the palpability of signs—the poem points up the "bond," or likeness, between language features and symbolizes the network of formal and cultural obligations that the poet must negotiate to bring a lyric into being.[14]

Frost sent an early version of "Bond and Free" to Sidney Cox in July 1913 with two other poems—"Misgiving" and "Good Hours"—both of which are metaphorical accounts of the figure of the poet. That letter follows one sent to Cox two months before that discusses the problem of poetic vocation in a utilitarian society, as Mark Richardson nicely shows.[15] "Bond and Free" has much in common with both poems, demanding to be read as a meditation on poetry and the poetic profession. In it, Frost strives to assert his personal difference as a poet *and* to integrate into the decorums of society, just as the poem must accept the limits of language *and* achieve originality. The paradox expressed at the end of the poem—that Love's grasp is wide in its narrow circuit—is conspicuous for its phonemic sequencing, which twists the tongue that tries to sound it out, and distinctly genders the compromise that the poet must make. The draft that Frost sent to Cox does not include the final stanza, but perhaps the most telling change is that it figures both Love and Thought as female ("But thought has kicked her ankles free"), whereas the published version symbolizes Love as female and Thought as male.[16] In this way, Love more clearly represents lyric's "soft" (female) subject, which must be transformed and so made safe for the male poet in American literary culture. As Frank Lentricchia finds, "the lyric is sanctioned in modernist polemic when what is culturally branded (and denigrated) as essentially female is not done away with but married to the male principle"; in Frost's draft, Love (or traditional lyric), by partaking of masculine freedom, is made over, with "airy romantic ideality" opened up to "life-likeness" (or worldly experience).[17]

Forms of equivalence in addition to meter also shape in unmistakable ways a section of Frost's poem "Birches," which is published with "Bond and Free" in *Mountain Interval* and likewise is about the cultural construction of the "poetical" and its claims in a world of "fact." Near the beginning of the poem the speaker, who is marked as a poet, describes a wintry scene in a flurry of figurative language that boasts a high frequency of assonance and alliteration:

> They click upon themselves
> As the breeze rises, and turn many-colored
> As the stir cracks and crazes their enamel.
> Soon the sun's warmth makes them shed crystal shells
> Shattering and avalanching on the snow crust—
> Such heaps of broken glass to sweep away
> You'd think the inner dome of heaven had fallen.
> (*CPPP* 117)

Although Borroff contends that this passage features mimetic sound symbolism—the sound of ice shattering on the crusted ground mimed by the clustered phonemes /sh/ and /ch/—it is more expressive than mimetic, symbolizing a moment of heightened imagination and lyric intensity. The metaphor at the heart of the passage is as showy as the one that stamps "Bond and Free," and Frost adds more trope to the pile when he draws a visually striking image of the lasting effect of the ice storm on the trees:

> You may see their trunks arching in the woods
> Years afterwards, trailing their leaves on the ground
> Like girls on hands and knees that throw their hair
> Before them over their heads to dry in the sun.

In these four lines phonemic resonance is toned down a bit, but the language is no less "poetic." Moreover, the movement toward anapests, metrical feet in which stress is catapulted ahead of two unstressed syllables, imitates the act of hair being tossed forward in the sun; here we find not "the sound of sense," but, as Alexander Pope would have it, sound echoing sense. After issuing this simile, the speaker claims that what he has said is tangent to his purpose: "But I was going to say when Truth broke in / With all her matter-of-fact about the ice-storm." When the poem is published for the first time in the *Atlantic Monthly* in 1915, these two lines are followed by one that alludes to the special nature of the language to be used: "(Now am I free to be poetical?)" Frost's speaker takes the liberty of going on to imagine a fanciful scenario—that some boy has bent the birches low to the ground by swinging on them—and, as he does, alliteration and assonance recede. Of course, description in the lyric leading up to this parenthetical question has been intensely imaginative; indeed, it has been rich in figure and equivalence, clearly branded as a "poetical" construct. But the speaker's identification of what follows that question as the real "poetical" amounts to a redefinition of lyric in the modernist period, with the boy birch-swinger standing as a figure for masculine freedom whose "poise" points to the careful balance that the poet must strike between the romantic and the realistic. In retrospect Frost said that he prized "Birches" for its "vocality" and "ulteriority," terms that suggest both the discrepant phonologies of the two halves of the poem ("vocality") and its metaphor for contemporary poetic culture ("ulteriority") (*CPPP* 731).

In a slightly earlier poem that appears in *North of Boston,* sound symbolism figures not only the feminine "airy romantic ideality" of premodern lyric but also a dangerously unmoored political idealism at issue during World War I. "The Black Cottage" is, for the most part, unremarkable for its phonemic sequencing—that is, until we approach the end of the poem. The narrator and the minister, the latter of whom does most of the talking, reflect on an abandoned cottage, which stands both in and out of time; it is described as "a special picture" and is presented to us as an art object: "He [the minister] made as if to hold it at arm's length / Or put the leaves aside that framed it in" (*CPPP* 59). In subtle ways, Frost already is calling our attention to the aesthetic concerns of the poem ("framed") and the political issues entailed in them. The minister recalls the simplicity and innocence of the woman who once lived in the cottage and considers the nature of truth in a changing world, coming to the conclusion that "Most of the change we think we see in life / Is due to truths being in and out of favor" (*CPPP*

61). As Jonathan Barron has observed, he doubts the theological ground for the nationalist ideals in which the woman believed, the woman having sacrificed her husband in the Civil War based on her conviction in "the principle / That all men are created free and equal" as put forth by the framers of the Constitution.[18] Figuring himself as "monarch of a desert land / I could devote and dedicate forever / To the truths we keep coming back and back to," the minister gives free reign to his imagination, weaving a description of a never-never land that shimmers with assonance and alliteration:

> So desert it would have to be, so walled
> By mountain ranges half in summer snow,
> No one would covet it or think it worth
> The pains of conquering to force change on.
> Scattered oases where men dwelt, but mostly
> Sand dunes held loosely in tamarisk
> Blown over and over themselves in idleness.
> Such grains should sugar in the natal dew
> The babe born to the desert, the sand storm
> Retard mid-waste my cowering caravans
> (*CPPP* 61–62)

This phonemic patterning coincides with a highly literary language at a significant turn in the poem—the minister's mental retreat from reality to a world of his own making—and serves to critique the purely fictive domain of poetry as well as his unprincipled idealism. When the minister abruptly cuts himself off, confronted by reality, that patterning recedes momentarily. By the final line, it resumes as assonance in the repeated phoneme /o/:

> He struck the clapboards,
> Fierce heads looked out; small bodies pivoted.
> We rose to go. Sunset blazed on the windows.

These sentences are as artful as those in the minister's flight of fancy, if less obviously so, and symbolize the framing of reality by the imagination. Frost's use of parataxis—a grammatical figure to which I will return—points up the uncertainty of actuality, as no causal links appear to explain relationships to us, and assonance serves here as a sign of the masculine (modernist) poetic, which is not to be walled off, but made to act upon the things of this world.

Written in 1938, Frost's "The Silken Tent," a Shakespearean sonnet awash in "harmonised vowels and consonants," similarly encodes segmental units, and it, too, is as much about the sounds of poetry and the making of the sounds of poetry as it is about the ostensible subject (in this case, the admired woman of grace):

She is as in a field a silken tent
At midday when a sunny summer breeze
Has dried the dew and all its ropes relent,
So that in guys it gently sways at ease,
And its supporting central cedar pole,
That is its pinnacle to heavenward
And signifies the sureness of the soul,
Seems to owe naught to any single cord,
But strictly held by none, is loosely bound
By countless silken ties of love and thought
To everything on earth the compass round,
And only by one's going slightly taut
In the capriciousness of summer air
Is of the slightest bondage made aware.

(CPPP 302)

Here Frost does not try to simulate blank verse by separating rhyme pairs as Keats does in his sonnet about the sonnet ("If by Dull Rhymes"), a poem that figures rhyme as a device that shackles and, therefore, has an interest in evading the appearance of it. Rather, he uses assonance and alliteration—a fillet of internal rhyme—and closely knit rhyme pairs at the ends of lines to dramatize the fact that both the woman and the sonnet are free in their constraint. It is not until we reach the concluding lines that we are "made aware" of the "bondage," the couplet (*air : aware*) figuring the tie at its tautest. The appearance of many of the end rhymes in the poem represents the paradoxical condition of freedom in limitation, as many of the rhyme words do not look much alike, despite sounding similar (*breeze : ease; pole : soul; heavenward : cord; taut : thought*). The morphologies of these words disguise the ties that bind, supporting the conceit that shapes the entire poem. That these rhymes depend as much on the eye as the ear for their full figurative effect further conflicts with the priorities of Frost's principle of "the sound of sense."

John Hollander has suggested that in "The Silken Tent" Frost may be troping a phrase from Keats's "I Stood Tip-Toe," a poem in which he compares metrical discourse to "silken ties" ("the soft numbers in that moment spoken / Made silken ties that never may be broken.")[19] While Frost does does draw a connection between "numbers" and the "silken ties of love and thought" in his sonnet, he also imbues the poetic function of language with figurative significance. Not only is this poem "ostentatiously metaphorical," as Frost observed during a reading of it; it also vaunts an ostentatious sound structure that foregrounds its literariness.[20] Through the music of its words, the poem acts as a meditation on the gendered equipoise of lyric, with the male poet charged with knotting together love and thought (the same figures we find in "Bond and Free") in an effort to bind his beloved to the earth, which, he tells us in "Birches," is "the right place for love" (as it is, Frost claims, for poetry and the poet).

Frost's range of poetry attests to the fact that sublexical linguistic sounds carry important semantic meaning over and above the meanings generated by suprasegmental contours; it also shows the importance of verbal syntactic schemes, which often become significant figures in his poetry, notwithstanding Frost's detraction from them in his theory of form. When Frost lets Cox know of his preference for the sentence that conveys a striking intonation as opposed to the one that monotonously bears a message, he suggests that grammar is the least of his concerns: "It may take some time to make people see—they are so accustomed to look at the sentence as a grammatical cluster of words. The question is where to begin the assault on their prejudice" (*SL* 140). Of course, Frost recognizes that intonation is "entangled somehow in the syntax idiom and meaning of a sentence," but he draws attention away from grammar because he associates it with the rigid rules and regulations governing formal writing (*SL* 107). And surely he is right that to be a "precisian in syntax" is to fail to appreciate idiomatic turns of phrase that express a wealth of emotion without always being grammatically correct.[21] However, when Frost "damn[s] grammar" outright in his polemical outbursts, he shapes the course of criticism of his poetry, and it is rare to see investigations of his grammatical constructions apart from considerations of tone (*SL* 99). Even when he is not so fierce, he affects a nonchalance about the string of language (as opposed to the "string" of the "sentence-sound"), informing a group of college students: "You can be rather loose in your syntax as far as I am concerned" (*SL* 111).[22] In fact, though, Frost is anything but loose in his syntax, and his rhetoric fails to predict the figures of grammar—many of them politically charged—that inflect his verse.

Indeed, in some poems Frost purposefully distorts natural word order in an effort to mime local meaning, violating his own stated desire in a statement on "the sound of sense" "never [to] use a word or combination of words that I hadn't heard used in running speech" (*SL* 102). In "Mowing," for example, the grammatical confusion that confronts the reader in the sestet primarily represents the speaker's momentary mental turmoil, his confusion when met with a threat to his masculinity and his art (really one and the same):

> Anything more than the truth would have seemed too weak
> To the earnest love that laid the swale in rows,
> Not without feeble-pointed spikes of flowers
> (Pale orchises), and scared a bright green snake.
>
> (*CPPP* 26)

The relation between the second verb ("scared") and the subject ("earnest love") is nearly lost in this tangle of syntax. Between them lie two prepositional phrases (each occupying a full line) and the parenthetical naming of the flowers at the head of the line. The appearance of the "Pale orchises," not to mention the orderly swale and green snake, suggests that the world of fact provides aesthetic satisfactions that are real and concrete, and so preferable to fancies. Here again Frost considers the problem of being a male poet at a time when most men of letters felt that poetry—and the arts generally—had been feminized to the point of flaccidity. The choice of orchis, which derives from the Greek word for "testicle," is not accidental, showing that Frost is deeply concerned about words in themselves and the meanings they communicate.[23] (Both Katherine Kearns and Karen Kilcup mention Frost's use of the orchis in the early lyric "Rose Pogonias," where, Kilcup points out, the flowers "are at once representations of female eroticism and coded metaphors for male sexuality.")[24] It is an adherence to "truth"—the hard facts of life—that Frost suggests will allow him to resituate the profession of poetry within a masculine arena—one far removed from "lady-land," which is what the preserve of fancy is labeled in "West-Running Brook" (*CPPP* 237).

In the first stanza of "The Onset" Frost's combination of words is even less like anything he ever "*heard* used in running speech." Although he does not note the discrepancy between the form of Frost's poem and his theory of form, Richard Poirier has observed that "the syntax of the whole stanza—a long and complexly subordinated sentence—is derivatively but loudly Miltonic," and Frost's nod to Milton through his grammatical scheme amounts to a crucial layer of meaning:[25]

> Always the same when on a fated night
> At last the gathered snow lets down as white
> As may be in dark woods, and with a song
> It shall not make again all winter long
> Of hissing on the yet uncovered ground,
> I almost stumble looking up and round,
> As one who overtaken by the end
> Gives up his errand, and lets death descend
> Upon him where he is, with nothing done
> To evil, no important triumph won,
> More than if life had never been begun.
> (*CPPP* 209)

In the first half of this passage the sinuous syntax tropes the snake-like hissing of the snow on the ground, but it does more than that: it suggests the complicated twists and turns of the speaker's "errand"—a word, Poirier notes, "from the Latin *errare*—mission, error, wandering all at once"—and signifies Frost's abiding concern for etymology.[26] The grammatical subordination here (we do not reach the subject of the main clause until the sixth line) figures the subordination of the speaker to the ominous circumstances of his surroundings. At the beginning of "Directive," another quest poem, Frost similarly defers the main clause, requiring us to pick our way through a maze of prepositional phrases much as the imagined adventurer, led by a guide "Who only has at heart your getting lost," must triumph over indirection to secure salvation:

> Back out of all this now too much for us,
> Back in a time made simple by the loss
> Of detail, burned, dissolved, and broken off
> Like graveyard marble sculpture in the weather,
> There is a house that is no more a house
> Upon a farm that is no more a farm
> And in a town that is no more a town.
> (*CPPP* 341)

The past, though once as complex as the present, has been sheared to simplicity, but our way back to that past is roundabout, much as parables are: the speaker asserts at the end of the poem that not everyone will locate the grail, which is "Under a spell so the wrong ones can't find it, / So can't get saved, as Saint Mark says they mustn't" (*CPPP* 342).

In "Mending Wall" grammatical parallelism, as opposed to syntactic involution, shapes many of the speaker's statements and symbolizes the central image of the poem—two men walking along a wall, "One on a side," repairing the damage done by winter; moreover, it can be read as staging a potent political debate. The following phrases and sentences in the poem exhibit syntactic balance: "To each the boulders that have fallen to each"; "And some are loaves and some so nearly balls"; "He is all pine and I am apple orchard"; "walling in or walling out." Although Frost claims that the statement "He is all pine and I am apple orchard" is to be heard in a tone of "Idiomatic balance," presumably the tone we are to hear in the other grammatically counterpoised expressions as well, that balance is also there to be seen—a phonological as well as an inscriptional presence (*CPPP* 689). That presence also takes on political significance, as in 1945 (just after World War II and in the midst of questions about American involvement in world affairs that the war raises), Frost states, "I played exactly fair in it [the poem]. Twice I say 'Good fences make good neighbors' and twice 'Something there is—.' You can make it national or international."[27] Here the balance of utterances in the poem—two on a side—suggests Frost's political ambivalence, that is, his own uncertainty about what posture America should strike, and demonstrates his willingness to get new meanings out of his poems—and the forms of his poems—in light of changing historical circumstances.

Anaphora, a particular form of parallelism that brings metrical and syntactic frames into alignment, shapes prominently several of Frost's better-known poems, but his strategic use of it, which attests to his keen interest in "the grammatical sentence" as much more than "merely accessory" to "the vital sentence," has not received sustained critical attention. Frost almost never mentions the pattern, in part because he knows that it serves as a major prosodic form in much free verse and, as we have heard him try to persuade, "I have nothing in common with the free-verse people. There is no more distressing mistake than to assume that I have." One of his poetic parodies of *vers libre,* where he expresses his ambivalent feelings toward Pound, reveals the connection in his mind between anaphora and nonmetrical poetry:

> I am a Mede and Persian
> In my acceptance of harsh laws laid down for me
> When you said I could not read
> When you said I looked old
> When you said I was slow of wit
> I knew that you only meant
> That you could read
> That you looked young
> That you were nimble of wit . . .
>
> (*SL* 85)

Here, in the absence of meter, anaphora dominates, as Frost repeats several times at the beginnings of lines the words "When you" and "That you." He even refers to the poem as a "Whitmanism," a term that signifies Frost's recognition of Whitman's use of anaphora to structure his extensive catalogues as well as Whitman's paternal relation to Pound. But as Frost well knew, it is not just free verse poets who rely on that pattern. Huntington Brown notes in the *Princeton Encyclopedia of Poetry and Poetics* that Shakespeare was one of its most skilled practitioners, using it for purposes of eulogy, as in John of Gaunt's speech: "This royal throne of kings, this sceptred isle, / This earth of majesty, this seat of Mars, / This other Eden." Shakespeare also employs it for expressions of nostalgia, as when Richard, later in the same play, orates: "With mine own tears I wash away my balm, / With mine own hands I give away my crown, / With mine own tongue I deny my sacred state [etc.]."[28] In each of these instances, anaphora appears in the context of blank verse, but Frost looks askance at these passages: "There are the speaking passages and the rhetorical passages to choose from [in Shakespeare's work]. When I think of successful poetic drama I think of the speaking passages. They are the best of Shakespeare to me—lean, sharp sentences, with the give and take, the thread of thought and action quick, not lost in a maze of metaphor or adjective" (*I* 61). In other words, Frost says he prefers the "sentence-sounds" that the speaking passages convey as opposed to the drawn out discourse of declamation.

In the unusual instance when Frost does mention the pattern of anaphora, he strives to subordinate it to his theory of tone in poetry. Drawing a distinction between "intoned poetry" (what free verse poets write) and "intonational poetry" (what he writes), he defines the former by its linguistic recurrences:

I went to church, once (loud laughter)—this will sound funnier when I tell you that the only thing I remember is the long line of "Nows" that I counted. The repetition grew tiresome. I knew just when to expect a "Now," and I knew beforehand just what the tone was going to be. There is no objection to repetition of the right kind,—only to the mechanical repetition of the tone. It is all right to repeat, if there is something for the voice to do. (*RFW* 143)

Frost allows that anaphora, which is used in religious and devotional poetry, constitutes a legitimate prosodic form so long as there is no neglect of "the sound of sense." Although he says he does not mind that scheme ("It is all right to repeat"), his statement is hardly a ringing endorsement of it. Referring to anaphora again in the midst of a discussion of Carl Sandburg, Frost claims to know better than that poet the basis of his prosody: "Old Carl tries hard to write without form, but he has a form without knowing it. When he repeats himself, as he sometimes does, he is following a certain form, a slight form."[29] Frost defends free verse from the charge of formlessness based on its use of anaphora, but at the same time belittles that pattern ("a slight form"), remaining silent about its figurative potential.

Frost's poetry, however, demonstrates how he often allegorizes the scheme of anaphora, suggesting his sense of the symbolic relation between that prosodic feature and particular cultural forms and social performances. In his sonnet "Acquainted with the Night," Frost employs that pattern to dramatize the speaker's act of surpassing—his transcendence of the city limits—and his subsequent, if uneasy, reintegration into human society:

> I have been one acquainted with the night.
> I have walked out in rain—and back in rain.
> I have outwalked the furthest city light.
>
> I have looked down the saddest city lane.
> I have passed by the watchman on his beat
> And dropped my eyes, unwilling to explain.

I have stood still and stopped the sound of feet
When far away an interrupted cry
Came over houses from another street,

But not to call me back or say good-by;
And further still at an unearthly height
One luminary clock against the sky

Proclaimed the time was neither wrong nor right.
I have been one acquainted with the night.
                                        (*CPPP* 234)

The repetition of the first-person pronoun "I" at the beginning of seven of
the lines asserts a solitary position, and the lack of communication between
many of the lines reinforces that sense of loneliness (an effect of line-
sentence counterpointing that I will explore in the next chapter). In addition to lexical repetition, Frost relies on the repeated use of the present perfect tense, which identifies an action either as one that began in the past and
is still going on in the present or as one that is finished at the time of speaking or writing; through that ambiguous grammatical form, he hints that
the spirit that moved the speaker to transgress might not have subsided
and, consequently, that his reincorporation into society is tenuous at best.
For the most part, Frost does not arrange statements in subordinate and
main clauses in this poem, preferring instead a sequence of simple parallels,
or parataxis. Robert Alter has shown that parataxis is a formal emblem of
"the vigorous movement of biblical writing away from the stable closure of
the mythological world and toward the indeterminacy, the shifting causal
concatenations, the ambiguities of a fiction made to resemble the uncertainties of life in history."[30] In "Acquainted with the Night" parataxis represents the lack of closure that the speaker feels (his sense of alienation as
yet unresolved) and his resistance to the need to subordinate his eccentricity. The night with which he is acquainted figures the uncertainties of life in
history, with the speaker's faith in his ability to negotiate between the demands of society and the sanctity of the self shaken. In addition to anaphora, another form of repetition shapes this poem, as the final line echoes
the first: "I have been one acquainted with the night." This linguistic framing of the poem enacts its theme: an individual walks outside the frame of
polite society, under a clock that sets no schedule of human intercourse,
only to return to the fold, even if temporarily.

In "Good Hours" anaphora again appears to trope a night walker's effort to overcome social estrangement. That the poem closes the American
edition of *North of Boston,* its terminal position emphasized by being set
in italics, is a joke on Frost's part, since one of its dominant patterns—

anaphora—constitutes a "figure of repeated beginnings," even as it gestures toward his own poetic makings in a workaday world indifferent to them.³¹ In the poem we find the speaker trying to make a new beginning after a foray beyond the pale of the town:

> I had for my winter evening walk—
> No one at all with whom to talk,
> But I had the cottages in a row
> Up to their shining eyes in snow.
>
> And I thought I had the folk within:
> I had the sound of a violin;
> I had a glimpse through curtain laces
> Of youthful forms and youthful faces.
>
> I had such company outward bound.
> I went till there were no cottages found.
> I turned and repented, but coming back
> I saw no window but that was black.
>
> Over the snow my creaking feet
> Disturbed the slumbering village street
> Like profanation, by your leave,
> At ten o'clock of a winter eve.
>
> (*CPPP* 102)

As in "Acquainted with the Night," the repeated "I" points up the speaker's loneliness as well as his extreme egoism. Here, though, we find not the present perfect, but the past tense, which clearly signifies that the condition that led to transgression is not ongoing. The poem narrates the speaker's liminal standing, and in the course of the narration we sense the play between hypotaxis and parataxis, a dialectic that signifies the twin impulses to cede to and outstrip social constraints. The subordination of the first and early second stanzas denotes the speaker's (illusory) sense of connection to a larger community—that, though by himself, he is not alone ("And I thought I had the folk within"). In the lines that follow, however, we experience an aggressive paratactic style that emblematizes the same speaker's disconnection from that community upon his entrance into no man's land, despite his feeling of fellowship. Upon his decision to reintegrate into society ("I turned and repented, but . . ."), hypotaxis returns to figure stable closure as against the ambiguities and uncertainties of life. But here, too, Frost's grammatical display is ironic, since the speaker seems to chafe at the self-suppression that is a precondition for social engagement.

Two other poems by Frost that end in parataxis—in particular, anaphora—use that scheme to stage the threat of death and the attempt to fend off that threat, and in them national political meanings run just beneath the surface. The speaker of "Bereft," published in *West-Running Brook* with the note "As of about 1893," is in a panic about his vulnerability in the face of invidious forces at work in the world, and the close of the poem impresses upon us through lexical repetition that exigency:

> Something sinister in the tone
> Told me my secret must be known:
> Word I was in the house alone
> Somehow must have gotten abroad,
> Word I was in my life alone,
> Word I had no one left but God.
>
> (*CPPP* 230)

The phrasal repetition ("Word I") at the head of three of the last four lines expresses the speaker's sense that the world is closing in on him, as he cannot even break out of linguistic formation. It is not just the tone that is sinister, then, but also the grammatical figure of anaphora, which signifies the assault on the solitary victim. By dating the poem as he does, Frost harks back to the desperate time when he appealed to his future wife Elinor to leave college to be with him, and she refused. But he also may be alluding to a political moment when working-class Americans felt threatened as a result of their isolation from each other in the face of big business. As the populist platform of 1892 reads, "A vast conspiracy against mankind has been organized on two continents" (a reference to the fact that silver had been demonetized to add to the purchasing power of gold by decreasing the value of all forms of property as well as human labor), and "The urban workmen are denied the right of organization for self-protection."[32] In "November"—another poem in which anaphora is politicized—Frost describes the waste of leaves at the end of fall and our deluded sense of our own conservationist ethic through that pattern, even as he comments on the escalation of world war, a theme driven home by the date "1938" inscribed at the end of the poem in *A Witness Tree* (1942):

> Oh, we make a boast of storing,
> Of saving and of keeping,
> But only by ignoring
> The waste of moments sleeping,
> The waste of pleasure weeping,
> By denying and ignoring
> The waste of nations warring.
>
> (*CPPP* 326)

The accretion of syntactic parallels symbolizes the fact that every new day will bring with it mounting destruction, but Frost's recycling of the phrase also suggests his desire to stem the tide, to find a way around conflict. That the poem runs one line beyond the traditional scope of the sonnet is grimly ironic: Frost's superfluity points to the abundance of resources soon to be squandered by men in a world consumed by war.

Frost's attention to the figurative (and social and political) dimension of rhetorical devices apart from tone of voice also is told in his calculated use of chiasmus, or the crisscrossing of elements in a line or sentence. In the fourth and fifth lines of his early poem "Mowing," he features that figure when his speaker tries to hear what his scythe has to say: "Perhaps it was something about the heat of the sun, / Something, perhaps, about the lack of sound—" (*CPPP* 26). In these lines the pattern stands as an image of the speaker's indecision, but it also mimetically represents the visual phenomenon of the movement of the scythe through the field, each stroke mirrored in its back-stroke. Indeed, as we find, chiasmus in his poetry often serves as an emblem of physical and mental reflection. In "The Mountain" an old man says of a spring on top of a mountain, "it's warm / Compared with cold and cold compared with warm" (*CPPP* 48). Frost crosses syntax here to graph the figure of analogy, as when we compare one thing to another, we cross them in our minds. A bit earlier in the same dramatic dialogue Frost writes a line that is an instance of both chiasmus and epanalepsis (Greek, "a taking up again"), a pattern of self-enclosure in which the first and last words of a line are identical: "Hor is the township and the township's Hor." Hor is the name of the local mountain, and the old man remarks that "[t]he boundary lines [of the town] keep in so close to it" that the town is synonymous with it. Through syntactic mirroring, Frost shows that the town is so hemmed in that it cannot see beyond itself; grammar gives us a picture of that self-containment. As the old man says of his own statement "it's warm / Compared with cold and cold compared with warm," "all the fun's in how you say a thing." Beside this line in Elizabeth Sergeant's copy of his collected poems, Frost wrote: "'And the chance it gives you for tones of voice.'"[33] Although Frost is led again to "the sound of sense," much of the fun of this poem is in images for the eye as well as for the ear.

In other poems Frost also creates momentary pictures through that grammatical arrangement, which particularly lends itself to displaying the poetics of vision. In the second stanza of "Spring Pools," Frost includes a striking chiasmus that symbolizes the reflective capacity of water and of the human mind: "These flowery waters and these watery flowers" (*CPPP* 224). The pattern appears again in "For Once, Then, Something" to depict the fracture of a mirroring surface: "Water came to rebuke the too clear water" (*CPPP* 208). Here a drop of water falls, disturbing the still well water; the two reflect each other at the point of contact (Water . . . /k/ . . . to : too . . . /k/ . . . water). The rippling of the water denies revelation, and epanalepsis tropes the denial of visionary power, as syntax circles back on itself and locks out all but the already known. In addition, Frost's use in the poem of the grammatical construction "Me myself"—a personal pronoun followed immediately by a reflexive pronoun—constitutes an unwritten pun on the reflective surface of the water and the egoistic nature of the speaker. In "Two Look at Two" the line "She saw them in their field, they her in hers" reports a couple's encounter with a doe (*CPPP* 212). This mutual act of seeing—eyes looking into eyes, fields of vision crossed—is represented by the crossing of syntax (She . . . them : they . . . her); meanwhile, the title presents a case of epanalepsis, cutting a figure of reciprocal engagement. In "All Revelation" Frost inscribes the line "Eyes seeking the response of eyes," enacting yet another mutual visual event: looking down the verse line, a word finds at the other end a consoling image of itself (*CPPP* 303).

Frost finds other figurative uses for these reflective forms in poems representing social and political performances. In his lyric "Tree at My Window" chiasmus and epanalepsis graph the speaker's desire for security in a threatening world. Frank Lentricchia has observed that the poem constitutes "Frost's most self-conscious treatment of landscapes, interior and exterior. . . . Frost feels so strongly that the outer landscape is not congenial to the self: the sash, at night, must be lowered, we must stay enclosed for our own good."[34] The patterns of enclosure that shape the fetishistic renaming of the tree in the first line ("Tree at my window, window tree") signify the speaker's self-encapsulation—his social and cultural disconnection—as well as the analogical crossing at the heart of the poem, with the speaker comparing his internal disturbance to that of the wind-swept tree (*CPPP* 230). Frost's Revolutionary War poem "The Gift Outright" also contains both patterns, as the following two lines reveal: "The land was ours before we were the land's"; "Possessed by what we now no more possessed" (*CPPP* 316). In both instances, grammatical units shift in function down the verse line. As figures of containment, the schemes represent what the poem is saying: Americans once were "Possessed by" Great Britain, ostensibly renouncing that colonial power in revolution; for a long time, however, they continued to be contained by their cultural, if not political, reliance on the motherland. Frost remarked during a reading of the poem that "It all lies in the first line" ("The land was ours before we were the land's") (*I* 158). Even if we concede its undeniable phonological effect, much of the line's rhetorical flair comes from its emblematic design.

Despite Frost's adamance that intonation is his only prosodic concern ("All I care a cent for is to catch sentence tones that haven't been brought to book"), his poetry proves otherwise, revealing Frost's attention to a wealth of forms—many of which carry political weight (*SL* 191). It remains, however, to take a more careful accounting of Frost's construction of tone of voice in view of the powerful inscriptional presence of his poetry.

II

One of the problems presented by Frost's concept of intonation is his refusal to concede that, at most, a poem is a text of hints at voicing. In acknowledgement of this fact, Antony Easthope states that "Intonation can only be defined for speech, not writing, since writing can always be spoken aloud in different ways. . . . Even though punctuation and typography may help, it isn't easy to illustrate a tone-unit on the page."[35] Likewise, the linguist Dwight Bolinger asserts that "points of emphasis made so naturally by the human voice can only be suggested in writing. . . . The ordinary printed page is intonationally deprived."[36] The intensity of Frost's desire to overcome the deficit of the printed page leads him to deflect from the reality that, as John Hollander maintains, "poems are neither purely spoken utterances nor inscriptions," but straddle the two.[37] In England Frost wrote in his notebook: "You must remember that no sentence is quite on the page anyway. The sentence concept that holds the words together is supplied by the voice" (*PJ* 101). Certainly, it is fair to say that as readers we must supply a voice to words on a page, but it is extreme to say that the sentence is not on the page; indeed, it is both on and off the page, graphed on the axes of sight and sound. In another notebook entry, Frost records his conviction that "Writing must disappear as speech becomes more far reaching" (*PJ* 80). Here he imagines inscription yielding wholly to the spoken word, the page and its marks withering away in the face of an encroaching orality. His idealization of that vanishing act signifies his reluctance (in theory) to commit fully to a scripted medium, and accounts for his promotion of the ear over the eye in his principle of "the sound of sense": "The imagination of the ear is more peculiarly poetical than the imaginative eye, since it deals with sound[,] which is what poetry is before it is sight" (*PJ* 119).

Frost's habit of using the word "say" rather than "read" to characterize his oral performance of poems suggests the degree to which he seeks to override the mediation of print. Louis Untermeyer, for one, yields to Frost's authority, observing of his poetry: "Here we have speech so arranged and translated that the speaker is heard on the printed page; any reader will be led by the very kind and color of these words into reproducing the actual speech in which they are supposed to be uttered."[38] Despite such claims, no representation of speech rhythm is fully clarified on the page, as "voice" remains in writing a fictive, not a literal, construct, with a simultaneity of tones and interpretations possible in silent reading if not in public performance.

In his theorizing of "the sound of sense" Frost attempts to rule out ambiguity, asserting that intonation contours in his poetry are not susceptible to misinterpretation. In a notebook, he claims that "[t]he sentence must never leave the reader in doubt for a moment as to how the voice is to be placed in it" (*PJ* 118). To John Bartlett in 1916, he sounds even more dogmatic, once again insisting that the poet's task is to reproduce unequivocally human speech contours:

There are tones of voice that mean more than words. Sentences may be so shaped as definitely to indicate these tones. Only when we are making sentences so shaped are we really writing. And that is flat. A sentence *must* convey a meaning by tone of voice and it must be the particular meaning the writer intended. The reader must have no choice in the matter. The tone of voice and its meaning must be in black and white on the page. (*SL* 204)

Referring to a line in "Home Burial," Frost brushes aside the hermeneutic issue: "I am not bothered by the question whether anyone will be able to hear or say those three words ('If—you—do!') as I mean them to be said or heard. I should say that they were sufficiently self expressive" (*SL* 130). Despite his claims, tones of voice on the page often are not "sufficiently self expressive," and, as we will see, many of Frost's poems capitalize on the undecidability of voice.

Some critics have tried to smooth over this extreme rhetoric, imagining Frost as a poet who, in his writings about "the sound of sense," appreciates tonal ambiguity; however, they can only do so by misreading him. Barbara Packer cites Frost's praise of Emerson's sentences "that may look tiresomely alike, short and with short words, yet turn out as calling for all sorts of ways of being said aloud or in the mind's ear" to support her claim that the sentences in Emerson's essays are difficult to pin down as a result of an "indeterminacy of tone"; as she believes, Frost's comment illustrates the fact that "Emerson's sentences can usually be read in more than one way."[39] In fact, though, Frost says something quite different—that all of Emerson's sentences are structured similarly and yet each demands a different, unmistakable tone of voice. Packer invokes Frost to defend "the old aural-oral world in which eloquence flourished" as opposed to "the print-centered, visually oriented world in which it languishes and dies," even though Frost is not composing primarily for oral performance, as Emerson was, or, more recently, as Vachel Lindsay and many Beat and Black Arts Movement poets often were.[40]

While most of Frost's critics have not challenged his more hyperbolic claims, which have become the basis of interpretations of his work, some artists who were his contemporaries did. Although Frost's contention that the voice on the page must and can be clearly indicated dates from his earliest writings about "the sound of sense," his vociferousness grows as he begins to distance himself from the very same modernists he had tried to keep pace with in London. Reacting against the canonization of poems such as Eliot's *The Waste Land* (1922) by the New Criticism in the academy, Frost launches an attack on poetic ambiguity with his theory of "the sound of sense" leading the charge. His contention that there is only one way to hear tone of voice in writing came under friendly fire from a fellow writer, Gamaliel Bradford, who articulated his concern in a letter in 1924:

You left me a lot to think of Sunday. . . . Among other things, I reflected a great deal upon your suggestions as to the fundamental quality of style and the importance of the acted element, that is, of the element of utterance. When, however, you come to applying all this to the art of the writer, I am not so sure that I quite follow you. It is probable that every writer hears his own composition as well as sees it. But the subtle possibilities of variation in the matter are so wide, that I can hardly feel that you are right in feeling that any one interpretation out of many can possibly be imperatively indicated. Take the Hamlet line you instance:

So I have heard, and do in part believe it.

[It is] a line, by the way, constantly quoted in my family. I can imagine half a dozen ways of reading that, and I am not at all sure which would satisfy Hamlet or Shakespeare. (*SL* 298–99)

Bradford draws a distinction between writing and speech ("utterance"), insisting that there is a difference in our ability to indicate tone of voice in these two forms of expression. He agrees that a writer may have a definite and precise intonation in mind when he sets down words on the page, but refutes the idea that that intention absolutely can control interpretation.

Bradford was not alone in criticizing Frost's position. The actress Florence Eldridge March betrayed her misgivings after Frost made similar claims during a roundtable discussion on "Poetry and Intelligibility" at a 1935 writers' conference in Colorado. Thompson recorded the encounter between March and Frost in this way:

As soon as she met Frost, she asked if he really believed there was only one way to read a good poem. Yes he did. Oh no, Mr. Frost, you must know better than that, for if that were true then all actors and actresses reading lines from Shakespeare's best plays would read them in much the same way—or at least in as nearly the same as possible. But they never do that. Instead, they demonstrate in their performances that there are many different ways to read—and to interpret—one and the same poetic passage. Frost answered pleasantly by saying that if such ambiguities occurred in any of Shakespeare's plays, the fault must lie with Shakespeare as poet. You mean, said Florence Eldridge, that you can do with words what Shakespeare didn't do? Smiling, Frost answered, yes. Not amused, Miss Eldridge abruptly turned her back on the poet and walked away.[41]

This incident illustrates Frost's perverse pleasure in antagonizing opponents; he clearly is reveling in his contrariety. But it also signifies how deeply he believes in the writer's ability to fix intonation contours definitely on the printed page and for all time ("Some doubt that such tones can long survive on paper. They'll probably last as long as the finer meanings of words") (*SL* 130). Attributing tonal indecision to imprecise writing, Frost remarked in a lecture that "if we let *playwright* represent the bad writer of plays, and dramatist the good writer of plays, the playwright was the one who had to teach the actors how to speak the lines. And the dramatist was the one who could go off and die and actors would get the tones just right."[42] However, as Henry Fielding shows in his novel *A Journey from This World to the Next* (1743) not even Shakespeare is capable of such precision, as the narrator finds him arbitrating debates in the underworld over "ambiguous passages in his works."[41]

During the panel that March attended, Frost took aim at ambiguity, which he delightedly derided in the work of his modernist peers. As Thompson reports: "When his [Frost's] turn came for making his own case for poetic intelligibility, he advanced his favorite theory: if the poet will only be careful in ordering his lines, so that they convey the sound of sense, he can make each poem completely intelligible: there will be only one correct way to read the poem, and it will be intelligible, in only that one way, to all intelligent listeners."[44] The phrase "to all intelligent listeners" resonates, asserting as it does that only those with a well-tuned ear will be able to hear what is definitely and precisely marked on the page. Frost's attempt to distance himself from the "extreme modernists," who, he says, "do not care whether their communication is intelligible to others," comes, then, with its own elitism (*I* 80).

Although he suggests that he is led to his extreme position that tone of voice in writing is unambiguous as a result of his displeasure with modernist disjunctive poetics—with the prevailing poetry of obscurity and obfuscation—the oral emphasis of his poetics is perfectly consistent with that in modernist aesthetics generally. We already have taken account of the imagist concern for spoken speech, perhaps most forcefully stated by Amy Lowell: "Poetry is a spoken and not a written art."[45] Furthermore, Mark Morrisson has revealed the relationship between elocution, verse recitation, and modernist poetry in prewar London, illustrating the privileging of "the oral over the visual, the pure voice over the 'artificiality' of music-hall spectacle and poetry written 'for the page,'" and it is telling that Frost's first London literary outing is to the opening of Harold Monro's Poetry Bookshop, which was created as "a center for the oral performance of poetry by poets" and where Frost met Frank Flint.[46] Indeed, the poetic priorities that Flint propounds are identical to Frost's. For the March 1914 issue of Monro's magazine *Poetry and Drama,* Flint translated a speech by Henri Ghéon in which he praised the new practice of verse recitation preceding a play, insisting, "We read too much with our eyes."[47] Similarly, Monro, promoting the practice of verse recitation in his magazine in December 1913, laments that "Every year humanity continues to use its ears less and to trust more to its eyes."[48] For all of these modernists, the written text threatens the purity and transparency of the poet's voice, and their effort to promote what Richard Bradford has called a "phonocentric ideal of presence" is precisely what Frost seeks to promote through his theory of form.[49]

Frost's certainty that tones of voice in his poetry are unmistakably rendered illuminates his view of "authority" in writing—a view that contradicts the findings of poststructuralist theorists such as Foucault and Derrida, who pronounce on the absence of the author in print. As Foucault believes, "To give a text an Author is to impose a limit on the text, to furnish it with a final signified, to close the writing."[50] Frost tries to impose just such a limit on his poetic texts when he asserts his ability as author to control meanings through the modulation of tone of voice. Derrida, too, strenuously questions whether authorial "intention" "is able to govern the entire scene and system of utterance," determining that it is not.[51] In his critique of the second half of Plato's dialogue *Phaedrus,* in which Socrates condemns writing and praises direct speech, Derrida argues that the notion that writing is in all cases inferior to oral communication—what he believes to be a general tendency of Western philosophy—because it is less direct, less comprehensible, and less ambiguous denies the fact that no mode of communication is free from misinterpretation, ambiguity, and appropriation by another person independent of its author's intentions. As he insists, all the problems that Plato identifies for writing apply to speech as well, but Frost sees it differently (or so he says), arguing the priority of speech (what Phaedrus terms "the living, breathing discourse of the man who knows") over writing (seen merely as a system of alien, arbitrary, lifeless signs).[52] To Derrida's claim that "Writing can never be totally inhabited by the voice," Frost would reply that, in fact, it can be, and it is only when writing is so inhabited that the absence of writing is transformed into an authentic living presence.[53] Although Frost at one level cherishes ambiguity and even hints outside of his theorizing that there are limits to an author's ability to legislate meaning ("The poet is entitled to all the meanings the reader can find in his poem"), his statements about "the sound of sense" stand against poststructuralist accounts of the ambivalence of the inscripted voice and fully reveal his involvement in "the politics of poetry," as he works to distinguish himself from the high modernist cult of "difficulty."[54] His polemic, though, does not match his poetry, which, if not as obscurantist as some modernist writing, nonetheless resists easy interpretation, in large part as a result of tonal equivocation.

In *The Printed Voice* Eric Griffiths demonstrates that British Victorian poets "record a wide gamut of dismay about the prosodic ambiguity of the printed word," so Frost's wrestling with the problem is not unique. Ironically, as William Allingham reports, Tennyson, whom Frost dismisses with Swinburne for his lack of concern for the music of tone of voice, "spoke a good deal about the want of some . . . fixed way of indicating a poet's intention as to the pronunciation of his verses."[55] Both Tennyson and Frost desired to transcribe speech unambiguously, then, but of the two only Tennyson admitted that the printed page was not capable of securing proper voicing. Consequently, Tennyson complained that only he could read his poetry aloud correctly, while Frost insisted that anyone could read him correctly simply by listening closely to the poem on the page. Only rarely, and outside of expositions of "the sound of sense," did Frost concede the deprivations of the printed page, as he did implicitly to John Haines, who revealed, "I had a newspaper on which he [Frost] scribbled symbols indicating how it [Frost's poem 'Putting in the Seed'] should be read."[56] Such symbols are conspicuously absent from Frost's published poetry, as he refuses to score words on the page in such a way as to demonstrate the particular pitch curve of an utterance that would help to clarify the mood or emotion intended. Although he tells Cox that "diacritical marks" cannot "fix" a pronunciation, he uses them with Haines to show what the sentence unaided cannot (*SL* 108).

Despite Frost's insistence that his sentences are sufficiently self-expressive, his readers are often hard pressed to interpret intonation contours in his poetry and resort to his oral performances in order to help them do so. In explanation of the editorial policy that guides *The Poetry of Robert Frost* (1969), Edward Connery Lathem admits that he often used oral evidence based on Frost's recordings "to remove ambiguity or bafflement," citing several examples "which unpunctuated would be potentially troublesome."[57] Others were as ready to bow to Frost's utterance. After hearing Frost "say" his poems, the critic Carl Van Doren confessed: "the sound of his voice for the first time explained his poetry to me. I had, somehow, read the words as universal English, like any other poem's. But now I found that they were Yankee words and without their true intonation had never said to me half they meant."[58] Referring to Van Doren's reaction, Robert Newdick has stated that "Lesser but equally honest readers point out specific lines and passages that they have read appreciatively but not quite correctly until after hearing Frost read them either in person or in the Columbia University or Erpi phonographic recordings of his readings"; taking up a line from "Birches" ("Until he took the stiffness out of them"), he confidently asserts the proper pronunciation based on Frost's oral emphasis: "Which word in that line is properly to be stressed the more in reading it, 'stiffness' or 'out'? The correct response is 'out.'"[59] Newdick's use of the word "correct" signals his reverent attitude toward these tape recordings; for him, Frost's pronunciation of the poem is the only valid one. Of Frost's reading of a line in "Stopping by Woods on a Snowy Evening," Newdick again insists that only one cadence satisfies the textual conditions: "one instantly recognizes the rightness of his . . . tempo. . . . But even Louis Untermeyer, who regularly dwells on the poem in his most popular lectures, reads the lines without making it clear the wholly admirable differences in tempo that Frost wrote into them."[60] But Newdick wanted to have it both ways; after noting that it is impossible to read some of Frost's lines "correctly" if you have not heard Frost read them aloud, he illogically concludes, "Frost went on, in the same Norton lecture [1936], to express his conviction that the great art is to make the poem so that it cannot possibly be misread; and his thoroughgoing admirers insist that precisely this height of art is his."[61]

In an attempt to clear up ambiguities surrounding Frost's poem "Mowing," Seymour Chatman also draws on the evidence of Frost's oral performance with similarly confused results. Using Frost's reading of the poem as a control, Chatman operates according to the following dangerous premise: "The present analysis attempts to describe the verse line as it is actually 'performed.' It avoids the unfortunate assumption that performances involve 'exceptions' to some kind of norm. In fact, it suggests that the poem as document may be lifeless until it is actualized into sound pattern."[62] Here Chatman makes his own unfortunate assumption, which is to think that a poem must be orally performed in order to be actualized fully. It might be true to say this of a poem that refuses to submit to the status of fixed aesthetic object—for instance, a talk-poem by David Antin—but it is not true of Frost's verse, which appears in print without protest. In effect, Chatman, like Frost, denies that a poem is mapped in relation to the two axes of utterance and inscription. Although he claims that "the poet's reading need be no more authoritative than any other reader's," he goes on to confess that "two passages [of the poem] were clarified for me when I analysed the junctural features of Frost's performance."[63] Believing that a reader can "misinterpret a poem . . . by using an inappropriate intonation pattern," Chatman further notes that "punctuation often fails to guide the reader with any accuracy to the junctures a poet may have had in mind"; he even corrects Frost's punctuation of "Mowing" in light of his listening, suggesting that "it might have been wiser" in lines 11–12 "to encompass everything from 'not' to 'orchises' in parentheses, and to represent the apposition of 'Pale orchises' with a comma."[64] Chatman's suggestion that Frost's oral performance of the poem should take precedence over the poem on the printed page is extreme, and he fails to take into account the fact that Frost does not always read a poem in the same way. Stanley Burnshaw has noted the variability of Frost's public recitals: "[A]s any number of frequent listeners knew from his platform readings, in 'saying' his poems Frost was inconsistent as he was in other respects, sometimes racing through verses as though over-anxious to end the performance quickly."[65] Thompson, who heard Frost read on many occasions, calls attention to the same inconsistency in vocalization and even sees how that inconsistency refutes the poet's theory of form: "Frost himself provided the best disproof of his own dogmatic claims that he could rigorously control meanings by poetically arranging words so that there could only be one convincing way to hear them. His own changes of mood and attitudes often caused him to read his poems in different ways, and thus give them different meanings."[66] However, in his study of Frost's poetry entitled *Fire and Ice* (1942), Thompson never mentions the discrepancy, assenting to Frost's claim that "'There is only one way to read each word'" in well-written dialogue.[67]

Samuel Levin argues against Chatman's privileging of the poem in performance, although he agrees with him that ambiguities can be resolved in light of it. That "The very act of [oral] performance more often than not forces the reader to resolve ambiguities, to decide between alternatives" is, however, not necessarily a desirable occurrence: "One can argue that ambiguity is built into poetry, and that resolution of this ambiguity represents not a service to a poem, but a disservice."[68] In *A Survey of Modernist American Poetry* (1927) Laura Riding and Robert Graves similarly contend that the repunctuation of a piece of writing (they use a sonnet by Shakespeare as an example) can work to close down meanings, to congeal interpretation through a more precise definition of vocal contour.[69] Another critical duo, William K. Wimsatt, Jr., and Monroe C. Beardsley, signal a related caution against making too much of oral performance: "There is, of course, a sense in which the reading of the poem is primary: that is what the poem is *for*. But there is another and equally important sense in which the poem is not to be identified with any particular performance of it, or any set of such performances."[70] Of course, the oral performance of a poem should not be dismissed out-of-hand. Such vocalizations can provide important clues to a writer's understanding of the prosody on which his or her work is based. However, the ambiguity of intonation that exists in writing should not be lamented or wished away. Indeed, as Jakobson contends, "Ambiguity is an intrinsic, inalienable character of any self-focused message, briefly, a corollary feature of poetry. Let us repeat with [William] Empson: 'The machinations of ambiguity are among the very roots of poetry.'"[71] The supremacy of the poetic function over the referential function does not obliterate the reference but renders it ambiguous, and, as we will see, Frost is no more able (or willing) to escape that fate than is any other poet.

Frost's refusal to concede the limitations of the printed page in the reproduction of speech rhythms led him to ignore in his theorizing those resources available to the artist desiring to specify more clearly, if not unambiguously, such rhythms. As we have seen, Easthope points to punctuation and typography as important cues to intonation. David Crystal cites the "necessity of punctuation in writing, or other graphetic cues (such as colour or type-size), in order to avoid ambiguity."[72] J. L. Austin, noting that suprasegmental contours are "not reproducible readily in written language," also finds that "punctuation, italics, and word order may help" to convey tone of voice, cadence, and emphasis, even if they are "rather crude."[73] Even Pound credits the assistance of such cues in representing intonation on the page, observing in a self-descriptive sentence in a letter to Hubert Creekmore (1939): "ALL typographic disposition, placing of words *on* the page, is intended to facilitate the reader's intonation, whether he be reading silently to self or aloud to friends."[74] Frost's sense that the high modernists are only in the business of cultivating unintelligibility in poetry does not square with Pound's remark, which expresses his interest in communicating a tone—and poetic message—clearly to the reader.

Despite the usefulness of such hints at voicing, Frost nonchalantly dismisses them in the course of theorizing "the sound of sense." To Leonidas Payne he claims "a sort of indifference to punctuation": "I dont mean I despise it. I value it. But I seem rather willing to let other people look after it for me. One of my prides is that I can write a fifty word telegram without having to use a single 'Stop' for the sense" (*SL* 370). Here he gloats that his ability to represent intonation contours precisely does not depend on punctuation, and his letters and notebook writings attest to his occasional disregard of it. In 1951, he sounds even more fierce, telling a Dartmouth College audience: "I hate to depend on punctuation at all."75 About ten years later in an interview in *Atlantic Monthly,* Frost blusters: "You don't have to know how to punctuate at all."76 If Gertrude Stein had made these statements, her prose poetry would support them, since she uses punctuation in it sparingly. Coming from Frost, though, this disavowal is strange, since he pays such close attention to the emphatic assistance of punctuation in his verse. In his polemic he either detracts from or dismisses punctuation, because he does not want to appear to be too heavily invested in the graphic surface of a poem; his poetry is, he claims, essentially a spoken art. Although he cites punctuation as a resource of the artist in his essay "The Figure a Poem Makes" (1939), he separates it out from the other resource of "dramatic tones of meaning," failing to indicate how punctuation figures in the construction of intonation contours—how it seeks to overcome the limitations of a print culture in the very devices of writing (*CPPP* 776).

Frost suggests the constitutive relationship between punctuation and tone of voice when he revises a set of utterances at a lecture that Sidney Cox attended:

"The dog has come into the room."
"I will put the dog out."
"He will come back again."
Those are dead. These are alive:
"There's that dog."
"Out you brute!"
"Here he comes, right back."

In his report of the lecture to his mother, Cox says, "I am not sure of that last one. But I think you will observe that he is right in saying that the tone is down there in black and white."77 Here he concedes that Frost is not able to represent tone unambiguously in every case, even as he succumbs to Frost's extreme rhetoric ("the tone is down there in black and white"). That punctuation can help clarify the tone of voice intended is indisputable, however, and we find in these new and improved sentences an expressiveness lacking in the originals.

Frost himself was quite scrupulous about punctuation in his poetry; he recognized its strong rhetorical function—its ability to reduce the range of voicing possibilities—and worked with printers to assure that junctural features were scored properly. Joseph Blumenthal of the Spiral Press attests that "The act of making the book, of putting his words into the imperishability of type on paper that would go out to a critical world, could not be for Frost a routine and impersonal matter"; specifically, he reports that in going over page proofs, Frost advised that a dash be inserted into the second line of "To a Young Wretch" ("As take his gun—rod—to go hunting—fishing"), asking, "Doesn't that break it up better than a comma after rod?"[78] Of course, such a hands-on approach does not mean that Frost can banish tonal ambiguity from the written page, but it does suggest his desire to use all available rhetorical resources to carry across his meanings to his readers.

Frost's professed indifference to punctuation does not predict his practice or the controversy that erupted, and still rages, over Edward Connery Lathem's editing of *The Poetry of Robert Frost*. In 1982, Donald Hall criticized Lathem's liberal editorial policy, citing two lines from "Home Burial" that he claims are ruined as a result of undue tampering. The version in *Complete Poems* (1949) is punctuated in the following way: "What is it you see / From up there always—for I want to know."[79] Lathem's version of the same two lines reads somewhat differently: "What is it you see / From up there always?—for I want to know." Hall finds Lathem's repunctuation guilty of changing the tone of voice Frost intended:

The idiom, grammar, and pacing embody the husband's state of mind. He feels his wife estranged and he wants the sensitivity he lacks. As Frost punctuated it, the husband begins the speech as a question which he interrupts with a demand: "—for I want to know." Lathem alters and diminishes Frost's characterization of the husband by supplying the question mark. . . . Of course if a reader charges through "Home Burial" as if it were *Newsweek,* Lathem's question mark does little harm; but if the reader hears the poem in the mind's ear, then the question mark raises the pitch of "From up there always," sentence-sound is altered, and the husband's voice becomes gentler and less demanding.[80]

As this passage reveals, Hall recognizes the significance of punctuation in the reproduction of intonation in writing and the effect that that reproduction has on our construing of character. His remark about reading practices in a capitalist culture expresses his view that the language of news reportage, especially that found in mass-circulation magazines, is unremarkable for its "sounds of sense." Indeed, his invocation of "the sound of sense" in defense of his criticism of Lathem signals the extent to which Frost's theory continues to motivate. In his further analysis of "Home Burial," Hall accuses Lathem of altering the pitch of other utterances as a result of changes in punctuation, and criticizes most of the editorial changes on the grounds that they disturb Frost's carefully contrived "sentence-sounds," correctly arguing that editors "must not punctuate by performance."[81] Gerald Burns makes a similar charge, but at the same time falls under Frost's spell in defense of his position, complaining of "Lathem's hyperconservative commas, largely unnecessary in a poet who prided himself on writing lines you *couldn't* misread."[82] To assert that Lathem's editorial procedures are ill-advised does not require us to agree with Frost that tones of voice on the page are unambiguous; rather, when we see the damage that Lathem has done, we should be convinced that punctuation matters greatly in the inscription of speech cadence, regardless of Frost's statements to the contrary.

Frost's belief that suprasegmental contours in his poetry are well defined without the assistance of supplemental cues led him to rail against poets who try to clarify intonation on the printed page by means of such devices: "Some have proposed inventing a notation to make sure the tones intended[.] Some have tried to help themselves with adjectives in the margin. But the sentences themselves, whatever else they are, are a notation for indicating tones of voice" (*PJ* 134). In particular, Frost decries "Sidney Lanier's musical notation of verse" and in the second of his Charles Eliot Norton Lectures at Harvard disparages Vachel Lindsay when he says that "'One mad theorist' gives reading directions with his poems" (*RFPP* 263).[83] He again refers derisively to Lindsay's cues in a 1959 interview with Cleanth Brooks and Robert Penn Warren: "'Say this in a golden tone,' he says. You ought not to have to say that in the margin" (*I* 201). In his notebook, too, Frost is careful to distinguish his method from theirs, reverting once again to his theory of sentence form: "Poets have lamented the lack in poetry of any such notation as music has for suggesting sound. But it is there and always has been there. The sentence is the notation" (*PJ* 114).

Ironically, though, Sidney Lanier's prosodic treatise *The Science of English Verse* (1880), which Frost read in 1895, predicts Frost's interest in "the sound of sense" and his determination to control the sound of the poem. Lanier states there that tune "appeal[s] to some of the subtlest and least understood operations of the human soul," and finds, with the aid of Herbert Spencer, that "the greater part of expression is carried on by means of melodies rather than words": "every affirmation, every question, has its own peculiar tune; every emotion, every shade of emotion, has its tune; and such tunes are not mere accidents but are absolutely essential elements in fixing the precise signification of words and phrases. . . . Further still: these tunes not only affect the signification of words, but they greatly modify the meaning of the same words, so that a phrase uttered according to one tune means one thing, according to another tune another thing.[84] Lanier's view that it is "the sounds of the human speaking-voice, in which the art of verse finds its primary material" accords with Frost's concept of "the sound of sense" and its role in poetry.[85] His example of a German comedy in which the two words "Come here" are uttered in different tunes by characters in different situations could just as well be Frost's: "The play just cited shows . . . that the variations of pitch which accompany all spoken words are, in the strictest sense of the term, tunes: that they are definite successions of tones, so definite as to be remembered and reproduced by the actress (in the case given) and as to be remembered and instantly recognized by the audience: for how else would the propriety of each different tune to each different situation be discovered by the hearers, the words always remaining the same?"[86] As Jed Rasula notes, "Logocentrism prevails in Lanier's vision of written poetry as prelude to sound" (Lanier states that "Print and writing are systems of notation for the tone-colors of the human speaking-voice").[87] The same is true of Frost's vision. But, as Rasula correctly sees, Lanier's poetry does not live up to his theory: "Despite the radical implications of some of Lanier's suggestions, in his own poetry as in nearly all Victorian versifying, 'sound' is still in retainer to a sensibility mired in a soporifically melodious sense of rhythm."[88] It is this variance that leads Frost to denigrate Lanier's poetic example.

No matter what he says outside of his verse, Frost relies on graphetic cues to help define intonation contours in his poetry, even if he does eschew marginal and musical notation. William Pritchard has called attention to a line in "Stopping by Woods on a Snowy Evening" with which Lathem interferes by adding a comma after "village" that does not exist in any other publication of the poem: "Whose woods these are I think I know. / His house is in the village, though." Pritchard rightly finds that this change, though seemingly slight, alters drastically our understanding of character: "In the case of 'Stopping by Woods' the substantive change in tone introduced by the editor's emendation of a comma before 'though' . . . turns the speaker into a coyly twinkling fellow with all too much of a clever tongue lodged in his cheek. Robert Frost was more impersonal than that, and his jokes were harder to catch."[89] Donald Hall and Frank Bidart point to another unhappy change—this one to Frost's lyric "To Earthward"—that they say affects not only the rhythm of the poem, but its basic meaning. Hall reports that in the poem "there is a new comma which extends the pause at the end of a line—and which, as it happens, destroys the paralleling of syntax and therefore the sense of the stanza."[90] Frost originally wrote:

> Now no joy but lacks salt
> That is not dashed with pain
> And weariness and fault

As Hall finds of this original scripted performance, "Frost hurtles passionately from line to line, making this poem as overtly emotional as anything in his work. Feeling is diminished by Lathem's comma after 'salt'—and the sense vanishes":

> Now no joy but lacks salt,
> That is not dashed with pain
> And weariness and fault

Of the same passage Bidart states that "Suddenly 'is' becomes parallel to 'lacks,' and the lines say that every joy is 'dashed with pain.' This is not only wrong, but self-contradictory: if every joy 'lacks salt' it cannot be 'dashed with pain.'. . . . [I]n the name of textual clarity Lathem has ruined a crucial stanza."[91] Neither, however, takes the opportunity to call into question some of Frost's claims about "the sound of sense"; instead, Hall finds that Frost's boast that he can write a fifty-word telegram without punctuation signifies that "Frost admired self-reliance even in sentences."[92] As compelling as this fiction may be, it does not match prosodic facts.

Although Frost's dicta warn against inscriptional devices, then, the performance of his poetry tells a different story. In addition to his careful deployment of punctuation, Frost uses italics with some frequency to attempt to clarify intonation contours. Although John Hollander notes that "because of its conventionality, accentual-syllabic verse can do its own sort of italicizing," that it is possible to "use versification to resolve . . . syntactic ambiguities," Frost does not place full faith in the ability of meter to fix tone of voice.[93] Despite this fact, he insists in his theorizing of "the sound of sense" that italicization is a crutch—one unworthy of the true poet: "It is only as the poem and the sentence within the poem exceed statement (not fall short of it) that poetry arises. . . . One sentence must speak to another till the accents begin to single out particular words for notice[,] without italics" (*PJ* 70). In a letter to Edwin Arlington Robinson, Frost reiterates this view in praising Robinson's play *The Porcupine:* "I wonder if you agree with me that the best sentences are those that convey their own tone—that haven't to be described in italics" (*SL* 180). While these comments to Robinson could be read as the statement of an ideal, Frost's frequent use of italics in some of his best poetry (and some of his best sentences in that poetry) compromises his position, as it indicates that metrical notation alone often cannot designate the feeling behind an utterance.

As early as *A Boy's Will* Frost uses an expressive typography to make his emotional register clearer. The poem "In Neglect," which Frost told Pound was about his grandfather's disinheritance of him and his wife, features an italicized word in the final line in order to impress a sardonic tone:

> They leave us so to the way we took,
>   As two in whom they were proved mistaken,
> That we sit sometimes in the wayside nook,
> With mischievous, vagrant, seraphic look,
>   And *try* if we cannot feel forsaken.
>   (*CPPP* 25)

Although the metrical pattern places stress on *try* as a result of its position in the line, Frost feels that that emphasis is not enough; the typographical inscription of pitch makes more evident the fact that the couple in the poem are mocking those who cast them out, disdainfully imposing on themselves a feeling of dejection that the disinheritance itself could not. In "In Hardwood Groves" he again uses that type—this time to insist that unwavering principles underwrite the operations of nature. The poem records the speaker's view of falling leaves and his recognition of the necessity of that fall, which, ironically, ensures that life will go on, since fall will lead to rebirth and yet another fall:

> They must go down past things coming up.
> They must go down into the dark decayed.
>
> They *must* be pierced by flowers and put
> Beneath the feet of dancing flowers.
> However it is in some other world
> I know that this is the way in ours.
>   (*CPPP* 34)

The italicization of the word *must*—a word that already has been used twice in the pattern of anaphora (here a figure of nature's repetitions) set in the preceding stanza—exposes the event as mandatory (the immutable laws of nature) and signals the anxious urgency of the speaker, as assurance yields to plea, since the failure of the fall will mean the end of his existence.

Italics also play a prominent part in Frost's dramatic monologues and dialogues, and all but two of the poems in *North of Boston* mark tones of voice with it. In "Mending Wall" the skeptical and teasing attitude of the narrator comes into focus through that script: "*Why* do they make good neighbors?" If we read that statement with a feeling for metrical stress, we probably are more apt to hear it as a serious query—deeply quizzical as opposed to highly ironic. The tone of voice is not fully resolved, but not wholly open either. In "The Fear" Frost also uses italics to clarify utterance to a large extent:

> He's coming toward us. Joel, *go* in—please.
> Hark!—I don't hear him now. But please go in.
> (*CPPP* 90)

Without the graphetic cue, it would be difficult to know the wife's mood. A reader might hear the line with emphasis on "in" ("Joel, go *in*—please"), and probably would be more likely to hear it in this way than with emphasis on "go" in light of the metrical pattern. Frost's scripting of it helps show that the woman is not barking an order at her husband, but rather beseeching him to leave her alone with a man from her past.

Italics appear in Frost's later lyric verse as well, where it similarly aids in the definition of character and drama. The manuscript version of Frost's poem "Happiness Makes Up in Height for What It Lacks in Length" contains an underlined word that points up a meaning not as available in the published version, which does not include italicization. In the original copy the speaker explains that while the world looks to him an ominous place, he has had a change of heart about it as a result of a day's journey with his beloved:

> I verily believe
> My fair impression <u>may</u>
> Be all from one day
> No shadow crossed but ours
> As through its blazing flowers
> For change of solitude
> We went from house to wood.[94]

Frost's highlighting of the modal helping verb throws into relief the question of whether and to what extent the speaker's mood shapes his reality, as he wonders "whence / I get the lasting sense / Of so much warmth and light" in such a "stormy stormy world." He sends the manuscript of the poem in a letter to Cox, where he tells of his wife's illness ("a severe attack of grippe"): "Elinor is my chief anxiety. She has to stay out of much that goes on—not out of all."[95] In the poem Frost seems to be reflecting on their own happier days together, before Elinor's health takes a turn for the worse (a year after he sends it, she is operated on for cancer), and it is perhaps his memory of one such happy day that allows him to escape a sense of all-encompassing darkness. Through the underscored modal part of speech in the original version, he calls attention to the subject of the poem—how mood figures in our perception of our world.

Sometimes Frost italicizes a word in a poem not to help specify a tone of voice, but to highlight through a visual prosody the figurative significance of that word in the poem. In "For Once, Then, Something," Frost marks for special emphasis the first word of the seventh line: "*Once* when trying with chin against a well curb" (*CPPP* 208). In scanning the line, we assign stress to *Once,* recognizing an initial reversed foot, but accord it no more prominence of pitch perhaps than any other word in stressed position. By italicizing the adverb, Frost lets on the emblematic importance of it in the scheme of the poem: what happens to the speaker is a singular event; he never before looked into the well and received a sign, and never has since. In "Birches" Frost likewise calls attention to an often neglected part of speech—the preposition—through italics: "I'd like to go by climbing a birch tree, / And climb black branches up a snow-white trunk / *Toward* heaven, till the tree could bear no more" (*CPPP* 118). In a recorded reading of the poem, Frost does not alter the pitch of his voice when he reaches the word *Toward;* his pronunciation of it is in keeping with its unstressed position in the metrical line.[96] Here, then, italics would seem to operate as visual supplement rather than aural cue, with the preposition *Toward* highlighted as mode of transit in a poem that is about the transit—not the translation—from one world to the next. By failing to stress that italicized word in this reading of it, Frost signifies his interest in graphic elements that are as much for our eyes as for our ears, betraying his concern for the poem written on the other side of a closed door.

In rare instances at the end of his career, Frost italicizes parts of words in poems for humorous effect as he comments on national and class politics. In a brief lyric originally entitled "The Astronomer," he emphasizes the suffixes of three cognate words in calling attention to the American fascination with space exploration as of the late 1950s:

> But outer space,
> At least this far,
> For all the fuss
> Of the popul*ace,*
> Stays more popul*ar*
> Than popul*ous.*
>   (*CPPP* 477)

Here the italic type encourages us to place emphasis on these endings, which signify the differences between words whose roots are the same and between words that sound identical (in the case of the homonyms "populace" and "populous"). The poem is a witty play about our reach exceeding our grasp, about our national aspirations outstripping science. If we read the poet as "The Astronomer," we find that Frost explores language much as the astronaut explores space; the poet's exposure of similarities *and* differences in language figures the American public's simultaneous familiarity with *and* distance from the infinities. In "How Hard It Is To Keep from Being King When It's in You and in the Situation" italicization lights up part of a word to distinguish one pronunciation from another and to lay bare the class politics of pronunciation itself. The ex-King says "*Quintes*-sence"; the man who buys him at auction laughs at his mistake, remarking, "It seems you call quint*ess*ence *quint*essence." The ex-King chalks it up to class difference: "I'm a Rhodes scholar—that's the reason why. / I was at college in the Isle of Rhodes" (*CPPP* 464). In this exchange Frost pinpoints the central drama of the poem (summed up by the rather lengthy title), as he makes a joke of the idea that how we say what we say tells all about who we are and who we might become.

A final typographic feature—the capitalization of all the letters of a word—appears in a couple of Frost's late political poems; although uncommon, these moments further indicate Frost's tacit acknowledgment in his poetry of the intonational deprivation of the printed page and his effort to overcome it. In "Kitty Hawk" the speaker, meditating on the flight of Orville and Wilbur Wright, probes the human desire to be first, asking, "What did men mean by / THE original?" (*CPPP* 442). Here a definite article gains emphasis to indicate the singularity that men and nations seek, including in the space race in the 1950s when the poem was published ("And the radio / Cried, 'The Leap—The Leap!' / It belonged to US, / Not our friends the Russ") (*CPPP* 448). In the poem "A Reflex," Frost employs italics in questioning man's knowledge in the face of new scientific research: "What / ARE we to believe? / That there is an It?" (*CPPP* 476). The upper case "ARE" is meant to suggest that our understanding has been sorely tested; the rise in pitch signals a confusion and panic on the part of the speaker, who does not know what recent scientific discoveries prove, if anything, about the nature of the universe. That the cryptic pronoun "It" is so far removed from its rhyme pair (located seven lines above) points to our anxiety about finding similitude in our world. Through such prosodic events, Frost illustrates the importance of the graphic element in his verse as well as his ideological affinity with other modernist artists on the matter of sound in poetry, despite the increasingly oppositional tenor of his theory of form.

III

As we have seen, despite Frost's confident claims that he can reproduce intonation contours on the printed page without the assistance of graphetic cues, his poetry demonstrates his reliance on a range of devices meant to clarify utterance. Notably, though, these devices do not rule out ambiguity altogether, even if they do help to delimit the range of potential vocal contours. Indeed, Frost often tries to capitalize on the intonational deprivation of the written word in his poems. As Eric Griffiths finds, "The intonational ambiguity of a written text may create a mute polyphony through which we see rather than hear alternatively possible voicings, and are led by such vision to reflect on the inter-resonance of those voicings."[97] Frost's slighting of the faculty of vision in his theory of form suggests a lack of concern for such indeterminacies, but our experience with his poetry suggests their absolute importance. On the silent page, we are offered opportunities not available through the spoken word; we are able to try out a range of tones that would satisfy the conditions established by a text, to turn lines in different expressive directions, without ruling out all but one. Although one Frost critic has claimed that "There is no poet of whose voice we are surer than Frost's, no poet whom we hear more distinctly as we read," tonal indecision often thwarts such certainties, productively opening up the text to the reader's imagination as it opens up questions about the politics of his poetry.[98]

Only on the rarest of occasions did Frost admit the open-endedness of voice in black and white. As Sidney Cox recalled, in a 1916 lecture he "admitted there were cases of ambiguity about the sound images, but convinced us that they were not more numerous than those of ambiguity about visual images."[99] Here Frost insists that while ambiguity might not be averted fully, it is kept to a minimum and so does not get in the way of his ability to convey his meanings; he does not acknowledge that tonal ambiguity is the foundation on which many of his most complicated and rewarding poems rest. A few years later, Frost is taken aback by those who believe he rules out ambiguity in poetry, and in the privacy of his notebook he mentions more positively the persistence of ambiguity in life and art: "The Buffalo papers said I made an attack on ambiguity. The Syracuse papers said I was suffering from hasty recognition. (false recognition.) I had tried to show how unavoidably ambiguous we are most of the time in word, phrase, sentence, tone, deed and even situation" ("Notebook" 156). Of course, this claim undercuts his many statements about "sentence sounds" up to this point and is far more tenable than the extreme statements found elsewhere: we *are* unavoidably ambiguous most of the time in word, phrase, sentence, tone, deed, and situation. It is surprising that Frost felt his position had been misrepresented by the papers, since his avowal in his notebook does not bear any resemblance to his public polemic (as he told a Harvard audience in 1936, "A poem should be read as written").[100] The fact is, though, that some of Frost's most successful—and most challenging—poems do not secure proper voicing, leaving it to readers to construct divergent meanings out of his ambivalent speech rhythms.

The ambiguity of the printed word should have been brought home to Frost in 1915. After watching a theatrical production of "The Death of the Hired Man" by "The Am. Dram. Soc. (Ink.)" in Boston that year, Frost complained of the actors' interpretation of character through tone of voice, especially that of the husband: "The thing about that, the danger, is that you shall make the man too hard. That spoils it. That's the error the people made: they made the man too hard. And all our thinking turns on that" (*LU* 16; *CPPP* 763). As these remarks indicate, Frost believes that there is only one way to "hear" Warren in the poem, and that to hear him otherwise constitutes an "error." However, there is nothing on the page that mandates the degree or quality of the husband's hardness. The tone of voice to be assigned the following two sentences spoken by him is far from fully resolved: "'When was I ever anything but kind to him? / But I'll not have the fellow back,' he said." With the minimal marker, "he said," we are left with much to imagine. His question could be heard as indignant, peremptory, or beseeching, while still satisfying metrical conditions. But what does it matter, one might ask, whether we construe the man's statements as more "hard" or more "soft"? Frost's contention that "all our thinking turns on" our "correct" interpretation of tone makes clear his sense that our perception of the meaning of the poem is strongly affected by the answer to that question. And, indeed, much does turn on our interpretation of tone, but Frost has made it so that we can hear a statement as spoken in various ways. Again, there are limits to the range of possible intonation contours; we do not hear Warren as joyful in the passage quoted above. But to admit these limits is not to admit that there is one and only one way—and that way authorized by Frost—to construe "voice" in his poems. Griffiths explains the impact of such tonal ambiguities: "when a reader faces and tries to voice an intonationally ambiguous line, he is asked to reflect on the pull one reading rather than another exerts on him, and to ask why it does so. He comes to know himself in the act of becoming convinced that he knows the fictional speaker."[101] Frost's ambiguous lines and sentences incite such self-knowledge, requiring us to come to terms with our own attitudes as we draw toward or away from a speaker based on our soundings of tone.

The silent drama of "The Death of the Hired Man" bears out Griffiths's remarks. Mark Richardson has dismissed the poem for its "formulaic" treatment of gender, pointing to a correlation Frost makes between sentiment and tone in the poem and his personal political views:[102]

They think I'm no New Dealer. But really and truly I'm not, you know, all that clear on it. In *The Death of the Hired Man* that I wrote long, long ago, long before the New Deal, I put it two ways about home. One would be the manly way: "Home is the place where, when you have to go there, / They have to take you in." That's the man's feeling about it. And then the wife says, "I should have called it / Something you somehow hadn't to deserve." That's the New Deal, the mother's love. You have to deserve your father's. He's more particular. One's a republican, one's a Democrat. The father is always a Republican toward his son, the mother's always a Democrat. Very few have noticed that second thing; they've always noticed the sarcasm, the hardness of the male. (*CPPP* 885)

In this 1960 discussion Frost revises himself, suggesting that "the sarcasm, the hardness of the male" has crowded out appreciation of the tone of feminine kindness, not that the man has been misheard as "hard." Evidently, Frost, like his readers, is susceptible to hearing his poem differently in light of changes in attitude. Here he fixes tone in order to define more clearly the ideological poles in his construing of the poem as a political allegory. Ironically, though, it is this sharp distinction between the tones of husband and wife that Frost criticizes the Boston actors for making. While Richardson is correct to point out that Frost stereotypes gender in these remarks about the poem, the negotiation of gender in the play of tone in the poem itself is more nuanced than Frost's retrospective account suggests. Citing that account, Karen Kilcup finds that Frost reveals "a strikingly politicized sense of gender relations" in the poem and ultimately embraces the feminine perspective.[103] I would agree that Frost politicizes gender in the poem, but it is less clear that the empathic feminine voice wins out; as Frost himself insists, both the manly and feminine perspectives assert claims on our sympathies, and it is for us to weigh them in turn.

How we hear the sentences by husband and wife that we read on the page determines in large part what we think of the characters and the sentiments they express, and some of Frost's most astute critics disagree about what precisely they hear. Richard Poirier finds the wife's statement, "'I should have called it [home] / Something you somehow haven't to deserve,'" annoyingly "sententious."[104] Reuben Brower, on the other hand, hears a tone of "gentle plainness" in that last line.[105] I can imagine the statement as moralizing and as tender in various readings of it, and in different expressive turnings of the line I reflect on the pull one reading rather than another exerts and consider why it does so. Does the woman sound as if she is correcting her husband, teaching him how to temper his justice with mercy? Or is she offering up an alternative definition of "home" that is not meant so much as a reproof of her husband's as it is an affective supplement to it? To what extent is she preaching and to what extent gently coaxing? The quality of the relationship between husband and wife is revealed in the answers to such questions.

Sidney Cox says that Frost spoke of "The Death of the Hired Man" as "a little drama in which the gradual change in Warren is shown," but readers (who are also imaginative hearers) are divided about just how much Warren evolves in the course of the dialogue.[106] Katherine Kearns notes his emotional progress when she finds that at first "Warren's concerns are economical and his attitude is juridical, and it is only when he is brought to remember that Silas could impose a small but perfect order in building a load of (usable, marketable) hay that he begins to be deterred from anger."[107] Here are the lines to which she refers:

> "I know, that's Silas' one accomplishment.
> He bundles every forkful in its place,
> And tags and numbers it for future reference,
> So he can find and easily dislodge it
> In the unloading. Silas does that well.
> He takes it out in bunches like big birds' nests.
> You never see him standing on the hay
> He's trying to lift, straining to lift himself."
> (*CPPP* 43)

In contrast to Kearns's interpretation of this speech, Brower refers to it as a "slightly acid tribute," suggesting his belief that Warren's sarcastic tone in these lines is consistent with the "juridical" tone apparent in earlier exchanges.[108] One of these exchanges also prompts Brower to remark on the man's "hard"ness:

> "What did he say? Did he say anything?"
> "But little."
>   "Anything? Mary, confess
> He said he'd come to ditch the meadow for me"
> "Warren!"
>   "But did he? I just want to know."

As he finds, "Her tone is begging and explanatory, her 'Warren' here and later pressing the personal is very unlike his stern 'Mary,' calling the defendant to the bar."[109] Brower's interpretation of Warren's tone is not unwarranted, but it is certainly possible to imagine his voice as not "stern" but teasing—a tone that is meant to call the hired man to the bar more than his wife.

Based on his reading, Brower comes to the opinion that "Mary's character like her husband's grows more distinct as she builds out the picture of Silas," with one pitted against the other in this drama of tone. He specifically refers to the "harsher turns" of Warren's concluding speech, believing that the "wife's voice is entirely different" from the husband's—a difference maintained throughout the poem: "But though their feelings converge [in the end], their last words are thoroughly characteristic, hers questioning, his brief, hard, and final, though much is unsaid."[110] Kearns, on the other hand, contends that whereas early on in the poem Warren "thinks legalistically, in terms of imperatives whose violation would result in some punishment," his tone softens as Mary continues to talk; ultimately, she credits "Mary's great power to move Warren toward empathy," and finds that "Such yielding as Mary would awaken in her husband is nonetheless a form of unmanning, almost a kind of bewitchment, as if she would bring Warren to be as ineffectual in worldly terms as the 'son' Silas whose case she pleads."[111] Brower's and Kearns's divergent interpretations point to the ambiguity of these "sentence-sounds" and reveal the pull between the values of justice and mercy in the poem and in the world.

In "Home Burial," another dramatic dialogue in *North of Boston*, scripted utterances similarly can be turned in different ways, and these coexistent tonal possibilities profoundly affect our interpretations of character and gender politics in the poem. Since Frost rarely consented to read "Home Burial" in public, most of those who would seek to pin tones to his own reading of it are left with nothing to go on but the printed page. Ambiguity of voice not only exists in the poem; it is thematized there as well: Amy's accusation, "There you go sneering now!" prompts her husband's denial, "I'm not, I'm not!" an exchange that suggests that tone of voice can be mistaken even in speech, especially at heated moments. Although attitudinal markers in a poem (for example, "mocked gently") may enforce a particular tone, such markers are infrequent in Frost's dramatic verse, and, consequently, ambiguities proliferate. With this in mind, we would be wise to scrutinize Frost's statement about the emotionally charged sentence that ends "Home Burial": "I am not bothered by the question whether anyone will be able to hear or say those three words ('If—you—do!') as I mean them to be said or heard. I should say that they were sufficiently self-expressive" (*SL* 130). While it may be clear that the words are said in a fit of desperation, just how much fury is entangled in them is in question, and that undecidability of tone presides over the action of the entire poem.

Other statements in the poem betray the same ambivalence, a condition that complicates our laying of sympathies. To the husband's plea, "'Don't—don't go. / Don't carry it to someone else this time,'" Richard Poirier responds, "if he [the husband] is insensitive, he is at least not without gentleness," and further finds that "he is less peremptory than is she: 'Don't, don't, don't, don't,' she cried."[112] As Poirier believes, the husband's "reasonable beseeching" is pitted against the wife's "physical and spiritual lack of outgoingness, forthcomingness."[113] While I would agree with the view of the husband as "beseeching" and the wife as non-forthcoming, I can imagine hearing these words by husband and wife differently. In the two sentences that Poirier defines as "less peremptory" than the wife's speech, I also can hear peremptoriness, frustration, pique (*not again!*). In the wife's concatenation of "don't"s I can pick up a highly pathetic beseeching; in fact, I am able to hear each "don't" in a different tone as each registers a different agony. Frost once remarked that "the four 'don't's were the supreme thing" in the poem, and they are if by that he means the height of ambiguity of expression.[114]

Through this tonal ambivalence Frost explores cultural attitudes about gender and bereavement and forces us to come to terms with our own. Although he identifies "The Death of the Hired Man" as the "elegy" in *North of Boston*, "Home Burial" more fully stages the work of mourning the dead (*RFW* 82). As we have seen, the different responses of husband and wife to the death of their child, and, consequently, to each other, provoke different attitudes in readers. Do we understand the bereft woman as engaged in what Freud calls "normal mourning," or is she enacting the work of "melancholic" mourning, as she resists solace, lashing out at her husband and wishing for her own death?[115] In other words, do we feel that she is going through a stage on her way to surpassing her grief, or that she is mired in a grief that is not to be consoled, that is bound to destroy herself and her marriage? To the extent that we feel she is normative, we tend to extend sympathy to her, to upbraid the husband for his callous remarks. To the extent that we feel she is "psychotic," we probably take the side of the husband, who we imagine is trying to save her from her own extreme condition.[116] Confronting the ambiguous tones of the poem, we come to our own conclusions about what constitutes reasonable reaction to loss, or whether reason is a thing to be considered in the face of loss, as we identify with one or the other (or both) speakers.

Moments of vocal indecision shape other dramatic narratives in *North of Boston* as well and compound the (political) meanings that they convey. One such poem is "Mending Wall." During a public reading of that poem, Frost remarked on the aphorism that is twice spoken by the neighbor: "You know, I've read that so often I've sort of lost the right way to say, 'Good fences make good neighbors.' See. There's a special way to say [it] I used to have in my imagination, and it seems to have gone down. You say it in two different ways there."[117] Frost's confession that he has not been able to retain the intonation that he originally had in mind suggests the inability of the printed page to record unambiguously tones of voice; here he reveals that he has lost his own intention. Nevertheless, he continues to believe that there is a "right way" to say the sentence, when in fact there are several possible ways. The first appearance of the famous aphorism comes in reply to the narrator's taunt:

> My apple trees will never get across
> And eat the cones under his pines, I tell him.
> He only says, 'Good fences make good neighbors.'
> (*CPPP* 39)

In 1915, when the tone is fresher in his mind, Frost advises that this instance should be heard as expressing "Incredulity of the other's dictum" (*CPPP* 689). But how much sarcasm is entangled in the speaker's quotation of his neighbor's statement? The tone is held in suspension, allowing us to imagine it as said with either a shrug or a sneer. The second inscription of the maxim comes at the end of the poem and is introduced by the narrator's description of the relationship between neighbor and cliché:

> He will not go behind his father's saying,
> And he likes having thought of it so well
> He says again, "Good fences make good neighbors."

We might hear this second voicing of the aphorism differently from the first, as Frost says we should, perhaps imbuing it with a self-satisfied tone, but no tone is perfectly clear. Of course, none of the imaginable tones is flattering to the neighbor: when we hear it one way, we condemn him as smug and self-congratulatory; when we hear it another way, we write him off as a blockhead ("an old-stone savage armed").

However, there is wisdom in the sentence, as Frost himself acknowledged on more than one occasion, and his identification with both speakers ("Maybe I was both fellows in the poem")—his refusal to take sides ("I make it a rule not to take any 'character's' side in anything I write")—further complicates our interpretation of tone (*I* 257; *SL* 138). The narrator is, after all, the one who proposes mending the wall *and* the one who questions the need to do so. The tone is tricky here, as is the situation. How are we to take the speaker's criticism of his neighbor if he himself is in some way behind the expression? How light-hearted is his criticism or how heavy-handed? Reginald Cook has said that in a reading of "Mending Wall," Frost stressed the sentence, "I'd rather he said it for himself," in the following lines, which speculate humorously on the forces that topple the wall:[118]

> I could say 'Elves' to him,
> But it's not elves exactly, and I'd rather
> He said it for himself.

Nothing on the page indicates that we should emphasize this remark, but if we do, certain meanings come to hand, for instance, that it is not so much the content of the phrase, as it is the neighbor's uncritical absorption and echoing of it, that galls. Stanley Burnshaw describes the situation of the poem in the following way: "Two 'contradictory' speakers, both of them 'right' up to a point, and only when they are joined is the poem resolved— and then in an 'open-endedness.'"[119] But to see this confluence one must hold to a certain interpretation of tone in the poem. It would be just as easy to reject fully the position of the neighbor, since the printed page does not reveal definitely the speaker's sympathy with the essence of the aphorism. Frost grants us leave to accept or reject the neighbor's message based on the tones of voice we project onto the lines and, in doing so, forces us to probe our often conflicted attitudes about personality and inter-personality, and, on a political level, about nationalists (those who want walls) and "One-worlders" (those who want none), a tension that Frost claimed in 1955 the poem was about.[120] The "open-endedness" of tone requires us to judge for ourselves where the point of intersection between the positions of the two speakers lies, and our inflection of the lines no doubt will depend upon our feelings about political conditions at the time we read, or reread, the poem.

Despite such ambiguous tones, critics are quick to fix attitudes to statements in Frost's poetry and pin their interpretations of meaning in the poem on them. The final quatrain of "Come In" is a case in point, as the tone of the speaker's refusal of the thrush's call asking him to "come into the woods and lament" resists easy classification:

> But no, I was out for stars,
> I would not come in.
> I meant not even if asked,
> And I hadn't been.
> 			(*CPPP* 304)

Of these lines, Marie Borroff writes: "In a dramatically expressive reading, there will be a slight rise of pitch on *I* and *stars* in the first line and on *meant* and *asked* in the third. The most striking sentence sound comes in the elliptical phrasing of the last line: 'I hadn't been,' a reduction of 'I hadn't been asked.' The last chief syllable of the poem, *been,* must be read with weak stress and a corresponding drop in pitch. Both the contracted form 'hadn't' and the expression 'out for stars' have the distinctive ring of everyday speech."[121] Surely, Borroff's interpretation of tone in this stanza is valid, as Frost does not provide italics to assist us. However, one might hear the expression "I was out for stars" without a slight rise of pitch on *I* and *stars,* and instead as "I was *out* for *stars.*" In Borroff's version, the utterance assumes a defiant tone, with the speaker boldly asserting himself when confronted by an invitation to self-extinction. In the other version, the line takes on a more jaunty tone, as if to suggest that it takes no special effort not to succumb. The title itself predicts this ambivalence, as we cannot be sure whether the phrase is to be heard in a casual colloquial voice (Come In), or as full-throated and ominous (*Come In*).

Assigning tone of voice in the last stanza of "Come In" is difficult because the tenor of the metaphor is unclear. Is the poem about the speaker's refusal to bow to grief? (In the period leading up to the first publication of the poem in February 1941, Frost had lost a daughter, son, and wife.) Is it about his refusal to join with other modernist poets in their "difficult" poetics? Is it about his rejection of political leftists who lament social conditions in America? The tonal ambiguities at the end of the poem thwart resolution of these questions. If we read it as a refusal to wallow in loss, we might hear the sentence in the way Borroff does, as the speaker attempts to safeguard his ego in the face of a potentially all-consuming grief. If we read it as a rebuke to unpatriotic forces, we might hear it otherwise, with the speaker rather blithely turning his back on them as holding no special interest: "But no I was out for stars." By enforcing neither of these interpretations, Frost lets us hear the sentence on the page variously and imagine the range of contexts that could give rise to such utterance.

Such shiftiness of speech rhythm has occasioned a great deal of critical wrangling, and the controversy that erupted when the renowned literary critic Lionel Trilling announced at Frost's eighty-fifth birthday party that he is "a terrifying poet" owes much to the "problem" of tone in Frost's work.[122] The two poems that Trilling cites—"Neither Out Far Nor In Deep" and "Design"—exemplify both the ambiguity of tone and the opportunities that that ambiguity afforded Frost. "Neither Out Far Nor In

Deep" narrates an epistemological crisis, but it is not immediately clear what the poem is in fact about and, thus, how it should be heard:

> The people along the sand
> All turn and look one way
> They turn their back on the land.
> They look at the sea all day.
>
> As long as it takes to pass
> A ship keeps raising its hull;
> The wetter ground like glass
> Reflects a standing gull.
>
> The land may vary more;
> But wherever the truth may be—
> The water comes ashore,
> And the people look at the sea.
>
> They cannot look out far.
> They cannot look in deep.
> But when was that ever a bar
> To any watch they keep?
>   (*CPPP* 274)

One is left to wonder whether that final stanza is optimistic or pessimistic. Is it a cheering statement of Frost's "attitude and belief that man will never conquer nature but that he will never cease trying" or rather a sneering at the masses, who are visually and critically impaired, but who refuse to acknowledge that fact, foolish in their futile quest (*CR* 115). Is the word *they* in that stanza pronounced with "deadpanned contempt" or are the final lines spoken with a rouse?[123] One critic has noted that in the poem Frost recognizes "the essential limitations of man, without denial or protest or rhetoric or palliation," but that he "doesn't say it [the last stanza] unpleasantly—he says it with flat ease, takes everything with something harder than contempt, more passive than acceptance. . . . The tone of the last lines—or, rather, their careful suspension between several tones, as a piece of iron can be held in the air between powerful enough magnets—allows for this too."[124] This condition of tonal indecision points up a complexity of attitude and meaning at the heart of the poem, and compels us to search out our attitudes about our fellow man, our sense of our capabilities in an often inscrutable world—a world that will not yield up its mysteries to either telescope or microscope (the two instruments that Frost says he alludes to in the lines "They cannot look out far. / They cannot look in deep").[125]

Like "Neither Out Far Nor In Deep," "Design" is about our ambivalent relation to the universe—a relation figured through ambivalent speech

contours—and our sense of purpose in it. In the final lines of the poem—
the sestet of the sonnet—we find a series of questions and a final statement
that confound interpretation of the speaker's mood:

> What had that flower to do with being white,
> The wayside blue and innocent heal-all?
> What brought the kindred spider to that height,
> Then steered the white moth thither in the night?
> What but design of darkness to appall?—
> If design govern in a thing so small.
>
> (*CPPP* 275)

Does the first question sound like "ordinary annoyance at a fact that
doesn't fit in," or does it sound honestly quizzical?[126] Is the next question
("What brought the kindred spider . . .") heard as in "a voice of lost innocence," or does it mark the speaker simply as dumbfounded.[127] At issue is
whether the speaker has been touched by the "darkness" of the world or
whether he remains unknowing—and at sea—in his grappling with the
mysteries of his surroundings. The cadence of the final question—"What
but design of darkness to appall?"—is as elusive, leaving us to decide for
ourselves whether the speaker expresses sheer incomprehension or rather
deep suspicion at the shape of things. One critic has referred to "the sooth-
ingly humorous hesitation" of the last line of the poem, a "hesitation that
points to something many readers may find less agreeable than design of
darkness, to no order whatever," but it, too, is ambiguous, and could be
taken as more serious than humorous, a frightening reminder of the possibility of teleological breakdown.[128] Frost's claim that "Design" is "very
undramatic in the speech entirely," that "It's a kind of poker-face piece,"
suggests some of the problems that the poem's hearers are up against.[129]
But that description of it is also misleading, since it is not that the poem is
tone dead, but rather that its elusive tones keep us guessing, just as we are
left unsure whether a higher force shapes our ends.

The tonal inter-resonance of "The Road Not Taken"—another case in
which Frost plays it close to the vest—similarly has perplexed readers, and no
wholly adequate account of the auditory dynamics at the end of the poem has
been forthcoming, despite much work on the part of critics to lay bare the
irony involved in those lines. Here is what the speaker of the poem declares:

> I shall be telling this with a sigh
> Somewhere ages and ages hence:
> Two roads diverged in a wood, and I—
> I took the road less traveled by,
> And that has made all the difference.
>
> (*CPPP* 103)

Frost himself revealed that in the first line of the last stanza tone is difficult to ascertain, cautioning, "See, the tone of that is absolutely saving. You've got to look out for it, though. See."[130] William Pritchard comments on the discrepancy between Frost's poetics and the intonational ambiguity at work in the poem, mapping its biographical coordinates:

Yet Frost had written Untermeyer two years previously [in 1915] that "I'll bet not half a dozen people can tell who was hit and where he was hit in my Road Not Taken," and he characterized himself in that poem particularly as "fooling my way along." He also said that it was really about his friend Edward Thomas, who when they walked together always castigated himself for not having taken another path than the one they took. When Frost sent "The Road Not Taken" to Thomas he was disappointed that Thomas failed to understand it as a poem about himself; but Thomas in return insisted to Frost that "I doubt if you can get anybody to see the fun of the thing without showing them and advising them which kind of laugh they are to turn on." And though this kind of advice went exactly contrary to Frost's notion of how poetry should work, he did on occasion warn his audiences and other readers that it was a tricky poem.[131]

Which kind of laugh are we to turn on when we see that the speaker has falsified the record, pretending in his old age that he took the road less traveled, despite the fact that earlier in the poem we learn that "both [roads] that morning equally lay / In leaves no step had trodden black"? Do we laugh with derision when the speaker stands exposed as a revisionist, or is the laugh we turn on gentler—one directed as much at ourselves as at the speaker of the final lines? If we hear the final statement as heartfelt, absent a moralizing strain, we probably regard the speaker with some sympathy, as symbolic of the human propensity to construct fictions to justify choices made in clouded circumstances. But if it strikes our ear as sententious, we are more likely to laugh at his expense, to mock his pretentiousness. Frost permits us to hear the final statement in at least these two ways, perhaps at different stages of our life, even as we register its irony, and so encourages us to come to terms with our vexed attitudes about what it means to fashion a personal history, to represent life as worth living.

As such poems testify, moments of epistemological and eschatological crisis often are shaped by tonal ambiguity in Frost's poetry, which is keenly aware of the limits (and possibilities) of our comprehension of our world. Frost is not a "spiritual drifter," as Yvor Winters alleged, but a poet committed to undermining easy confidences about our moral position.[132] In "For Once, Then, Something" Frost depicts someone who tries to find a way to know (and know he has known) such a moral absolute as Truth. The speaker seems to be an object of ridicule for pursuing absolutes without a proper faith—a person blinded by egotistical concerns ("Others taunt me with having knelt at well-curbs"). But that figure is not fully imagined; we do not receive a profile that would help us determine with certainty the attitudes and emotions behind his utterances. It is unclear how he feels about the taunting that he receives and how his search for "Something more of the depths" is shaped by it. The questions leading up to the phrase in its final appearance only muddy the water: "What was that whiteness? / Truth? A pebble of quartz?" How are we to hear these questions? Does he ask them in an agitated tone? Is he profoundly disturbed or gently quizzical? The disparity between "Truth" and "A pebble of quartz" suggests that he has glimpsed either something essential or something wholly inconsequential. Does his tone reflect the crushing distance that lies between them? Is he exasperated by the refusal of his world to yield full meaning to him, or excited by what he has been shown? The epistemological problem that the poem presents— "How can we know Truth if at all?" and "How do we know if we have known Truth?"—is never finally resolved. Originally, the poem was titled "Wrong to the Light"; Frost changes it to the polyvocal "For Once, Then, Something" in order to highlight the uncertainty of vision and stimulate the reader to face the perplexities of his relationship to nature and God.

The same suspension of tone shapes the conclusion of Frost's lyric "The Most of It," a title that is clipped from a colloquial utterance (the poem was originally called "Making the Most of It") and that we can hear in at least two ways—as much or little, as cheery or deflated—as we measure our expectations against the realities of our world. When we say in life we will "make the most of it," we either express through our tone a weary resignation to our fate (we will do the best we can with meager resources) or an enthusiastic acceptance of matters as they lie. In the poem a man's quest for "counter-love, original response" from the universe ends in an ambiguously coded buck ("nothing ever came from what he cried / Unless . . .") that crashes through the water in front of him. The final phrase of the poem compounds this ambiguity, as we are told that the buck

> landed pouring like a waterfall,
> And stumbled through the rocks with horny tread,
> And forced the underbrush—and that was all.
> (*CPPP* 307)

It is not quite clear here how we are to regard the speaker's attitude toward the response he gets to his call and, therefore, how we should say "—and that was all": does the pitch fall on "all" to suggest disappointment or does it rise in signal of wonderment? The intonation is not indicated by the "notation" of the sentence and, consequently, the meaning of the buck's crash remains uncertain. It either represents an "original response," even if not human, in which the speaker can take satisfaction, or mocks his wish for "counter-love," thwarting his desire for human colloquy. William Empson argues that the word "all" is "as suited to absolute love and self-sacrifice as to insane self-assertion," and Frost's use of the word here invokes that range of attitudes.[133] Ultimately, there is not a "right" way to speak the final phrase, because there is not a simple solution to the speaker's dilemma: the buck is something and nothing; it comes in the wake of the man's appeal, but it may or may not betoken the thing for which he is searching. Richard Poirier has argued that in the poem "to be told 'that was all,' does not, needless to say, mean that 'all' is nothing," that the final words "are addressed not to the inadequacy of the buck to live up to the spectator's sentimental expectations but to the incapacity of the spectator, and of us, to find any way to account for the buck, its power and fantastic indifference."[134] I would say rather that Frost's tonal play allows us to weigh the significance of the buck for ourselves—to see it both as something and nothing—in our various soundings of the phrase that the mute polyphony of "all" allows.

Like "The Most of It," the title of Frost's thanatopsis "Away!" represents a segment of a larger statement, this one derived from a song—the chorus of the old chantey *Shenandoah* ("I'm—bound—away!"). Abstracted from that phrase, however, its tone becomes highly ambivalent and, as such, provides an ironic counterpoint to the poem that it introduces. The exclamatory expression from the song appears in full in the penultimate stanza:

> Unless I'm wrong
> I but obey
> The urge of a song:
> I'm—bound—away!
> (*CPPP* 427)

The same sentence appears in Frost's *A Masque of Mercy* (1947) with the helpful stage direction that Jonah "*quotes it to the tune*" of the song (*CPPP* 396). But "Away!" is not a theatrical script, and Frost does not include such a cue. Despite this fact, one is likely to conjure up a wistful air with that song in mind when the sentence is met with in the poem, as that mood is in keeping with the sentiments expressed by the speaker, who, happy with this world, simply chooses to explore the (not so) final frontier:

And I may return
If dissatisfied
With what I learn
From having died.

But if, as I have suggested, the full line "I'm—bound—away!" would seem to indicate a particular intonation contour, the mere title "Away!" does not. In remarks about the poem at a reading at the Bread Loaf Writers' Conference (June 30, 1958), Frost lets on that the intonation of the title is not fixed in his mind, but wonderfully suggestive of a range of attitudes: "[H]ere's a little death [poem]—just for the fun of it. This is a real death poem. It's called—I guess I call it 'Away'—'Away'—'Away.' [Giving the word different intonations] That would make you suspicious to begin with."[135] The transcript does not tell what tones of voice he tried out, only that he turned the word in three different expressive directions. If said wistfully, it would make one suspicious of the poem as about death, since we usually do not think of our demise in terms of that emotion. But one can imagine other turnings, for instance, toward fear (*Stay away!*) and pleasurable excitement (*Up and away!*), whose coexistence also makes one suspicious, disturbing our stereotyped notion of death. Rereading the title in light of the poem, we find that the ambivalent tone expresses an ambivalent view of mortality, for the speaker, who is given to imagine death as reversible.

The title of Frost's poem "'Out, Out—'" calls attention more obviously to its status as borrowed text, alluding to the famous soliloquy by the title character of Shakespeare's drama *Macbeth* upon learning of the death of his queen, and its probing of the political issue of child labor calls on us to measure our own political natures in turn. As with the two poems just discussed, important questions are raised even before reaching the body of the lyric as to how to hear the words on the page. An actor on the stage would be forced to choose how to say these words ("Out, out, brief candle!"), invoking the sting of death either through a clipped, bitter pronunciation, a drawn-out melancholy one, or some other tone on the spectrum between these two poles. In any event, the expression serves as an ironic comment on what follows: Macbeth's metaphorical and philosophical turn ("Life's but a walking shadow, . . .") is foreign to Frost's poem, which is set in a place where such consideration is a luxury that the characters cannot afford. The indeterminacy of the initial vocal contour is matched by the final tone of voice displayed in the poem: "No more to build on there. And they, since they / Were not the one dead, turned to their affairs" (*CPPP* 131). Are these final lines contemptuously said, "a bitter comment on the callous indifference to human suffering"?[136] Or is there poignancy entailed in the flat remark? How we hear the end of "'Out, Out—'" ultimately depends on our personal sympathies and attitudes, as Sidney Cox discovered: "Some of my optimistic acquaintances think the close [of "'Out, Out—'"] uncomfortable. In other words it is too sincere for them, and they fail to sense the tender sympathy."[137] Here he suggests that some who want the world better than it is cringe at the conclusion, but those, including himself, who take the world as it is, find in those same lines a current of "sympathy" for the conditions that give rise to the boy's untimely death. In defense of the poem to his friend Alice Ray, who had expressed qualms about it, Cox further remarked, "I know how you feel about the last line. But that isn't Mr. Frost. That's life. I don't know anyone who has more of the right sort of tenderness than Mr. Frost. It shows in the [tenth] line 'Call it a day I wish they might have said.' You say 'I like it and still I don't.' That's exactly how I feel about life."[138] How Cox feels about life conditions his hearing of "tenderness" in the poem, and he is right to say that when we read the poem we cannot help but reflect our own political response to the world and suffering in it.

Indeed, in several of Frost's poems that exhibit tonal ambivalence he represents an elusive public politics through them, registering his ideological ambivalence and compelling us to search out our own sympathies when we come into contact with them. Sometimes, irony in Frost's political verse is hard to see, and there often are no clues (unlike in "The Road Not Taken") to go by. For instance, in his early poem "My Giving" that he sent in 1911 to Susan Hayes Ward, he plays both sides of the political question. On the face of it, the poem asserts a solidarity with industrial workers that the speaker of "Good Relief" (a poem of the same period that I address in the first chapter) cannot muster—one that would have pleased Ward; on the other hand, the speaker in the poem could be heard as mocking the idea of full-blown sympathy for the dispossessed:

> Here I shall sit, the fire out, and croon
> All the dismal and joy-forsaken airs,
> Sole alone, and thirsty with them that thirst,
> Hungry with them that hunger and are accurst.
> No storm that night can be too untamed for me;
> If it is woe on earth, woe let it be!
> (*CPPP* 518–19)

Is this an ironic expression or does the plaint come across as sincerely felt? Probably its tonal resonance depends on the politics of the hearer, on how far one believes caring should go.

Later during the Depression Frost again writes poems in which we may or may not hear the voice on the page as ironic, and that ambivalent condition holds his politics in abeyance. In "Provide, Provide" in *A Further Range* it may be clear that the speaker is exhorting self-protection, but his precise attitude to the problem of our security is not immediately apparent:

> The witch that came (the withered hag)
> To wash the steps with pail and rag
> Was once the beauty Abishag,
>
> The picture pride of Hollywood.
> Too many fall from great to good
> For you to doubt the likelihood.
>
> Die early and avoid the fate.
> Or if predestined to die late,
> Make up your mind to die in state.
>
> Make the whole stock exchange your own!
> If need be occupy a throne,
> Where nobody can call *you* crone.
>
> Some have relied on what they knew;
> Others on being simply true.
> What worked for them might work for you.
>
> No memory of having starred
> Atones for later disregard,
> Or keeps the end from being hard.
>
> Better to go down dignified
> With boughten friendship by your side
> Than none at all. Provide, provide!
> (CPPP 280)

Stanley Burnshaw points to this poem as one that bothers our notion of Frost's conservatism, as it "confounds oversimple judgments" by virtue of the fact that "though [the poem is] 'sung' by a single speaker, the contradictory voice is heard through implications that cannot be missed."[139] I would argue, however, that the tonal implications may well be missed and that Frost invokes a reticence on the written page to figure his political openness and to make room for our own political involvement. Randall Jarrell has said that for him the poem "is full of the deepest, and most touching, moral wisdom—and it is full, too, of the life we have to try to be wise about and moral in."[140] But is the speaking voice purely poignant, or do we find in it a "bitterly sarcastic" note?[141] Does it mock the striking scrubwomen at Harvard that Frost said the poem is about, or rather does the speaker mock himself by exhorting Americans to provide for the future at a time when for many merely providing for the moment is in question? Although Jarrell claims that the poem has a "conclusiveness" about it, it is ultimately inconclusive in its political posture, not a simple screed directed at the sentimental humanitarianism of the New Deal.[142] In readings of the poem, Frost often quipped after the final line, "Or somebody else'll provide for you! . . . And how'll you like that?"[143] Here Frost shows his political hand more fully, revealing in his oral performance of the poem an animus against the welfare state that the poem on the page withholds.

Before the dawn of the New Deal, in his poem "The Egg and the Machine" (1928), Frost addressed the rapidly changing economy and the political forces involved in it through a similarly ambiguous speaking voice—one that seems so flatly expressive that we are kept guessing as to whether it is at points ironic. The title announces an opposition between the natural and the man-made, and in the poem the speaker blasts the incursion of industrial forces into the rural setting, inveighing against what Leo Marx has termed "the machine in the garden":[144]

> He gave the solid rail a hateful kick.
> From far away there came an answering tick,
> And then another tick. He knew the code:
> His hate had roused an engine up the road.
> He wished when he had had the track alone
> He had attacked it with a club or stone
> And bent some rail wide open like a switch,
> So as to wreck the engine in the ditch.
>
> (*CPPP* 248)

Here Frost activates "the trope of the interrupted idyll"—a trope that shapes the work of some important nineteenth-century American writers responding to the new industrial economy.[145] In the poem the locomotive is imagined as a steam monster reminiscent of the shrieking mill: "Then for a moment all there was was size, / Confusion, and a roar that drowned the cries / He raised against the gods in the machine." The speaker's hatred of it prompts a belated wish that he had sabotaged the rails "So as to wreck the engine in the ditch," a statement that raises questions about the man's political identity. At the time Frost wrote the poem, it was widely believed that the International Workers of the World (I.W.W.) sponsored acts of sabotage; Bill Haywood, Wobbly organizer in the 1912 textile strike in Lawrence, Massachusetts, is credited with saying, "Sabotage means to push back, pull out or break off the fangs of Capitalism."[146] In addition, the poem was entitled "The Walker" when it was first published—the same title as a poem by Arturo Giovannitti, an Italian-born writer and orator who came to Lawrence early in the strike to take charge of strike relief. Giovan-nitti wrote his poem in prison after being jailed for his involvement in the strike, and it was published in a pamphlet issued by the I.W.W. in 1913. It is quite possible that Frost's rail-walker is meant to be an I.W.W. itinerant worker, especially in light of the fact that "Most of them beat their way by freight car from one place to another, and railroad companies estimated that there were half a million hoboes riding the rails, walking the tracks, or waiting at railroad junctions to catch onto a train, at any one time."[147]

The climax of the poem holds in suspension Frost's attitude toward the man and his proposed act of sabotage. Following the track of a turtle (as opposed to the artificial steel track that the engine rides), the man finds a buried nest and arms himself with turtle eggs, preparing to throw them at the train engine's headlight upon its next approach:

> "You'd better not disturb me anymore,"
> He told the distance, "I am armed for war.
> The next machine that has the power to pass
> Will get this plasm in its goggle glass."

The "war" that he stands ready to wage conjures up the reality of warfare between labor and capital raging in America at the time, but his insufficient arsenal may be seen as mocking his position. Yvor Winters faults Frost for expressing in the poem his "sentimental hatred for the machine," thereby associating the poet with the title figure.[148] But just what is Frost's relation to the armed man? Does he identify with his desire to draw limits to the spread of industry? Or is he being ironic, trying to point up the futility (and hilarity) of union attempts to disrupt industry? (The landmark Railway Labor Act of 1926 emphasized collective bargaining and mediation over settlement of wage disputes by a federal board, and Frost may be suggesting that such legislation is fruitless, that each individual must measure himself against industrial forces at work in the world.) When asked about the poem, Frost denied any bias, stating that he was not "taking sides" and that whether he was leaning toward the organic or the mechanical (two political alternatives) "is for you to choose."[149] As these remarks indicate, his is no "sentimental hatred of the machine," but rather a careful weighing—and ambivalent staging—of the impact of the new industrial order through elusive tones of voice.

Elsewhere, too, undecidability of tone—or vocal latency—in Frost's poetry is implicated in class politics, as for one lower-class audience the oral performance of a poem from *A Further Range* effectively congeals its conservatism. Although it has been said of "Two Tramps in Mud Time" (1934) that "line after line speaks itself in the mouth with the turn and tone unmistakably intended; the poem reads itself," the fact is that in the poem on the page a rich ambiguity of tone requires readers to search out Frost's personal political philosophy—and, more importantly, their own—in their encounters with it (*CR* 114). It is possible to hear the ending as "rather sententious," as Malcolm Cowley does, with the narrator cautioning,[150]

> But yield who will to their separation,
> My object in living is to unite
> My avocation and my vocation
> As my two eyes make one in sight.
> Only where love and need are one,
> And the work is play for mortal stakes,
> Is the deed ever really done
> For Heaven and the future's sakes.
> (*CPPP* 252)

But in what manner is the speaker moralizing here? Is he trying to teach us a lesson or merely trying to content himself with a lesson he has learned? Our answers to these questions depend on whether we hear (and see) the narrator talking aloud to us or musing to himself. A teacher of the poem told Cowley that his students from poor families in the Alleghanies were made "vaguely uncomfortable when they heard it read aloud."[151] Their uneasiness no doubt arises from the sense they get that the narrator speaks the words in the poem, since the words are read aloud to them, that he is unsympathetically sermonizing upon sight of the displaced workers who want his job for pay. If, however, we imagine that the words are self-directed, comprising an interior monologue, or tacit text, it becomes possible to interpret the passage—and the message of the poem—differently. If unspoken, the speaker can appear less harsh, more pragmatic, his personal philosophy not foreclosing offerings of charity.

In this chapter we have observed the discrepancies between how Frost says his poetry operates and how it actually operates in a range of poems from throughout his career. Thus far, I have discussed primarily the unit of the sentence, the same unit to which Frost consistently draws our attention. In order to interrogate his formalism—and the politics of that formalism—fully, however, we must move away from that unit of discourse, turning light on the unit of the line—a unit that he is persuaded to say less, not more, about in the interest of "the sound of sense."

CHAPTER THREE

The Politics of the Visual Line

The sentence is everything—the sentence well-imagined.
—FROST TO SIDNEY COX, 1915

I

In the heat of theorizing Frost claims that the only prosodic technique he cares anything about is the counterpoint of rhythm and meter. Moreover, he claims that all power lies in the unit of the sentence, which carries suprasegmental speech contours: "The sentence is everything—the sentence well-imagined" (*SL* 151). Of course, Frost's insistence on meter presupposes the unit of the line, since meter is a function of it, but he rarely mentions that unit in intersection with the sentence. Despite his reticence, the straddling of lines by syntax in Frost's poetry constitutes a major form; indeed, his use of line-sentence counterpointing is systematic throughout his career. Probably one reason that he shies away from such a discussion is that enjambment frequently constitutes a basic organizational mode of nonmetrical verse. In light of early confusions about his prosodic practice, and his lifelong valorization of metrical composition, Frost would have resisted calling attention to that procedure, especially in his own work. Another reason behind his reluctance stems from the fact that enjambment is primarily visual. Although it is true that if we have a good ear we can hear enjambment in blank verse and, more easily, in rhymed metrical verse, because we can predict when a line will break, our impressions of these cuts in syntax will be fleeting. Only when we see the system of the sentence as it interferes with the system of the line can we comprehend fully the meanings that a poet like Frost depicts.[1] In his theorizing, though, he denigrates those who are well-equipped to inspect the operations of such counter-pointing, promoting "the ear reader" over "the eye reader," who, he claims, "is a barbarian"; while he primarily means here that one must read with attention to the nuances of sound and not simply skim for facts, his hierarchy implies that visually based prosodic effects are not of the utmost importance (*PJ* 18; *CPPP* 809).

Snide comments about enjambment as it functions in nonmetrical poetry are scattered throughout Frost's letters and critical prose and stake out his suspicions of that rhetorical form. In a letter to a friend, he cannot resist ridiculing enjambment as a main principle of measurement, wondering how a poet would know how "to cut lines unhocuspocusly" without the baseline of meter (*SL* 306). Suggesting that there is no rationale to guide the breaking of lines in free verse, Frost distances himself from such sleight-of-hand. To Richard Thornton in 1931, he reports receiving a "sinister" letter from Harriet Monroe demanding he reduce the price of his poems, and he laments his involvement with her and other proponents of free verse, whom he tars for their neglect of form: "[O]nce you are in with the lawless in verse rum or dope you cant get out and live. I know too many of their secrets about breaking lines where they break them not to be dangerous running at large" (*SL* 375). In the next chapter I will examine more fully the social and political implications of free verse that Frost hints at here ("the lawless in verse rum or dope"); for now, I want to call attention to his linkage of free verse and radical line-breaking, a linkage fueled by a politics of enjambment dating from the eighteenth century, when that prosody was tied to an ideology of license and misrule by conservative cultural critics.[2]

Despite Frost's strong association of enjambment with the (dis)organization of free verse, which led to his wariness about speaking of it, on rare occasions he was willing to admit that line-sentence counterpointing could be meaningful as a prosodic pattern in metrical poetry. In 1921, Frost wrote to his friend, John Erskine, about Erskine's blank verse poem "Metaneira": "You never fail to get something out of the relation of sentence to line" (*RFW* 99). This statement leaves unexpressed precisely what rhetorical effects are managed through such a relation, but Frost at least cracks the door, acknowledging the Miltonic tradition of enjambed blank verse in which the poem stands. In 1933, Frost wrote to his son Carol, commending his recent poetry for similar effects of line-sentence counterpointing: "Well you are getting a firmer grip on the art now in every way from rhyming up to packing in the ideas. (I ought to mention the way you vary the length and shape of the sentences in the lines and overlapping the lines to save

yourself from monotony also.)" (*SL* 391). Here he praises his son's variations in sentence structure, but goes against claims he makes in theorizing
"the sound of sense," where he holds as a virtue the poet's ability to express
different tones of voice in sentences that conform to the same general dimensions: "Sentences may have the greatest monotony to the eye in length
and structure[,] and yet the greatest variety to the ear in the tones of voice
they convey. As in Emerson's prose—and verse too" (*PJ* 131). Guided by
such remarks, critics like Reginald Cook have spoken out against the notion that the poet would be wise to vary the length and shape of sentences:
"Most writers have just one tone—a tone of statement. Others try to vary
this tone by lengthening or shortening the poetic sentences. Frost varies
the tone by using a dramatic image of speech, which is simply the precise
tone of voice by which the meaning in a word is communicated."[3] Notably,
it is only outside of his exposition of "the sound of sense" that Frost permits himself to credit the effects of variable line length and, in turn, line-
sentence counterpointing, even if he does not draw attention to the rich
and complex meanings available through that procedure.

In his introduction to Edwin Arlington Robinson's *King Jasper* (1935),
Frost signals his admiration for enjambment (although he does not use the
word) as it figures in Robinson's lyric entitled "Miniver Cheevy":

I remember the pleasure with which Pound and I laughed over the fourth
"thought" in

> Miniver thought, and thought, and thought,
> And thought about it.

Three "thoughts" would have been "adequate" as the critical praise-word then
was. There would have been nothing to complain of, if it had been left at three. The
fourth made the intolerable touch of poetry. With the fourth, the fun began.

(*RFPP* 350)

It is not just the verbal repetition in these lines that captures Frost's (and
Pound's) attention; it is also the manner in which the repetition appears:
"There is more to it than the number of 'thoughts.' There is the way the last
one turns up by surprise round the corner, the way the shape of the stanza
is played with, the easy way the obstacle of verse is turned to advantage"
(*RFPP* 350). By "the obstacle of verse" Frost can only mean the dynamics of
line terminus that orchestrate our encounters with syntax. The "shape" that
Frost alludes to here is not the "shape" of the sentence, but the rhetorical
shape of enjambment. Only late in his career does Frost hint at the possibility of line-sentence counterpointing at work in his own poetry: "I'm always

interested, you know, when I have three or four stanzas, in the way I *lay* the sentences in them. I'd hate to have the sentences all lie the same in the stanzas" (*CPPP* 890). But even here the arrangement of "sentences" into "stanzas" does not necessarily involve enjambment. Indeed, when Frost compliments himself on "The Peaceful Shepherd"—a three-stanza poem that is rather rigidly endstopped from start to finish—he uses those same terms to describe his performance: "Now, you see, what I'm interested in there is the three stanzas, to see if the sentences fall different ways in them. And I wonder if I get credit for that: to see if I can put a pretty sentence—a different sentence—lay them in their little stanzas."4

Throughout his career Frost evades discussion of the ways in which syntax is registered by the eye in lines and the significance of such surface patterning. For instance, when he says that Emerson's poem "Monadnoc" contains sentences of similar length, it would be more accurate to say that the poem is heavily endstopped, that line boundaries in the poem coincide largely with phrase and sentence boundaries, since some sentences occupy four lines and others as many as eight:

> Now in sordid weeds they sleep,
> In dulness now their secret keep;
> Yet, will you learn our ancient speech,
> These the masters who can teach.
> Fourscore or a hundred words
> All their vocal muse affords;
> But they turn them in a fashion
> Past clerks' or statesmen's art or passion.
> I can spare the college bell,
> And the learned lecture, well;
> Spare the clergy and libraries,
> Institutes and dictionaries,
> For that hearty English root
> Thrives here, unvalued, underfoot.
> Rude poets of the tavern hearth,
> Squandering your unquoted mirth,
> Which keeps the ground and never soars,
> While Jake retorts and Reuben roars;
> Scoff of yeoman strong and stark,
> Goes like bullet to its mark;
> While the solid curse and jeer
> Never balk the waiting ear.
> (qtd. *RFPP* 260–61)

If he holds these lines in high esteem, Frost found nothing to praise about the sentences that make up Wilfrid Gibson's poem "Solway Ford," remarking, "[L]ook at the way the sentences run on. They are not sentences at all in my sense of the word" (*SL* 151):

The empty wain made slowly over the sand;
And he, with hands in pockets by the side
Was trudging, deep in dream, the while he scanned
With blue, unseeing eyes the far-off tide:
When, stumbling in a hole, with startled neigh,
His young horse reared; and, snatching at the rein,
He slipped: the wheels crushed on him as he lay;
Then, tilting over him, the lumbering wain
Turned turtle as the plunging beast broke free,
And made for home: and pinioned and half-dead
He lay, and listened to the far-off sea;
And seemed to hear it surging overhead
Already: though 'twas full an hour or more
Until high-tide, when Solway's shining flood
Should sweep the shallow firth from shore to shore.[5]

What, one might ask, marks the real difference between these sentences and those in "Monadnoc"? Is it only their length (Emerson's poem does feature shorter sentences), or is it also the relation of syntax to line end? The running on of sentences and clauses in "Solway Ford" that Frost dislikes precipitates "hard" enjambment ("wain / Turned turtle"; "surging overhead / Already"; "flood / Should sweep"), which Emerson's poem evinces much less often.

Frost's reaction to Keats further suggests his misgivings about the rhetoric of enjambment, even in metrical verse. The one poem by Keats that he said he disliked was *Endymion,* and one likely reason for his qualms about that poem is that it "supplies some strong examples of e[njambment]," strong enough to be cited in the definition of "enjambment" in the *Princeton Encyclopedia of Poetry and Poetics* (*RFW* 75).[6] A passage from almost anywhere in the poem demonstrates Keats's reliance on that device:

Full in the middle of this pleasantness
There stood a marble altar, with a tress
Of flowers budded newly; and the dew
Had taken fairy phantasies to strew
Daisies upon the sacred sward last eve,
And so the dawned light in pomp receive.
For 'twas the morn: Apollo's upward fire
Made every eastern cloud a silvery pyre
Of brightness so unsullied, that therein
A melancholy spirit well might win
Oblivion, and melt out his essence fine
Into the winds:[7]

In this passage, hard enjambments ("the dew / Had taken"; "to strew / Daisies"; "might win / Oblivion") split subjects from their predicates and predicates from their objects. William Carlos Williams, in contrast, liked

Endymion, probably in part because of this tendency toward hard enjambment, which predicts his own prosodic practice.[8] Even though Keats's
other poetry is not without instances of enjambment, in *Endymion* enjambment is rife, a fact that may explain Frost's exclusion of that poem from his
list of favorites.

Although Frost hesitates to embrace any poem that is systematically enjambed, several poems that he says he admires for their "sentence sounds"
include prominent instances of line-sentence counterpointing. In a letter to
Sidney Cox, Frost points out "the beautiful sentences in a thing like
Wordsworth's To Sleep or Herrick's To Daffodils" (*SL* 151). Herrick's "To
Daffodils," which Frost holds up as exemplary for its "shape of stanza," includes a number of hard enjambments:

> Fair Daffodils, we weep to see
> You haste away so soon:
> As yet the early-rising Sun
> Has not attain'd his noon.
> Stay, stay,
> Until the hasting day
> Has run
> But to the even-song;
> And, having prayed together, we
> Will go with you along.
>
> We have short time to stay, as you,
> We have as short a Spring;
> As quick a growth to meet decay
> As you, or any thing.
> We die,
> As your hours do, and dry
> Away
> Like to the Summer's rain;
> Or as the pearls of morning's dew
> Ne'er to be found again.[9]

In the first stanza, Herrick cuts a subject off from its predicate in three different lines: "Sun / has not attain'd"; "day / Has run"; "we / Will go with
you." The flow of syntax through line termini represents the flow of time,
which the speaker cannot stanch. However, Frost does not allude to these
syntactic run-ons, unless it is when he hails the poem's "shape of stanza"; as
he makes clear in "The Constant Symbol," though, he primarily means by
this phrase the modulation of the metrical pattern from one line to the next:
"He may use an assortment of line lengths for any shape of stanza like Herrick in 'To Daffodils'" (*CPPP* 788). Although he does not say anything about
sentences overlapping lines here, such radical extensions and contractions of

the metrical line suggest the likelihood of overlapping. Notably, too, the phrase "shape of stanza" is the same one that Frost uses in his description of "Miniver Cheevy," which he explicitly commends for its line-sentence counterpointing.

In addition to Herrick's poem, Frost mentions Wordsworth's sonnet, "To Sleep," as a poem of "beautiful sentences." Although Wordsworth wrote three sonnets bearing this title, Frost would have been most familiar with the version included in Francis Palgrave's anthology of English verse, *The Golden Treasury* (1861):

> A flock of sheep that leisurely pass by
> One after one; the sound of rain, and bees
> Murmuring; the fall of rivers, winds and seas,
> Smooth fields, white sheets of water, and pure sky;
>
> I've thought of all by turns, and yet do lie
> Sleepless; and soon the small birds' melodies
> Must hear, first utter'd from my orchard trees,
> And the first cuckoo's melancholy cry.
>
> Even thus last night, and two nights more I lay,
> And could not win thee, Sleep! by any stealth:
> So do not let me wear to-night away:
>
> Without Thee what is all the morning's wealth?
> Come, blessèd barrier between day and day,
> Dear mother of fresh thoughts and joyous health![10]

In this poem not only must subjects look to the following line for their verbs ("bees / Murmuring"; "birds' melodies / Must hear"), but an adverb is positioned on the line below the verb that it modifies ("do lie / Sleepless"), in signal of the dislocation the speaker feels from lack of sleep. While the sentences in "To Sleep" are not all of the same length, many of them do bend "round the corner," a rhetorical effect Frost seems to appreciate despite his posturing.

In fact, Frost makes plain in his theorizing of "the sound of sense" that he is interested not in line-sentence counterpointing, but rather in the creative opportunity presented by a sequence of endstopped lines, since he believes these latter provide the best test of a poet's ability to imagine intonation contours: "The thing that gives you variety in a poem is to vary in tone the phrases used. Why, think of the intensity of dramatic expression that would vary twenty end-stop lines! . . . [Milton] steps right into it: 'Fly, envious time, till thou run out thy race.'"[11] It is telling that Frost quotes the first line of Milton's poem, "On Time," to justify his theory, since Justus Lawler points up the meaningfulness of the pattern of enjambment in the poem. The first line is endstopped as are (to a greater or lesser extent) the lines immediately following it:

> Fly, envious Time, till thou run out thy race:
> Call on the lazy leaden-stepping hours,
> Whose speed is but the heavy plummet's pace;[12]

But this passage does not set the form that the rest of the poem follows. Beginning with the eleventh line, hard enjambment prevails:

> Then long Eternity shall greet our bliss
> With an individual kiss;
> And Joy shall overtake us as a flood,
> When every thing that is sincerely good
> And perfectly divine,
> With Truth, and Peace, and Love, shall ever shine
> About the supreme throne
> Of him, t' whose happy-making sight alone
> When once our heav'nly-guided soul shall climb,
> Then all this earthy grossness quit,
> Attired with Stars, we shall for ever sit,
> Triumphing over Death, and Chance, and thee, O Time.[13]

As Lawler remarks of these lines: "Time, we are told, shall cease upon the honied middle of the night, as the temporal 'overflows' into the eternal; or rather, Milton emphasizes, eternity shall overflow and encompass time."[14] Frost, though, does not acknowledge these lines or the line-sentence counterpointing that shapes them, limiting his remarks to the beginning of the poem, which countenances his claims about "the sound of sense." Because enjambment often has little to do with the reproduction of tone of voice, Frost simply ignores the technique and the poetry that showcases it in the course of his theorizing.

In his discussion of Milton's "On Time," Frost also points to one of Shakespeare's plays that he claims includes a striking intonation contour within a single endstopped line: "If music is the food of love, give me excess of it." Although this opening sentence of *Twelfth Night* may inspire a reader to conjure up one or more expressive cadences, Frost does not get the sentence quite right—a sentence that in fact is not limited to one line: "If music be the food of love, play on, / Give me excess of it."[15] As George Wright has demonstrated, the play of phrase and line in Shakespeare's iambic pentameter attains great dramatic force,[16] and one might argue that the enjambment between the first two lines of *Twelfth Night* signifies the "surfeiting" that the Duke desires, as syntax indulgently spills over into the next line. Further illustrating the mastery of Shakespeare's line-sentence counterpointing, Lawler says of Sonnet 151 that "the enjambments are the central

pillar on which is erected the whole triumphant affair," with the hard enjambments of the second quatrain exemplifying the "fundamental medium
of transcendence" that is sexual love:[17]

> For, thou betraying me, I do betray
> My nobler part to my gross body's treason;
> My soul doth tell my body that he may
> Triumph in love; flesh stays no farther reason,

What Frost chooses to cite (and not cite) in defense of his aesthetic tells us
much about his personal sense of "the politics of poetry," but, as we will
see, it misleads about his actual formal practices.

Indeed, despite his evasions, Frost's poetry repeatedly shows how important line-sentence counterpointing is in the construction of meaning.
Reminding us of the long history of enjambment in metrical poetry,
Charles Hartman contends that it is "even more readily available in metrical verse than in free verse because the system of the line is more obviously
systematic. The steadiness of the meter strengthens the feeling of enjambment."[18] John Hollander recognizes the range of meanings that enjambments make available to us, arguing that they attain significance "for what
they reveal—about language, about the world, or because of when and
where, in the course of the poem" they occur.[19] Such a critical focus serves
as an antidote to those who would claim, as Edward Thomas did in a review of *North of Boston,* that Frost "would lose far less than most writers by
being printed as prose" (*IMO* 190). Not only does such a statement over-
look the crucial metrical effects in his poetry not directly related to intonation; it also treats as insignificant other expressive powers of lineation. It is
clear, though, that Frost's preoccupation with the unit of the sentence informs Thomas's position. Frost's *ars poetica* "In a Poem" makes unmistakable his point of emphasis:

> The sentencing goes blithely on its way,
> And takes the playfully objected rhyme
> As surely as it keeps the stroke and time
> In having its undeviable say.
> (*CPPP* 329)

Here phrase boundaries neatly match line boundaries, and line endings
(marked by rhyme) are imagined as nothing more than slight obstacles to
be overcome, not the richly representational zones that they often turn out
to be in Frost's verse. Again, this rhetoric has had its effect on Frost critics,
with Richard Poirier chastising Reuben Brower for praising a line of "Hyla
Brook" as "'the most exquisite line in the poem'": "It might well be, if we

were encouraged by syntax to read Frost by the line. But we are asked to read him at the very least by the sentence. For Frost, the sentence is the basic unit of voice in a poem."[20] The suggestion that we must attend to the intonation contours conveyed by Frost's sentences is correct, but it is also accurate to say that we respond to the unit of the line, which is not necessarily a unit of sense, as we read.

While agreeing with Hollander that the meanings of enjambment depend on what a poem has to say at the moment of its use, Lawler argues more generally that enjambment is mimetic and that in metrical poetry it signifies a gesture of human freedom and transcendence, and Frost's use of enjambment bears out Lawler's claim. When a sequence of endstopped lines is interrupted by a line that exhibits enjambment, a limit is broken that "shocks and delights" us: "Thus, a theory of enjambment will generally entail a theory of poetic surprise and, with certain qualifications, that will also be a theory of human transcendence."[21] Lawler points out both the universal truth that enjambment represents the surpassing of boundaries and the fact that it is fundamentally a visual form: "Since poetic structure is a kind of pictogram of poetic statement, one would therefore expect enjambment to occur when assaying that situation in which, after repeated frustration, the human subject suddenly experiences the overcoming of limitations and an expansion into something beyond those limits."[22] He goes on to remark that the "preeminent human experience of 'going beyond,' of 'overflowing,'" is "human sexual union," "one of the most prevalent and one of the most rich contexts of enjambment (though certainly *not* the only) for poets in the English-language tradition."[23] As his verse proves, Frost often deploys enjambment at moments when a limit is overcome, when our finite world is broken through, including in sexual consummation. Although it may not be the main principle of prosodic organization in Frost's poetry as it is in much free verse, enjambment has a crucial role to play, and Frost cultivates it quite consciously. Rather than simply attending to "the sentence within the poem," then, Frost's poetry attests to the fact that his division of those sentences into lines gathers figurative force (*PJ* 70–71).

Even as Frost's polemical devaluation of the visual line is driven by his view of modernist literary politics, his attention to it in practice enables him to trope not only human transcendence but contemporary social and political thought. Christopher Ricks has shown that line ends "can be a type or symbol or emblem of what the poet values, as well as the instrument by which his values are expressed," and such is the case with Frost.[24] Often we find in his verse that enjambment stands for a liberal ideology, and in the course of his career Frost uses it to paint the political philosophy of socialism—a philosophy he commonly contests—and, in a positive vein, to endorse democratic principles. He also engages that prosodic pattern to remark on the value of freedom and extravagance in literary and social spheres. Ironically, then, Frost avoids mention of enjambment in his poetics based on its association with liberal political views, but turns around and employs that prosody to invoke just such views (and, as I have suggested, not always negatively) in his poetry. On the other hand, when he writes verse that resists the pattern of enjambment, he usually goes in a conservative political direction, signifying through formal closure at line ends isolationism, resistance to New Deal programs and policies, and, in the Cold War, the containment of the spread of communism. Early in his career, though, endstopped lines are coded liberal, as Frost's pro-labor sonnets symbolize through the alignment of line and sentence the oppression of an immigrant work force by the unbending laws of industrial capitalism. As we might expect, too, with Frost prosodic happenings at line ends often are leavened by irony, a condition that makes their political valence hard to assess. In addition, mid-line pauses (or caesurae) frequently attain political significance in his verse, as they mark off Cold War geopolitical formations and become a (darkly humorous) sign of the annihilating force of nuclear technologies.

Ricks rightly urges a slowness and carefulness to reading if we are to appreciate the full effects of such linear design: "The eye and the ear . . . must be reconciled, neither lording it over the other. . . . Reading should itself be a type of the proper relation of eye to ear; and the poet's lines—the relationships which he creates between the single line and its accommodating passage—must effect such a relationship of eye and ear."[25] Of course, this kind of reading requires us to abandon Frost's own privileging of the ear, and, when we do so, we find that just as multiple meanings can coexist through ambiguous vocal posturing, so, too, can meaning be held in fruitful suspension through the suggestiveness of syntax at line ends.

II

Enjambment in Frost's poetry can be mimetic, intended to imitate an action or event in the world outside of the poem, or it can be expressive, standing for the mental or emotional orientation of the poet or speaker. Frost uses both types of enjambment throughout his career and repeatedly relates that scheme to issues of power.

For example, when Frost depicts the unleashing of the power of natural forces, he is able to represent their disrespect of limits in the rush of syntax through the boundary of the verse line. In "The Onset" he figures the coming spring thaw through that pattern, imagining a stream of water

> That flashes tail through last year's withered brake
> And dead weeds, like a disappearing snake.
>
> (*CPPP* 209)

Just as the melting snow runs sinuously through the debris, syntax winds through these lines, with one object of the preposition separated from the other. Earlier in the same stanza, Frost plants an expressive enjambment, as his speaker asserts hopefully the probability that he will outlast the assault of winter:

> I know that winter death has never tried
> The earth but it has failed

When we first encounter *tried,* we assume that it means "attempted" and not "tested," that the speaker is going to undeceive himself about the evil intent of the season (that is, that it *tried* to do harm). However, instead of finding an infinitive phrase at the head of the next line, we get a direct object ("The earth"). Suddenly, we realize that winter *has* tried to destroy us, but that it has tried and failed. When Frost forces us to reread *tried* as a transitive verb in light of the syntactic remainder in the next line, he calls attention to the agon of earthly existence, a meaning that is reinforced by the use of the Puritan term *errand* in the first stanza of the poem.

In "A Hillside Thaw," another poem about the turning of winter into spring and of ice into water, Frost again relies on a poetics of enjambment to depict the power of seasonal change. In the first stanza the speaker marvels at the thaw, and lineation represents that headlong flow:

> To think to know the country and not know
> The hillside on the day the sun lets go
> Ten million silver lizards out of snow!
> . . . .
> It looks as if some magic of the sun
> Lifted the rug that bred them on the floor
> And the light breaking on them made them run.
>
> (*CPPP* 218)

The movement of syntax between lines represents the water as it runs down the hillside, and the absence of caesurae dramatizes the fact that nothing impedes that wild descent. The first two striking enjambments divide a verb from its direct object ("not know / The hillside"; "let go / Ten million silver lizards"). The third appears when the speaker waxes metaphorical in describing the visual effect of rapidly disappearing snow; by separating subject from verb ("magic / Lifted"), Frost makes us run through the line end to complete the clause in imitation of the water overflowing the landscape. After these eight lines, when the speaker imagines trying to stop the water in its tracks, much softer cuts in syntax prevail.[26] In his early unpublished lyric "The Rain Bath," Frost similarly sets down run-on lines to highlight the brute force of the roaring wind and deluge of rain:

> Do you remember how in camp one day
> We boys awoke with shouts of joy to hear
> A fresh young gale in the forest plunge and rear
> And thrash our sylvan roof with boughs in play?
> . . . .
>   We flung the house door wide,
> Then waited till the rapid sky once more
> Turned darkest with the irrepressive tide,
> And then, when ripping leaves the wild downpour
> Was dashed to mist along the steps and path,
> We ran forth naked to the morning bath.
>
>   (*CPPP* 520)

The several turnings of syntax in this passage ("to hear / A fresh gale"; "rear / And thrash"; "sky once more / Turned darkest"; "downpour / Was dashed") symbolize nature's violence, which is answered, almost thwarted, by the boys' innocent exuberance. The appearance of *Turned* at the head of one enjambed line wryly remarks on the scheme that shapes this poetic performance—a scheme that forces us to recognize the boldness not only of nature but also of children who casually throw decorum to the wind.

Frost again reflects on the intersection of natural and social systems in "A Brook in the City," where syntax often spills over line boundaries in an attempt to represent the flow of the brook and its uneasy accommodation to urban forms. Before we glimpse the brook, though, we see the clash of two ways of life, symbolized by the disjunction of two man-made structures:

> The farmhouse lingers, though averse to square
> With the new city street it has to wear
> A number in.
>
>   (*CPPP* 213)

The first enjambment ("to square / With") splits a colloquial phrase in two, and the second enjambment divides a verb from its object ("it has to wear / A number in"). In this case these run-ons signify the violation of limits; as syntax bleeds from one line into the next, country things bleed into the modes of the industrial city. In these three lines, Frost also slyly comments on a visual aspect of his prosody apart from enjambment, with the words "averse" and "square" suggesting that the poem ("a verse") is itself forced to conform to a stanzaic shape (roughly a "square") that is not natural to it. When Frost next employs hard enjambment in the poem, it is to mime the play of water and its effect on objects in its course:

> I ask as one who knew the brook, its strength
> And impulse, having dipped a finger length
> And made it leap my knuckle, having tossed
> A flower to try its currents where they crossed.

Here Frost separates a compound object ("its strength / And impulse") and a compound verb ("having dipped a finger length / And made it leap"), causing the reader to cross over a line boundary in order to finish a phrase. In the other bold enjambment of the passage ("having tossed / A flower"), the verb hangs in air (much like the flower) before being caught up in the next line by its object. Crossing line with sentence, Frost draws a picture of the cross-currents of the brook. He also depicts the violent subjugation of that body of water, its unnatural imprisonment, through run-on lines: "The brook was thrown / Deep in a sewer dungeon under stone." In this instance, enjambment illustrates the descent of the brook, with the reversed foot ("Deep in") calling attention to the direction in which we must go, reading from one line down to the next. It also embodies Frost's sense of the direction in which we are headed as a society by calling up the threat that urban America and its stultifying forms pose to our personal freedom, our cherished individualism.

In "For Once, Then, Something," Frost again sets the line against the sentence to figure a body of water—one known not for its mobility but for its mirroring powers—and, in doing so, meditates on the relation of the individual to social systems as well as to abstract systems of knowledge and truth. When the speaker attempts to plumb the depths of a well in pursuit of the existential, he depicts himself as at odds with his culture and, thus, an object of ridicule:

> Others taunt me with having knelt at well-curbs
> Always wrong to the light, so never seeing
> Deeper down in the well than where the water
> Gives me back in a shining surface picture
> Me myself in the summer heaven godlike
> Looking out of a wreath of fern and cloud puffs.
>   (*CPPP* 208)

The *contre-rejet,* or continuation of the enjambed unit (literally, "throw-back"), tropes the speaker's experience of peering into the well, his image thrown back at him ("the water / Gives me back"); the syntactic break also represents his self-division and social dislocation. The other prominent enjambment of the passage ("so never seeing / Deeper down") mimes the dramatic action of the poem, forcing us to look down (to the next line) just as the speaker looks down (the well). Later in the poem, another hard enjambment occurs—this time when the surface of the water is disturbed: "One drop fell from a fern, and lo, a ripple / Shook whatever it was lay there at bottom." Here the fracture of subject and verb ("a ripple / Shook") is both mimetic and expressive, symbolizing the disjointing of the water's surface as well as the disjointing of the speaker's insight. Although Frost declares his interest in "recognizable" "sentence sounds," then, his poetry often generates meaning by making syntax momentarily unrecognizable through the rhetorical operations of enjambment.

Because Frost was so successful in setting the terms of discussion of his poetry, throwing attention on the sentence as opposed to the intersection of sentence and line, rarely do such enjambments attract comment. Several critics, though, have been led to remark on the mimetic and expressive line-sentence counterpointing in "Spring Pools," where the syntactic suspension points up the possible meditative propensity of the standing water:

> These pools that, though in forests still reflect
> The total sky almost without defect,
> (*CPPP* 224)

Although, as we have seen, Richard Poirier admonishes Reuben Brower for reading by line and not by sentence, Poirier is too good a critic not to read in just that way here, noting that "In the hesitation, just before turning into line 2, we can allow for the possibility that the 'pools' 'reflect' in the sense that they 'think'; but once we make the turn, the verb grasps its object, and 'reflect' means only 'mirror.' 'Pools' cannot 'reflect' the way the speaker can: they cannot remember the past in the present or meditate upon a destructiveness which is in any event a part of the spontaneous creative movement in which they participate."[27] Momentarily, then, we are made to feel that these pools might possess the human capacity to remember (an Ovidian universe in which organic material is invested with human psyche), but, as Poirier sees, when we round the verse line we find that the verb is in fact transitive, and so not indicative of thought process. However, our impression of the pools as in some sense human is not fully contradicted by the *contre-rejet.* The initial reading, which suggests the speaker's strong wish for correspondence, is not canceled out; rather, as John Hollander says about an enjambment in a poem by Blake, what we see is a "phantom image," a "blurred superposition of the two syntactic alternatives."[28] Indeed, Frost yields to the myth in the second stanza, attributing human mental ability to the trees that would "blot out" the pools ("Let them think twice . . ."). The hard enjambment of the first stanza that ushers in syntactic ambiguity enacts, then, the complex drama of man's ambiguous relationship to nature, particularly our desire to humanize it in an attempt better to understand it, to bring it in league with our sympathies.

Frost uses line-sentence counterpointing often to draw the dialectic between the human will to transgress, that is, our impulse to assert difference and break free of social constraints, and, on the other hand, our desire to enforce limits as a protection against the dissolution of the self. In "Trespass" a speaker declares ownership of a tract of land when confronted by an interloper, and varying degrees of enjambment represent the physical act of encroachment as well as the speaker's defensive maneuvers when his authority is threatened:

> No, I had set no prohibiting sign,
> And yes, my land was hardly fenced.
> Nevertheless, the land was mine:
> I was being trespassed on and against.
>
> Whoever the surly freedom took
> Of such an unaccountable stay
> Busying my woods and brook
> Gave me a strangely restless day.
> (*CPPP* 331)

The rigidly endstopped first stanza yields to a second stanza marked by a range of enjambments, with no marks of punctuation at three of four line ends. The most conspicuous cross-over occurs in the last line, which begins with a verb that must look back to the first line for its subject. In the first stanza the speaker asserts the legitimacy (even the propriety) of man-made boundaries; in the second he describes a man's refusal to acknowledge those boundaries and the anxieties that that lapse engenders in him. Finally, though, the stranger acknowledges the owner's rights, dramatically presented at the end of the poem by four endstopped lines reminiscent of the initial quatrain:

> Then came his little acknowledgment:
> He asked for a drink at the kitchen door,
> An errand he may have had to invent,
> But it made my property mine once more.

In this act of sociability not only are physical boundaries restored; the owner's mind is able to return to a point of order, as anxiety about his possession of his world (and about his self-possession) dissipates.

Frequently, Frost represents social transgression through physical acts of transcendence and employs line-sentence counterpointing to do so. For instance, in "Brown's Descent," enjambment pictures the smashing of boundaries when the title figure is blown downhill by a winter gale. Unable to get a foothold in the ice crust, he ends up two miles below his farm, his "slide" through obstacles in the landscape symbolized by epidemic crossings of line termini by syntax in that part of the poem: "could see / His lantern"; "make / His wild descent"; "the gale / Got him"; "he stove / A hole"; "he strove // And stamped"; "pursued / His journey"; "to risk / His neck"; "who saw afar / The figures"; "if I / should say"; "because / he couldn't climb"; "thaw / should take"; "the course / He steered" (*CPPP* 132–34). These radical enjambments signify the degree of Brown's physical *and* social extravagance (a neighbor who sees Brown in the distance exclaims at his being out "at such an hour of night! / He's celebrating something strange"). In the end, Brown capitulates to the forces that drove him, going back up the mountain the long way, and as his intransigence (or strangeness) fades, lines and phrases come into alignment: "He bowed with grace to natural law, / And then went round it on his feet, / After the manner of our stock."

In "Acquainted with the Night" Frost also uses enjambment to depict a man's foray beyond physical limits, a surpassing that stands as a metaphor for his straining against social structures. The syntactically parallel lines of the first tercet are rigidly endstopped; although the speaker reports in them his act of transcendence, the tight closure suggests that he is trying to exert some control over that experience, to draw attention to his own subsequent efforts to check that waywardness:

> I have been one acquainted with the night.
> I have walked out in rain—and back in rain.
> I have outwalked the furthest city light.
> (*CPPP* 234)

As the poem progresses, however, enjambments begin to pile up—a prosodic sign of the speaker's alienation from other people, his deep-rooted sense of eccentricity: "an interrupted cry / Came over houses"; "One luminary clock against the sky // Proclaimed the time was neither wrong nor right." In the final one-sentence noncaesural line ("I have been one acquainted with the night"), Frost represents the speaker's redoubled effort to assert his social conformity.

The related poem "Good Hours," which Frost wrote early in his career and which is about the dilemma of the artist who must struggle with the competing demands of self and society, dramatizes cultural disaffection through the same trope (a man who breaks the plane of a city limit in a late night excursion) and scheme. It is interesting to note that hard enjambment does not shape the penultimate stanza of the poem, as we might expect, since it is here that the speaker-poet recalls his vagrancy, his refusal to conform ("I had such company outward bound. / I went till there were no cottages found. / I turned and repented, . . ."). Ironically, the only truly startling enjambment occurs in the final stanza, where he narrates his return to social precincts:

> Over the snow my creaking feet
> Disturbed the slumbering village street
> Like profanation, by your leave,
> At ten o'clock of a winter eve.
>   (*CPPP* 102)

The enjambment "feet / Disturbed" signifies some unsettling trespass, as syntax creeps across the line boundary, just at the point where we would expect to find a coincidence of line and phrase boundaries to illustrate the speaker's reintegration into his community. By employing enjambment instead, Frost reveals that, while the speaker may be back in the fold, he is not sincerely "repent[ant]," as the tone of some of his remarks might suggest. Appearing to bow to bourgeois propriety, he retaliates against it, his impulse toward the unconventional undimmed.

If "Good Hours" is about the plight of the American artist, so, too, is Frost's early poem "Pan with Us," where that same artist figure must assert his independence from the English poetic tradition—a relationship figured, ironically, through line-sentence counterpointing, a prosodic form that strongly marks that tradition. The first three stanzas of the poem feature only soft enjambment, as the speaker, "pipes in hand," surveys the land ("In all the country he did command / He saw no smoke and he saw no roof. / That was well! and he stamped a hoof"). But as soon as he refuses to conform to conventional lyric modes, hard enjambment dominates, signaling his aesthetic disaffiliation and nationalization:

> He tossed his pipes, too hard to teach
> A new-world song, far out of reach,
> For a sylvan sign that the blue jay's screech
>   And the whimper of hawks beside the sun
>   Were music enough for him, for one.

> Times were changed from what they were:
> Such pipes kept less of power to stir
> The fruited bough of the juniper
>   And the fragile bluets clustered there
>   Than the merest aimless breath of air.
>   (*CPPP* 32)

In these stanzas, sentences are set against the line just as Pan sets himself against what he considers to be a listless poetic tradition. Objects are split from their verbs and compound objects from each other, and this linguistic disjunction symbolizes the disjunction between past and present conditions that necessitates a shift in procedure for the contemporary American artist. The final stanza also hinges on enjambment, as the poet frees himself to think of other ways to "play": "He laid him down on the sun-burned earth / And raveled a flower and looked away." Pan's surrender of his pipes leads to his speculative frame of mind, his creative freedom registered through the freedom of the sentence to range across these lines.

In other poems (both lyric and dramatic) written throughout his life, Frost's rhetoric of enjambment highlights mental exigency—the imagination freed from rational limit—and an often dangerous emotional surplus. In "Home Burial" Frost represents through the visual line the husband's emotional constriction, his refusal to let grief exceed culturally imposed bounds, as well as the overflowing grief of the wife, her refusal to be appeased and, thus, to conform to social standards. The wife's lament is scored on the page as follows:

> Friends make pretense of following to the grave,
> But before one is in it, their minds are turned
> And making the best of their way back to life
> And living people, and things they understand.
>   (*CPPP* 58)

Although the enjambments that shape this passage are not extreme, they stand out against the husband's sentences, which rarely exceed the ends of lines:

> "There, you have said it all and you feel better.
> You won't go now. You're crying. Close the door.
> The heart's gone out of it: why keep it up?
> Amy! There's someone coming down the road!"

In this dialogue Frost reveals the wife's transgressive mental state by having sentences transgress line boundaries; conversely, the husband's emotions are firmly held in check, with sentences neatly bedded in lines to designate his striving for order and control. While it may be true that the sentences they utter carry powerfully expressive (if not unambiguous) intonation contours, the impression those sentences make in lines is as crucial, standing as a figure for the psychological separateness of the two.

In "The Black Cottage" enjambment assumes a similar expressive function, as the minister's imagination of himself as "monarch of a desert land"—a land unaffected by the intellectual and social fashions of the day—and of his fictive kingdom (a description that I looked at in Chapter 2 for its phonemic sequencing) is strongly enjambed, a sign of the speaker's imaginative surplus. His final flight of fancy features these hard cuts in syntax: "or think it worth / The pains"; "but mostly / Sand dunes"; "should sugar in the natal dew / The babe"; "the sandstorm / Retard mid-waste." Together they graph the minister's romantic aspirations, his refusal to be bounded by fact. At the end of the poem, however, his insistently enjambed speech yields to the voice of his companion and, ultimately, that of the narrator, neither of whose utterances exhibit enjambment:

> "There are bees in this wall." He struck the clapboards,
> Fierce heads looked out; small bodies pivoted.
> We rose to go. Sunset blazed on the windows.
>
> (*CPPP* 62)

In this coda the wishful thinking of the minister is interrupted by his companion's statement of fact, "'There are bees in this wall,'" a sentence that fails even to reach the end of the line. Once the narrator takes over, we see sentences beginning and ending in the same line; there is no danger of syntax spilling over, as it does in the minister's monologue. The image of unlicensed talk that Frost achieves through enjambment yields to a rival image of closure and control, which denotes a return to realism (or empirical observation).

This expressive use of enjambment is not at all unusual in Frost's verse, which repeatedly represents mental and social extravagance by means of that device. In his dream-lyric "After Apple-Picking" in *North of Boston*, lines and sentences are often out of joint, dramatizing the strained psyche of the speaker, who has become enervated to the point of delusion from overwork. The poem begins with several prominent enjambments that force us to reread syntax in an attempt to piece together meaning:

> My long two-pointed ladder's sticking through a tree
> Toward heaven still,
> And there's a barrel that I didn't fill
> Beside it, and there may be two or three
> Apples I didn't pick upon some bough.
> But I am done with apple-picking now.
>
> (*CPPP* 70)

Frost starts off with a soft enjambment, dividing one prepositional phrase ("through a tree") from another ("Toward heaven"), both of which modify "ladder." The second enjambment ("fill / Beside") is also relatively tame, separating a verb from a prepositional phrase within the same clause. In the fourth and fifth lines, however, cuts in syntax are more sharp, with an adjective estranged from the noun it modifies. In fact, it is not at all apparent after reading the fourth line that the words "two" and "three" are adjectives and not direct objects (referring to additional barrels). This nonalignment of line and sentence occurs just as the speaker mentions the mental confusion he has experienced as a result of his labor. The sixth line, where he asserts his completion of his task ("But I am done with apple-picking now"), features an alignment of line and sentence that pictures his attempt to catch ahold of himself.

Throughout this poem, Frost plays with the possibilities of confusion that enjambment allows. After the sixth line, he slips back into enjambment just as his speaker slips into dream-memories of the work that has caused him so much mental and physical anguish:

> Essence of winter sleep is on the night,
> The scent of apples: I am drowsing off.
> I cannot rub the strangeness from my sight
> I got from looking through a pane of glass
> I skimmed this morning from the drinking trough
> And held against the world of hoary grass.
> It melted, and I let it fall and break.
> But I was well
> Upon my way to sleep before it fell,
> And I could tell
> What form my dreaming was about to take.

At the ends of several of these lines, meaning strains for completion. In certain cases, our encounter with a phrase on one line requires us to go back and revise our reading of the terminal word or phrase in a previous line. For example, the phrase "a pane of glass," which we initially take literally as a window pane, is turned into a figurative lens (a thin sheet of ice formed on the water in a trough) once we reach the *contre-rejet*. Perhaps most strikingly, "well," which is positioned at the end of a line, appears to be an adjective modifying "I." However, it turns out that "well" (a word in the colloquial phrase "well upon my way") is an adverb describing not the subject ("I") but the phrase "Upon my way." Although Frost sees that irony is possible in poetry when an intonation contour conveys a meaning at odds with the sense of the words ("I shall show the sentence sound opposing the sense of the words as in irony"), he does not credit the irony attainable through enjambment (*SL* 140). Here the speaker is not at all "well," either emotionally or physically; rather, he is in a limbo of half-sleep, and Frost relies heavily in the poem on the distortions of line-sentence counterpointing to figure the "over-tired" apple-picker's alienation from himself and the world around him. In cooperation with that prosodic feature, Frost's rhyme pairs look quite different but sound alike (*bough : now; off : trough; ache : take*). Hollander describes this kind of rhyme as one "where the ear and the eye intersect," and Frost's decision to make rhymes out of such visually dissimilar linguistic units relates to the dissonance that the speaker experiences ("I cannot rub the strangeness from my sight").[29]

However, alterations of consciousness are not always traumatic in Frost's verse; sometimes they perform emotional rescue, and the enjambments that shape descriptions of such feats mean to highlight the transcendence of the subject. In the eight-line poem "Dust of Snow" (1920) he uses enjambment to represent a dramatic slippage in his speaker's consciousness. Breaking syntax across line and stanza boundaries, Frost places his hardest enjambment at the center of the poem, at the very moment when the speaker records his psychic breakthrough:

> The way a crow
> Shook down on me
> The dust of snow
> From a hemlock tree
>
> Has given my heart
> A change of mood
> And saved some part
> Of a day I had rued.
>   (*CPPP* 205)

The first enjambment ("crow / Shook"), which divides a subject from its verb, reveals the shock that has occurred: there is something about the way the crow shook down the snow that causes outlook to change. The fact that the subject ("The way") of the sentence must wait to find its verb ("Has given") in another stanza, and across three lines, suggests just how radical the change is. This pivotal enjambment dramatizes the transcendence that the speaker undergoes; he has migrated from one mode of being to another. Our experience of reading syntax through these lines enforces that transition upon us. In "Away!" (1958) the speaker, like his counterparts in "Acquainted with the Night" and "Good Hours," is "out walking" when the poem begins and tells us that he "leave[s] behind / Good friends in town," a statement that is enjambed in order to picture his separation from these friends, his movement beyond the borders of the social. In contrasting his condition with that of "Adam and Eve / Put out of the Park," he uses enjambment again to symbolize our mythic break from Eden. However, the traveler in the poem does not just surpass a city limit; ultimately, he leaves earth behind for heaven, a transformation that takes him from the finite to the infinite. His estrangement, then, is not just from his friends, but from himself, as the event of death signifies a stunning self-surpassing:

> There is no one I
> Am put out with
> Or put out by.
>
> Unless I'm wrong
> I but obey
> The urge of a song:
> I'm—bound—away!
> (*CPPP* 427)

Here Frost breaks the "I / Am" without breaking the iamb, using enjambment within the boundaries of metrical verse, and the final hard enjambment of the passage ("I but obey / The urge") coincides with that ultimate act of transcendence. Notably, though, the final quatrain features only soft cuts in syntax ("And I may return / If dissatisfied / With what I learn / From having died") as a sign of the speaker's confidence in his ability to reintegrate body and soul. Along with the pattern of enjambment, the "tiny stanzas" of the poem (as Frost described them in public remarks) are seen and not heard, and so are not taken into account by his professed strict auditory aesthetic (*RFPP* 458). Although he does not explain the significance of this visual format, it would seem that the slightness of the stanzas is meant to announce the speaker's refusal to set up massive fortifications against death, thereby serving as a sign of his ease.

The transcendence that enjambment figures is sometimes sexualized, too, as Justus Lawler has observed, with one body breaking out of itself and into another, and Frost's erotically charged poetry puts that pattern to good use. For example, "Putting in the Seed" imagines human heterosexuality via the breakthrough of a plant into the earthly plane:

> You come to fetch me from my work tonight
> When supper's on the table, and we'll see
> If I can leave off burying the white
> Soft petals fallen from the apple tree
> (Soft petals, yes, but not so barren quite,
> Mingled with these, smooth bean and wrinkled pea),
> And go along with you ere you lose sight
> Of what you came for and become like me,
> Slave to a springtime passion for the earth.
> (*CPPP* 120)

Significantly, two of the enjambments in this sonnet relate to the faculty of sight. In the second line, Frost ends with the word *see,* giving an initial impression that he is speaking of a literal act of vision. But when we reach the next line, we find that *see* is, in fact, meant to be taken figuratively, as part of a colloquial phrase ("and we'll see / If I can leave off") that means "find out." The second instance of enjambment bearing on the work of the eyes features the terminal word *sight,* which again we are tempted to read literally; however, when we reread in light of the syntax of the following line, we discover that the word takes its place in yet another colloquial expression ("ere you lose sight / Of what you came for"), slipping from the literal to the figurative. This slippage imitates Frost's own metaphorical move in the poem from the theme of planting (literal) to the theme of "Love" (figurative). In his sonnet "Acceptance," Frost also leaves the word *see* hanging, and produces a similar rhetorical effect:

> "Let the night be too dark for me to see
> Into the future. Let what will be, be."
> (*CPPP* 228)

It is only after we read through the line (as *see* slips from literal to figurative) that we realize it is no mundane act of seeing that the speaker imagines, but rather visionary performance. Other enjambments in "Putting in the Seed" are intended to depict transgressive power. One phrase, "burying the white / Soft petals," splits two adjectives modifying the same noun. The final enjambment in the concluding couplet, "The sturdy seedling with arched body comes / Shouldering its way and shedding the earth crumbs," parcels out a verb phrase onto separate lines, upsetting our expectation of a prepositional phrase after *comes* (e.g., "comes / To life"). In this ultimate moment of transcendence, one charged with sexual significance, the seedling breaks through the earth to become a plant; in imitation of that action, syntax barrels through the line terminus, pointing up the primal force of nature and man.

"The Subverted Flower," a poem that recounts the aborted attempt of a boy to seduce a girl, likewise employs enjambment to represent sexual union and the transgressive power of human sexuality. The beginning of the poem is strongly endstopped, as the narrator stands off against the object of his desire:

> She drew back; he was calm:
> "It is this that had the power."
> And he lashed his open palm
> With the tender-headed flower.
> (*CPPP* 308)

As the boy closes in on the girl, the moment of transcendence approaching, the figure of enjambment rears its head:

> He flicked and flung the flower,
> And another sort of smile
> Caught up like fingers
> The corners of his lips
> And cracked his ragged muzzle.

His "flower" in hand, the boy leers, his boundless sexual energy figured by syntax breaking through the ends of successive lines ("smile / Caught up . . . / The corners . . . / And cracked"). To defend herself against his assault, "She had to lean away. / She dared not stir a foot." The end of hard enjambment signifies the girl's attempts to erect barriers between herself and this erotic, transgressive force. Frost shows her standing still, "Lest movement should provoke / The demon of pursuit." Here the splitting of verb and object again suggests the boy's libidinal exertions, the threat he presents to the virginal pursued. Finally, the girl sees the boy as debased by his sexuality—his "snout" cut "in half"—resembling a dog in his search for satisfaction, but she also recognizes that she has fulfilled the process of his degradation by her inability to see him as anything other than "beast." The further turnings of the poetic line ("what she could not see / Was"; "the flower might be / Other"; "Her own too meager heart / Had terribly completed") enact the drama of sexual subversion (literally, "a turning under") that the poem is about.

Frost figures not only sexual politics but also national politics through the prosodic pattern of enjambment, which during the Depression he applies to poems that negatively critique utopian socialism (what he sees as the flawed romantic notion of infinite progress) as codified (he believes) by Roosevelt's New Deal. If, as we have seen, Frost often expresses delight in transcendence outside of the political sphere, he castigates those politicos who would seek to transcend worldly limits in their quest for the perfectly just state. Frost's anti-utopianism is in full bloom in "The Lost Follower" (1936) included in the "Time Out" section of *A Witness Tree,* where he takes up the case of those who give up poetry for politics with the hope of instituting a utopia on earth. Playing on the title of Coleridge's poem, "The Lost Leader," which is about Wordsworth's increasing political conservatism and the danger that it poses to his poetry, Frost laments the socialist leanings that drive some out of poetry, finding that

> Some turn in sheer, in Shelleyan dejection
> To try if one more popular election

> Will give us by short cut the final stage
> That poetry with all its golden rage
> For beauty on the illuminated page
> Has failed to bring—I mean the Golden Age.
>
> (*CPPP* 325)

The hard enjambment "election // Will give" symbolizes the extravagant yearning for political perfection of these leftists. But, as Frost goes on to warn, no political measure can bring about the glorious end-time; as he says to these poets-turned-politicians:

> the millennium to which you bend
> In longing is not at a progress-end
>
> By grace of state-manipulated pelf,
> Or politics of Ghibelline or Guelph,
> But right beside you book-like on a shelf,
> Or even better god-like in yourself.

Notable in this passage is the shift from enjambment to closure at line ends, as Frost moves from representing a rival political point of view to picturing his own. Ultimate peace and prosperity is not attainable through politics ("On the lower plane of thought and opinion the poet is a follower"), he contends, but rather through faith and form in "the golden line / Of lyric" (*LU* 255).

Although I will consider endstopping more fully later in this chapter, it is important to observe here that other poems from this same period represent liberal political opinion in endstopped lines, rather than in radically enjambed lines, when they incorporate Frost's negative judgment of it. In "The Lesson for Today" (1938), for instance, the speaker refers condescendingly in tightly sealed lines to the desire of some to construct a utopia on earth:

> Earth's a hard place in which to save the soul,
> And could it be brought under state control,
> So automatically we all were saved,
> Its separateness from Heaven could be waived;
> It might as well at once be kingdom-come.
> (Perhaps it will be next millennium.)
>
> (*CPPP* 320–21)

In this passage Frost alludes to the specter of New Deal "state control," ridiculing those who would seek to eradicate suffering on earth through political means. The "trial by existence," Frost argues, cannot be preempted by some socialist agenda, and the staunch refusal of enjambment encodes Frost's disdain for the kind of progress he is describing—the same kind he speaks out against in his 1935 "'Letter' to *The Amherst Student*": "All ages of the world are bad. . . . Whatever progress may be taken to mean, it can't mean making the world an easier place in which to save your soul" (*CPPP* 739).

In poems published later in his career, Frost again turns to line-sentence counterpointing, this time constructing it as a political emblem of American democratic values, and through that emblem we are able to read his thoughts on contemporary class politics in America in all their complexity. In his blank verse eclogue "From Plane to Plane" (1948), enjambment signals the permeability of class boundaries in the post-World War II era by undoing social hierarchy in its blending of syntax. In the poem Frost comments on his visual prosody as he sets two farmhands talking. Upon first seeing the men in the field, we are told that

> They were giving corn
> A final going over with the hoe
> Before they turned from everything to hay.
> (*CPPP* 367)

These enjambed lines call attention to the blank space of the page—the turn of syntax—as the two men hoe down a row until its end, with the pun of *turned* reminding us that the Latin *versus,* which gives us *verse,* means a furrow, a turning of the plow. In the poem Frost compares the farmer's "method" of plowing in one direction only (walking back with his tool on his shoulder to till another row) to the technique of reading around a line end, our eyes descending from one linear plane to the next, as rows or lines of words turn from one to another. As Dick, a young man "fresh and full of college," informs Pike, a fifty-year veteran farmer:

> You do the way we do
> In reading, don't you, Bill?—at every line end
> Pick up your eyes and carry them back idle
> Across the page where we started from.
> (*CPPP* 368)

Here the words "line end" appear appropriately at the end of a line, and we reach the phrase "Pick up your eyes" only after we have picked up our eyes and returned them to the left margin. At the end of the next line, we again must "carry" our eyes "back idle" before arriving "Across the page where we started from." This method of reading is counterposed to one where the white space beyond the line end does not come into play:

> The other way of reading back and forth,
> Known as boustrophedon, was found too awkward.

Notably, enjambment does not mark this turn; instead, these lines enforce our pause at the right margin where we would begin the next line (reading from right to left) in that ancient form of writing ("boustrophedon").

Although "From Plane to Plane" is in part about "the sound of sense" and its indication of social position (at one point Pike imitates Dick's tone of voice), much of the poetic drama is communicated through silent line-sentence counterpointing, which undermines the social system that keeps the "Doctor," who employs these men, on a higher plane. Pike's insistence on walking back to the head of a row and not hoeing the rows back and forth stems from his refusal to give all to his employer, and enjambment shapes the moment when Pike,

>   having reached
>   The river bank, quit work defiantly,

Here enjambment amounts to a political gesture, as the merging of the two lines by syntax symbolizes the radical instability of social boundaries and class distinctions, with Pike refusing to abide by them. In his "walk of recreation back" he philosophizes: "'A man has got to keep his extrication.'" This sentence sits by itself on a line, a condition that expresses Pike's creed that one must keep something for oneself—that one must maintain some degree of independence. In the continuing dialectics of closure and flow in the poem, the narrator's enjambed description of the Doctor suggests an oppositional political perspective, as that professional's superior social status is not as sure as he believes:

>   Every time Dick or Pike looked up, the Doctor
>   With one foot on the dashboard of his buggy
>   Was still in sight like someone to depend on.
>   Nowhere but on the Bradford Interval
>   By the Connecticut could anyone
>   Have stayed in sight so long as an example.

In this passage, syntax overruns line boundaries with frequency, a condition that undermines the Doctor's paternalistic posture, as Pike and Dick fight "about equality" and the pressing question of "whether these professions [like the Doctor watching them] really work." The central enjambment of Frost's brief lyric "In Divés' Dive" in *A Further Range* carries similar political weight:

>   It is late at night and still I am losing,
>   But still I am steady and unaccusing.
>
>   As long as the Declaration guards
>   My right to be equal in number of cards,

It is nothing to me who runs the Dive.
Let's have a look at another five.
(*CPPP* 283)

The Declaration of Independence guarantees that we will be dealt with evenly, and enjambment figures that right, as syntax fuses the two lines ("guards / My right") in such a way that neither unit is advantaged, since the top line depends on the bottom line for completion of its meaning, and vice versa.

"From Plane to Plane," advertised as "A Christmas poem for physicians," was first published in the 1948 Christmas issue of *What's New,* a monthly magazine published by Chicago's Abbott Laboratories containing articles about medical conditions and new pharmaceutical treatments of them. Frost's poem appeared in that issue with several other literary pieces that figure the lower class and relations between the classes. In Karl Shapiro's poem entitled "The Thin Bell-Ringer," a "Santa of the spare" asks for alms beside his "cauldron of the unfed." James Hilton in his nostalgic sketch of Christmas in a mining town in England in 1912 (the first Christmas that Frost spent in England) similarly acknowledges the poverty in city slums. Norman Reilly Raine's short story "Peace on Earth—Goodwill to Men" features a clash between two sailors—the Highlander Captain Robertson, "master" of the ship, and the Lowlander Angus McGriff, "a lowly and impecunious Third Mate." The class struggle between the insubordinate McGriff and Robertson finally ends on Christmas morning, when Robertson feels "compunction" for his treatment of McGriff, expressing a "reluctant admiration for his fellow Scotsman, albeit a Lowlander." Frost's poem is in keeping with these other works, and, like Raine's story, is intended to impress upon readers (such as the Doctor) the need to reconsider the worth of those who do their manual labor and fight their wars. (Pike snarls at the privilege of the Doctor, knowing better than to appeal to those who never "fac[ed] bullets" for sympathy.) As George Lipsitz has observed, "Submerged tensions between competing interests surfaced in the postwar era, replacing national unity with vigorous internal disputes. Those who sacrificed and killed in pursuit of a better world found their loftiest aspirations betrayed by a society that demanded a continued sacrifice and aggression after the war. Under those circumstances, film noir dramas about isolation, lost time, guilt, frustration, powerlessness, and betrayal provided an appropriate cultural symbol."[30] Frost's poem provides an appropriate cultural symbol as well, and it seeks a remedy to those circumstances by reminding the professionals reading *What's New* of the equality of all people, with help from the prosodic equalizer of enjambment.

In "The Literate Farmer and the Planet Venus" (1941) Frost also uses enjambment to political effect, as he humorously remarks on the evolutionary tide that Darwin has revealed to us. The farmer in the poem tells a stranger who comes to his door seeking food and shelter that the star in the sky over his farm is in fact a giant lightbulb put there by Edison

> To give developments the final shove
> And turn us into the next specie folks
> Are going to be, unless these monkey jokes
> Of the last fifty years are all a libel,
> And Darwin's proved mistaken, not the Bible.
> I s'pose you have your notions on the vexed
> Question of what we're turning into next.

Surrounded by lines that are mostly endstopped, this passage stands out, as Frost uses the words *turn* and *turning* in enjambed lines to call attention to the genetic transformations that have culminated in man. The stranger at his door answers in enjambed lines as well:

> As liberals we're willing to give place
> To any demonstrably better race,
> No matter what the color of its skin.
> (But what a human race the white has been!)
> I heard a fellow in a public lecture
> On Pueblo Indians and their architecture
> Declare that if such Indians inherited
> The condemned world the legacy was merited.
> He had his ticket bought, his passage earned,
> To take the *Mayflower* back where he belonged
> Before the Indian race was further wronged.
> (*CPPP* 336)

The variance of metrical and syntactic frames ("I heard a fellow . . . / On Pueblo Indians . . . / Declare"; "inherited / The condemned world") formally enacts the racial equality that the man asserts, his liberal politics made apparent in the disintegration of linear boundaries—a disintegration emblematic of the man's disregard of traditional (racist) hierarchies.

Frost's "Bursting Rapture" (1948) further politicizes the poetic form of enjambment in light of the mounting farm crisis and the specter of nuclear holocaust in the Cold War. In the poem the speaker goes to a doctor to try to find a cure for his nervous condition, and Frost lineates his complaint as follows:

> The time had been when anyone could turn
> To farming for a simple way to earn;
> But now 'twas there as elsewhere, any gain
> Was made by getting science on the brain;
> (*CPPP* 362)

The first turn coincides with the speaker's expression that it is no longer easy to "turn / To farming," because that pursuit has been industrialized to such an extent that the family farm is no longer an economically viable entity. In the hard enjambment that follows ("any gain / Was made"), we are given to see that the condition of the family farmer has been radically altered, that his sense of security in his world has been shaken by encroaching science. Steven Diner has explained that American farmers long resisted scientific agriculture and that it was not until World War I, when increased crop yield was necessary to feed not only Americans but the Allies, that new methods of farming began to gain acceptance.[31] The mental "strain" that the speaker of "Bursting Rapture" suffers, which is depicted in the straining of syntax from one line to the next, represents, then, a political strain as well. In view of the sea change in agricultural methods that spells the demise of the family farmer, Frost here laments through blurred syntax programs and policies that would blur the distinction between the country and the city. In "A Roadside Stand," a poem in *A Further Range*, the speaker more obviously decries the "greedy good-doers" of the federal government whose plan is to resettle these farmers in villages "next to the theater and store," and, troubled by the desire of rural folk for city money, he is moved to say, "Sometimes I feel myself I can hardly bear / The thought of so much childish longing in vain" (*CPPP* 261). The enjambment, which pivots on the word *bear*, signals the fact that the speaker is at the breaking point, and it forecasts the line break at the end of "Bursting Rapture," where a fear that farming has become fully industrialized segues into a fear that unbounded science will wreck the security of the world; as the patient's doctor reassures,

> "There, there,
> What you complain of all the nations share.
> Their effort is a mounting ecstasy
> That when it gets too exquisite to bear
> Will find relief in one burst. You shall see.
> That's what a certain bomb was sent to be."

The prominent enjambed unit ("Will find relief") emblematizes an emotional tension as well as the uncontainable force of science in the form of the atom bomb, which in an act of political extravagance has been unleashed to end World War II and looms as an ominous presence on the Cold War landscape.

In his last book, entitled *In the Clearing* (1962), Frost's iambic dimeter poem "The Bad Island—Easter" gives enjambment yet another ideological twist, as in it he travels back centuries to explain the demise of the primitive culture that once flourished on Easter Island in the South Pacific in order to comment on contemporary political conditions. The speaker attributes that demise to the "guile" of a ruling elite, who told the people that they were free and "persuaded [them] to see / Something in it for them," that is, persuaded them to see that they were being governed well. Ultimately, "overtaxed / In nerve and resource / They started to wane," a depopulation that is intended to illustrate the devastating effects of any plutocratic government. Toward the end of the poem, Frost invokes the utopian land of William Dean Howells's socialist novel *A Traveler to Altruria* (1894), in which altruism replaces competition as the engine of the economy. The adjective is hyphenated across a line terminus in order to meet the demands of rhyme and lay bare the political meaning of the word: "altrur- / ian" (*CPPP* 459). Usually, one thinks of Cummings, Moore, or Williams in terms of such radical word-splitting enjambment, whose verse includes such formations as "e / yes" (Cummings), "ac- / cidental" (Moore), and "o- / dors" (Williams). When Frost fractures a word in this way, he does so in the company of an accentual-syllabic norm, but the results are no less striking to the eye. By divvying up the word "altrurian"—that is, having two lines share it—Frost enacts its socialistic sense and, in the context of the poem, denounces in joking fashion that ideology and its own plutocratic nature. The enshrinement of the Easter Island sculpture in Frost's poem ("They stood it in place / On a cliff for a throne") conjures up Stalinist public art and, thus, hints at democracy as a superior form of government to communism. Through radical enjambment Frost pokes fun at the radical politics he dislikes, even as he proposes a radical return to republican cultural values.

III

If Frost's uses of enjambment carry profound ideological resonances, so, too, does the intentional avoidance of enjambment in his poems. The determined conjunction of syntax and line boundaries often stands as a symbol for social and political isolationism or, alternatively, for conformity to established social codes and a conservative doctrine of self-reliance. The pro-labor sonnets that Frost wrote early in the twentieth century serve as one notable exception, however, as in those poems endstopped lines evoke the stifling effects of industrial capitalism on the working class from a liberal perspective. When syntax breaks but the line does not, resulting in a pause, or caesura, Frost also makes political points, weighing in on issues of national and international importance. Caesurae appear in Frost's lyric poetry to depict insufficiency, indecision, or interruption and in their careful placement provide trenchant analysis of political culture, particularly that of the Cold War.

If Frost figures seasonal flux through a pattern of enjambment in poems like "The Onset" and "A Hillside Thaw," he represents the poet's withdrawal from natural tempests—his social and cultural isolation—through insistent endstopping. In his early lyric "Now Close the Windows" the speaker, refusing to be swept up in the noisy chaos outside, seeks refuge and is immured much as these lines are:

> Now close the windows and hush all the fields:
>   If the trees must, let them silently toss;
> No bird is singing now, and if there is,
>   Be it my loss.
>
> It will be long ere the marshes resume,
>   It will be long ere the earliest bird:
> So close the windows and not hear the wind,
>   But see all wind-stirred.
>   (*CPPP* 33)

In the table of contents of *A Boy's Will* Frost glosses the poem as follows: "It is time to make an end of speaking." This statement, along with the closure at line ends, highlights the fact that the poem is about the closure of vocation, as the poet bars communication with nature, that power capable of energizing the poetical and prophetic voice. In "To the Thawing Wind," another lyric in *A Boy's Will,* Frost similarly shores up the integrity of his lines in representing the plight of the poet. Although the title might encourage us to think that we will encounter a poem boasting hard enjambments, since it suggests that the subject is the release of a frozen landscape, we find that the poem—mired in the moment—merely anticipates its coming. Consequently, the poem is shaped by a sequence of mostly endstopped lines, which symbolize the prison of winter that continues to hold the poet apart. The "thawing wind" is called forth to free him (and nature) from bondage:

> Come with rain, O loud Southwester!
> Bring the singer, bring the nester;
> Give the buried flower a dream;
> Make the settled snowbank steam;
> Find the brown beneath the white;
> But whate'er you do tonight,
> Bathe my window, make it flow,
> Melt it as the ice will go;
> Melt the glass and leave the sticks
> Like a hermit's crucifix;

> Burst into my narrow stall;
> Swing the picture on the wall;
> Run the rattling pages o'er;
> Scatter poems on the floor;
> Turn the poet out of door.
>
> *(CPPP* 21)

All but a few of these lines begin with an imperative verb form, as the poet moves from imagining what the wind will do to nature to imagining what the wind will do to him. The stops at the ends of all but one of the lines (in a handwritten version the semicolons in the poem are periods) emphasize the delimited condition of the speaker, who yearns for the spring wind in which poetic power resides, and ironically so, since it temporarily suspends his textual involvement and forces him to confront the world outside his window, where he will find material to nourish his creative activity.[32]

These two poems express a disconnection between the poet and nature through line-sentence alignment, as syntactic units are kept isolate, and Frost also relies on that prosodic formation to bring into focus the strained relations that sometimes exist between people. In "The Thatch" he describes a man's mental state after a fight with his wife—a fight that sends him outside to cool off. He is rigid in his refusal to be first to surrender, as is she, and the emotional isolation that this standoff produces is shown in lines that keep clauses to themselves:

> The light was what it was all about:
> I would not go in till the light went out;
> It would not go out till I came in.
> Well, we should see which one would win,
> We should see which one would be first to yield.
>
> *(CPPP* 231)

The tight closure here enacts the breakdown in communication between husband and wife, neither of whom is willing to open up to the other. The chiasmus ("I would not go in till the light went out; / It would not go out till I came in") adds to the sense of opposition, with the independent clause of the first line of the passage opposed to that of the second. The poem continues on for another twenty-six lines, and twenty-one of these are marked at the end by a period, comma, or dash; there is, needless to say, no rapprochement between the two parties. The only flow between lines occurs at the end of the poem, where Frost depicts the encroachment of rain into the broken dwelling where this stalemate once occurred:

> Its life of hundreds of years has ended
> By letting the rain I knew outdoors
> In on to the upper chamber floors.

Here the word "in" that goes with "letting" is pushed to the beginning of the following line; the enjambment stands out in the poem as a moment of rare overlap—the sort of communion that husband and wife in the poem are unable to hold, held off as they are from each other.

In "A Leaf Treader" Frost also pledges himself to strict line boundary integrity in order to depict the utter isolation of his speaker. Its lines, which swell to iambic heptameter proportion, indicate the long, unbroken stretch of his life's journey and his determined resistance to the transcendent experience of death. The exact coincidence of line boundaries and sentence boundaries coupled with the almost total lack of medial caesurae—an unusual scenario given the length of these lines—impresses on us the survivor's grim endurance:

> I have been treading on leaves all day until I am autumn-tired.
> God knows all the color and form of leaves I have trodden on and mired.
> Perhaps I have put forth too much strength and been too fierce from fear.
> I have safely trodden underfoot the leaves of another year.
> All summer long they were overhead, more lifted up than I.
> To come to their final place in earth they had to pass me by.
> All summer long I thought I heard them threatening under their breath.
> And when they came it seemed with a will to carry me with them to death.
> They spoke to the fugitive in my heart as if it were leaf to leaf.
> They tapped at my eyelids and touched my lips with an invitation to grief.
> But it was no reason I had to go because they had to go.
> Now up, my knee, to keep on top of another year of snow.
>   (*CPPP* 270–71)

Whereas the plight of the "over-tired" speaker of "After Apple-Picking" is rendered through hard enjambment and variable line lengths, the burden of the leaf treader is dramatized by a uniform extension of the metrical line. Although in "The Constant Symbol" (1946) Frost claims that lines of seven feet are out of bounds, he uses them quite effectively here to set a scene. In the same essay, he states that "Probably there is something between the mood and the vocal imagination (images of the voice speaking) that determines a man's first commitment to metre and length of line" (*CPPP* 789). Suggesting a correspondence between abstract metrical pattern and the rhythm of speech, Frost again obscures the iconic force of such a pattern, focusing exclusively on the auditory dimension. In "A Leaf Treader," though, we both hear and see these ranging lines, which illustrate the speaker's travail. The intentional avoidance of enjambment in the poem signifies that for the speaker there will be no release from his condition; indeed, his exertions are meant to keep him alive for another day.

With "A Leaf Treader" in *A Further Range* stands "There Are Roughly Zones," a poem with many lines that run well beyond the syllable count of typical iambic pentameter and with those lines mostly endstopped (sixteen of its twenty-one lines end in punctuation) to symbolize the fact that while we are bounded by nature, we often are inclined to challenge its laws. The poem begins with a one-sentence noncaesural line against which the lines following it are measured:

> We sit indoors and talk of the cold outside.
> And every gust that gathers strength and heaves
> Is a threat to the house.
>
> > (*CPPP* 278)

Here the one bold enjambment of the poem ("gust . . . / Is") signifies the danger that our man-made boundaries will be dashed by the force of the storm. As Frost goes on to reflect on the fate of a peach tree that has been planted in (and whose life is threatened by) a harsh climate, confinement of syntactic units is the norm:

> Why is his nature forever so hard to teach
> That though there is no fixed line between wrong and right,
> There are roughly zones whose laws must be obeyed.
> There is nothing much we can do for the tree tonight,
> But we can't help feeling more than a little betrayed
> That the northwest wind should rise to such a height
> Just when the cold went down so many below.
> The tree has no leaves and may never have them again.
> We must wait till some months hence in the spring to know.
> But if it is destined never again to grow,
> It can blame this limitless trait in the hearts of men.

In this passage we see lines bursting at their seams with syllables (one line has as many as fourteen), but phrases and clauses are kept roughly to a single zone (or linear plane). Taken together, these formal features hold the power to reveal Frost's belief that inevitably we will try to exceed limits imposed on us, but, as inevitably, we will be held in check by them.

Frost's alignment of line and sentence takes on symbolic value in the American political arena as well, as other poems in *A Further Range* reveal. Two of them—"On the Heart's Beginning To Cloud the Mind" and "The Figure in the Doorway"—belong to a new conservative documentary reportage that arises in the middle of the 1930s known as the "I've seen America" genre. William Stott has observed that "The 'I've seen America' book, a novelty in 1935, became the dominant nonfiction mode. Writer after writer told how, when, and where he 'discovered' America, how 'knowing' the country (that is, traveling it) provided his most vital education, and what America meant to him."[33] Expressing what is right with America—not just its economic deficiencies—this genre "tend[ed] to perpetuate the status quo, a fact radicals of the time were quick to notice and deplore."[34] Frost's speakers in these two poems see America but do not get too near their subjects; their refusal to interrogate should be read as a critique of the prying of journalists with leftist agendas through which case studies were filtered and, thus, as a ringing endorsement of the status quo.

In "The Figure in the Doorway" Frost's title figure is glimpsed by a man passing through the country on a train; its subtitle, *"or, On Being Looked at in a Train,"* turns the table, however, indicating that the speaker-sociologist is the one under observation, and surely the poem is concerned with both the poor and those inspecting the poor so closely during the 1930s. In the first four lines Frost uses enjambment to depict the succession of objects as they approach the speaker and trail off as the train speeds by. Although the enjambments are soft, they are quite conspicuous in a twenty-two-line poem that includes only one other line that is not endstopped:

> The grade surmounted, we were riding high
> Through level mountains nothing to the eye
> But scrub oak, scrub oak and the lack of earth
> That kept the oaks from getting any girth.
> (*CPPP* 266)

This panoramic "monotony" yields to a point of order—a "living man" whose "great gaunt figure" fills a doorway in a cabin. As Frost's speaker suggests, the tendency (in the 1930s) would be to see this man as a pathetic creature, one who suffers from "want." But the traveler resists such a projection, insisting on the free will and self-sufficiency of that individual:

> He had the oaks for heating and for light.
> He had a hen, he had a pig in sight.
> He had a well, he had the rain to catch.
> He had a ten-by-twenty garden patch.
> Nor did he lack for common entertainment.
> That I assume was what our passing train meant.
> He could look at us in our diner eating,
> And if so moved uncurl a hand in greeting.

Frost formally supports his statement of the man's self-sufficiency by having boundaries of line and sentence perfectly coincide: the man alone in the world is, Frost intimates, as self-contained as these lines, only two of which hold more than one clause, and those two featuring no subordination, a further sign of his independence. Syntactic parallelism reinforces the message that he is not in want—a "had," not a "had not." As Frost believes, this man has conformed to the limits of his environment and turned those limits to advantage. Frost's political message in the poem is clear: we should not assume helplessness in others, especially when we know nothing of their lives. The figure in the doorway epitomizes the determination to provide for oneself that he admires; he is in need of no New Deal. Of course, critics could (and did) accuse Frost of projecting his own ideologies onto the Depression-era landscape, and he runs the risk of being dismissed as a "train-window sociologist," a twist on W. E. B. Du Bois's pejorative tag "car-window sociologist" in *The Souls of Black Folk* (1903) applied to the person who does not examine closely the living conditions of African Americans in the rural South but purports to know all about them.[35]

"On the Heart's Beginning to Cloud the Mind" draws out this political credo, and a majority of its lines are also endstopped (thirty-seven of forty-five lines are tied off with some form of punctuation). It, too, features a train-riding speaker and similarly is about the need to gain a proper perspective on the country, to resist allowing one's emotions to occlude one's critical faculties. Out of his train window the speaker sees what he characterizes as a "flickering, human pathetic light" that is kept burning "It seemed to me, by the people there, / With a God-forsaken brute despair" (*CPPP* 265). However, he quickly corrects himself, imagining another scenario that he feels maintains the dignity of that desert people:

> But my heart was beginning to cloud my mind.
> I knew a tale of a better kind.
> That far light flickers because of trees.
> The people can burn it as long as they please:
> And when their interests in it end,
> They can leave it to someone else to tend.
> Come back that way a summer hence,
> I should find it no more no less intense.
> I pass, but scarcely pass no doubt,
> When one will say, "Let us put it out."
> The other with demur agrees.
> They can keep it burning as long as they please;
> They can put it out whenever they please.
>
> (*CPPP* 265)

This alternative tale is considerably more cheery, because it attributes a self-sufficiency and free will to these people; they are not shaped by their circumstances, but rather actively shape them. Four of these lines represent a single sentence; the others entail a discrete phrase or clause. The inscription "They can" at the beginning of the last two lines of the passage, which are also two independent clauses, illustrates his view that these people are not dependent on anyone or anything, that they are as autonomous as the syntactic formations that announce their freedom. Further on in the poem, we experience even tighter linear closure, as the speaker conjures forth the pleasant life that the couple must lead:

> Life is not so sinister-grave.
> Matter of fact has made them brave.
> He is husband, she is wife.
> She fears not him, they fear not life.

Here Frost presents four separate sentences on four separate lines. The final two lines contain caesurae and are syntactically balanced, allowing Frost to insist on the husband and wife's complementariness, their reliance only on each other. As at the two mid-line breaks in "The Figure in the Doorway," no subordination surfaces in these final lines (both of which contain two independent clauses) in recognition of the integrity of each and of their life as a married couple. Richard Poirier has noted that "Frost's train window poems . . . raise not merely phenomenological problems but questions of misreading, of necessary failures of perception," and he has called attention to Frost's "congenital circumspection about 'extra-vagance'—about making things up while 'in flight,' about inventing other people's lives without getting intimately involved with them."[36] This "circumspection about 'extra-vagance'" is recorded prosodically by his refusal of enjambment; his syntax, not at all extravagant, keeps conservatively to the limits of lines.

In "A Lone Striker," another poem in *A Further Range,* Frost further politicizes such alignment in representing his opposition to leftist forces seeking to secure the rights of workers through trade-unionism. The strict endstopping (of sixty-two lines, forty-eight end in punctuation) might come as a surprise, since the poem is about one worker's rejection of the regulated life of the mill, his release into the world of nature, a situation we would expect to see figured by enjambment. Notably, though, the subtitle—"*Or, Without Prejudice to Industry*"—insists that the man's walkout is not a vote against technological "progress." He is, after all, a "lone striker," not a fellow clamoring for general work-stoppage or seeking to throw a wrench in the machine. Frost takes pains through his prosody to show that he is no political radical:

> He knew another place, a wood,
> And in it, tall as trees, were cliffs;
> And if he stood on one of these,
> 'Twould be among the tops of trees,
> Their upper branches round him wreathing,
> Their breathing mingled with his breathing.
> If—if he stood! Enough of ifs!
> He knew a path that wanted walking;

He knew a spring that wanted drinking;
A thought that wanted further thinking;
A love that wanted re-renewing.
Nor was this just a way of talking
To save him the expense of doing.
With him, it boded action, deed.
(*CPPP* 250)

All but one of these lines are endstopped, and that one exhibits exceedingly soft enjambment. The conformity of phrase and line boundaries even as the speaker asserts his eccentricity is meant to suggest the double-edged message of the poem: one may choose not to conform, but one should not enlist others to do the same. Although these iambic tetrameter lines express a high degree of regularity, the lines with a surplus syllable (all those that end in a verbal such as "wreathing" or "doing") gently exceed the imposed limit, and this prosodic condition symbolizes Frost's view of the consistency between the system of industrialism and personal freedom, his allegation here that the former does not cancel out the latter, but rather permits dynamic individual expression within it (if only for those as relatively fortunate as he).[37]

If Frost's representation of himself as "a lone striker"—not just someone who figuratively "strikes out" on his own, but one who literally goes on "strike"—is not biased against industry ("The factory was very fine; / He wished it all the modern speed"), it is biased against the workers in that system of production, as the pro-labor sonnets he wrote in the first decade of the twentieth century are not. These sonnets come from an opposite perspective and, notably, use endstopped lines to impress a very different political point. In "When the speed comes a-creeping overhead" ten lines are marked by punctuation to signify what the tenth line states: "The music of the iron is a law." The law that has been laid down for the workers in the mill violates their natures ("But the task ne'er could wait the mood to come"); it is seen as unbending, just as it is by the speaker in "A Lone Striker," but here the tight closure at line ends suggests the brutal constrictions placed on the laborers, who are pictured as all but dead. Only at the end of the poem does enjambment prevail, with syntax slipping from one line to the next to illustrate the slipping away of souls:

And as upon the heavy spools that pay
Their slow white thread, so ruthlessly the hum
Of countless whirling spindles seems to draw
Upon the soul, still sore from yesterday.
(*CPPP* 511)

In "The Mill City" ten lines end in some form of punctuation as well, and no hard cuts in syntax appear. The endstopping here indicates the alienation both of the speaker from the workers he espies ("It was in a drear city by a stream, / And all its citizens were sad to me, —/ I could not fathom what their life could be—") and of those workers from their labor ("Then back at night, like drowned men from the sea, / Up from the mills and river hurriedly, / In weeds of labor, to the shriek of steam") (*CPPP* 509). The shift in political position from these two sonnets to "A Lone Striker" (written almost thirty years apart) is fully told in the radical revision of the ideological value of line-sentence alignment, as Frost uses it early on to encode a liberal politics and later on to encode his conservatism in the face of the New Deal and its efforts to safeguard workers' rights through such entities as the National Labor Relations Board.

Frost's politics are not always in plain view in his poetry, though, and occasionally when his figures seem least ideologically charged he is at his most partisan. "Nothing Gold Can Stay" stands as one striking case in point. It is a poem in short (iambic trimeter) lines from which we might expect some hard enjambment, since it is more difficult to keep syntactic units from spilling over line termini in such a situation; however, Frost works hard to keep such enjambment from occurring:

> Nature's first green is gold,
> Her hardest hue to hold.
> Her early leaf's a flower;
> But only so an hour.
> Then leaf subsides to leaf.
> So Eden sank to grief,
> So dawn goes down to day.
> Nothing gold can stay.
>   (*CPPP* 206)

It is seemingly ironic that the boundaries of phrasal units and lines should match up so neatly in a poem about transition, the change from one season to another. Why, one might ask, would Frost inscribe a sequence of self-contained lines that formally represent the opposite of seasonal "turning"? Why not bleed syntax from one line into the next in order to express the flow from one state of nature to another? The answer is that, through tight closure, Frost is able to depict the effort on Nature's part to "hold"—to try to resist the forces of change that inevitably will overpower her. Indeed, it is not just Nature, but the speaker, who wants to slow this death spiral, since Nature's subsiding foretells his own. Moreover, through that prosodic form Frost is speaking out on international political affairs in his sly way, and it is important to remember that this poem is composed in 1920, just after World War I has ended.[38] Feeling sure that "there are two or three more wars close at hand," Frost expresses a fierce nationalism at this time and, with it, an isolationist political position, an ideological development that I chart with respect to his theory of form in my final chapter (*SL* 255). "Nothing Gold Can Stay" tropes this position, suggesting through its isolation of syntactic units a refusal to become embroiled in global politics: just as Nature tries to resist the forces of change, so America must try to resist forces that would pull her beyond her borders, even if such resistance may be in vain. That the poem originally included lines that later became part of "It Is Almost the Year 2000," a poem that I discuss at the end of this chapter, points to another hidden political meaning, as Frost jabs at 1930s liberals who believe that the millennium is upon us on the evidence of the terrible times:

> In gold as it began
> The world will end for man.
> And some belief avow
> The world is ending now.
> The final age of gold
> In what we now behold.
> If so, we'd better gaze,
> For nothing golden stays.[39]

In this draft version, hard enjambment also is resisted, a formal condition that reads as an emblem of Frost's political resistance to socialist utopian thought.

Like "Nothing Gold Can Stay," "One Step Backward Taken" has lurking beneath the surface a political edge. In it, Frost depicts a person's stay against the chaos of life and, less obviously, the stay of the U.S. against proliferating global commitments in the nuclear age, as he revealed when on one occasion he said that the poem has "a figure for our times in it"—a figure for "the universal crisis" of World War II.[40] The poem begins with some relatively hard enjambments that depict the onward rush in danger of sweeping the man and his country away: "sands and gravels / were once more on their travels"; "Great boulders off their balance / Bumped heads" (*CPPP* 340). The isolationist theme is sounded formally in a momentary pattern of endstopped lines and exceedingly soft enjambment. When the speaker withdraws from that avalanche, however, phrase and line unit are more neatly in step: "But with one step backward taken / I saved myself from going. / A world torn loose went by me." In addition, the short (iambic trimeter) lines suggest the speaker's and nation's withholding, just as in "Nothing Gold Can Stay" that length of line symbolizes the shortness (or transience) of a season and of our earthly existence.

In poems about the political situation of the Cold War that are not so well disguised (and not often discussed because they seem so baldly stated),

Frost once again codes the strict alignment between lines on one hand and phrases and sentences on the other, but here his politics are more ambivalent, as he plays with the conservative position that communism must be contained in his own prosodic containments. The U.S. had renewed testing of atomic weapons in the summer of 1946, detonating two bombs in July at Bikini Atoll, and "It Bids Pretty Fair" (1949) responds to the nuclear arms race that that event sparks:

> The play seems out for an infinite run.
> Don't mind a little thing like the actors fighting.
> The only thing I worry about is the sun.
> We'll be all right if nothing goes wrong with the lighting.
> (CPPP 356)

Here Frost takes rather lightly global tensions and the extinction of mankind by nuclear war, finding more troublesome the extinction of the sun, that is, "God's last *Put out the Light*" (*CPPP* 229). Of course, what kindles these global tensions is the attempt to keep communism in check by the U.S. and its allies, and these endstopped lines invoke with a wink that international ideological struggle. Similarly, in "U.S. 1946 King's X," a poem first published in *Atlantic Monthly* in December 1946, Frost steadfastly refuses enjambment (with a mark of punctuation at the close of every line) in order to create a pictogram of Cold War containment policy and U.S. efforts through international organizations like the United Nations Atomic Energy Commission to halt the spread of nuclear weapons:

> Having invented a new Holocaust,
> And been the first with it to win a war,
> How they make haste to cry with fingers crossed,
> King's X—no fairs to use it anymore!
> (CPPP 362)

Trying to keep a lid on proliferation, these lines, in imitation of U.S. foreign policy, keep syntax from spreading, but the archness of them suggests Frost's clear understanding of American hypocrisy on this score.

Frost's poems communicate meaning not only through activities at the ends of lines, however; they also frame issues through prosodic activities in mid-line in the form of caesurae. Of course, it would be a mistake to assume that every time syntax stops short of the end of a line Frost invests that break with figurative significance. Often caesurae simply reflect the stops and starts of human speech. In "The Fear," for example, the wife says to her husband: "Joel, I won't—I won't—I promise you. / We mustn't say hard things. You mustn't either" (*CPPP* 91). The fissures in her discourse do not represent necessarily fissures in her consciousness, although her mental stability is in doubt; after all, her husband's sentences also stop and start mid-line, and he is much calmer than is she. Indeed, such breaks in the run of speech are so common in *North of Boston* that they become a target of E. E. Cummings's parody:

> Robert Frost I was quite wrong, and I will tell you why,
> And you will be surprised,—I'll wager that.
> You see it was like this. Yesterday I,
> Opening the kitchen door, saw our old fat[41]

Here line ends are tightly closed (the final line suggests a strong enjambment will follow, but in fact Cummings shifts to send up the style of another poet in his pastiche), and each line breaks in the middle, giving us a strong sense of the colloquial. Not infrequently, though, syntax breaking within a poetic line attains figurative significance—and political force—as Frost graphs through it our experience (and the threatened loss) of our world.

Caesurae in Frost's verse sometimes image the splintering of consciousness or the abrupt end of an individual's life, standing as a sign of personal extinguishing. In "An Old Man's Winter Night," for instance, mid-line halts imitate the psychic lapses of the endangered old man of the title:

> He consigned to the moon, such as she was,
> So late-arising, to the broken moon
> As better than the sun in any case
> For such a charge, his snow along the wall to keep;
> And slept.
>
> (*CPPP* 106)

The disjointed syntax within these lines provides an image of the "broken" moon as well as of the man's enfeebled condition. The final caesura, coming immediately after an initial foot, helps mark the man's sudden loss of consciousness: his light goes out and, when it does, a prosodic blankness yawns. In "Not to Keep," a poem about a soldier wounded in World War I who is shipped home temporarily to convalesce, caesurae represent agonizing twists and turns of mind—the psychic derangement imputed to the wife who is forced to piece together news of her husband's fate:

> They sent him back to her. The letter came
> Saying . . . And she could have him. And before
> She could be sure there was no hidden ill
> Under the formal writing, he was there,
> Living. They gave him back to her alive—
> How else? They are not known to send the dead—
> And not disfigured visibly.
>
> (*CPPP* 212–13)

The fragmentation of these lines signals not only her fragmented consciousness, but also the fragmented body—feared dead—that is sent back to be mended and then reassigned to political purpose. In "To E. T.," Frost's elegy for his friend Edward Thomas who was killed in World War I, we encounter a caesura at the moment he imagines Thomas's untimely death on the field of battle:

> You went to meet the shell's embrace of fire
> On Vimy Ridge;
> (*CPPP* 205)

Here the pause comes early in the line (immediately after the second foot), stopping us short, just as Thomas's life is stopped short.

In other poems Frost relies on caesurae to depict indecision—a speaker's groping through an unfamiliar landscape or toward self-knowledge (or both). In "A Boundless Moment" we confront a man who has stopped dead in his tracks and who is not sure of the lay of the land: "He halted in the wind, and—what was that / Far in the maples, pale, but not a ghost?" (*CPPP* 215). The comma and dash in the middle of the first line of this passage illustrate confusion, prompting us to pause just as the traveler does. "The Road Not Taken" also hinges on uncertainty—on the need to make a decision at a fork in the road—and it is stamped by caesurae at critical junctures throughout:

> And be one traveler, long I stood
>
> Then took the other, as just as fair,
>
> Two roads diverged in a wood, and I—
> (*CPPP* 103)

The walker is balancing options in his mind, and Frost represents the dilemma he faces by putting syntax on the scales. In the early poem "Mowing" lack of knowledge also is figured through a caesura: "What was it it whispered? I knew not well myself" (*CPPP* 26). A similarly coded rupture occurs in "The Exposed Nest": "Why is there then / No more to tell? We turned to other things" (*CPPP* 107). Here the turn from one thing to another is emblazoned by the turn in the middle, and not the end, of the line. These gaps dramatize the epistemological and existential crises faced by Frost's personae and rely in part on our perception of the poem on the page—its visual surface.

In later poetry these mid-line breaks often are more obviously politically inspired, as Frost positions himself with respect to the liberal ideology of the

New Deal and the new geopolitics of the Cold War. Published in 1942, "It Is Almost the Year 2000" registers Frost's view of the apocalyptic imaginings of leftists during the Depression. Looking forward to the dawn of the third Christian millennium, Frost mimes ultimate destruction through his prosodic arrangement. Only one caesura interrupts syntactic flow in the thirteen lines of the poem, signaling the catastrophic break that some say is imminent:

> To start the world of old
> We had one age of gold
> Not labored out of mines,
> And some say there are signs
> The second such has come,
> The true Millennium,
> The final golden glow
> To end it. And if so
> (And science ought to know)
> We well may raise our heads
> From weeding garden beds
> And annotating books
> To watch this end de luxe.
> (*CPPP* 328)

Those millennialists who fret about the darkness of America in the 1930s, who run around proclaiming the end of the world as a result of their conviction that times could not be worse and so human time must be about to give way to God's time, are mocked in the casual conclusion of the poem, where apocalypse becomes mere spectacle, with no thought of Final Judgment. The caesura in the eighth line stages end-time, with its hint of nuclear warfare, and it is appropriate that the poem appears in a section of *A Witness Tree* (1942) entitled "Time Out," a phrase that figures world destruction.

In the same book, the poem "Our Hold on the Planet" features a well-placed caesura that symbolizes the slight (but crucial) imbalance between nature's forces and our own in the world:

> There is much in nature against us: But we forget:
> Take nature altogether since time began,
> Including human nature, in peace and war,
> And it must be a little more in favor of man,
> Say a fraction of one percent at the very least,
> Or our number living wouldn't be steadily more,
> Our hold on the planet wouldn't have so increased.
> (*CPPP* 317)

In the first line of this passage syntax is divided unevenly, dramatically enacting the sense we sometimes get of being outgunned by nature. If the turn in the speaker's thinking had occurred at a line end, it would be unremarkable;

setting the turn at the end of the third poetic foot instead, Frost calls attention to the precariousness of the standoff. He links this contest to world war (the poem is published for the first time in 1940), asserting his belief that as horrible as that event may be, we will survive yet another round of mass killings. The sharp halts at line ends in the passage quoted above also lend force to Frost's charge, as clauses and phrases hold to themselves much as we have through great struggle managed to hold onto the planet.

In poems written during the Cold War, Frost humorously invokes Armageddon through breakdowns of syntax within lines. It is, to be sure, a black humor that leads him to reproduce in writing the moment of silence and blankness that results from nuclear explosion—a silence and blankness that is intended to give us pause (literally and figuratively) as we contemplate political forms that will impact the security of our world. Clustered in a section of *Steeple Bush* (1947) entitled "Editorials," Frost's Cold War poetic imaginings go undisguised as cultural criticism. In one of these poems, "The Broken Drought," a "prophet of disaster" forecasting the end of the world by drought is undercut when a light rain begins to fall; nevertheless, "in his heart he was unshaken sure," firm in his belief that man cannot survive much longer:

> The drought was one no spit of rain could cure.
> It was the drought of deserts. Earth would soon
> Be uninhabitable as the moon.
> (*CPPP* 363)

As measured against the one-sentence noncaesural line, of which the sonnet contains three, the second line in this passage startles, as it is the only line that features any degree of syntactic break within its boundaries and the only line to exhibit hard enjambment. By ending the short sentence when he does, Frost imagines the effect of drought—its curtailment of human existence on the planet—as tolled by the doomsayer. The syntactic run-over at the end of the line figures the impending nature of the crisis, with the verb left to the future. Although Frost does not specifically picture the prophet as a cold warrior, most of the poems it is grouped with explicitly are about Cold War politics and culture, making it difficult not to see the orator as sounding the note of hysteria brought on by the nuclear arms race.

In "No Holy Wars for Them" in "Editorials" another Frost speaker measures the political climate, spoofing the disparities between countries, some of which have attained superpower status and others of which are wholly inconsequential on the international scene. He begins the poem by perfectly coordinating line and sentence boundaries in order to depict for us the self-sufficiency of the superpowers; however, when he refers to the weak, non-militarized nations, that alignment fades:

> States strong enough to do good are but few.
> Their number would seem limited to three.
> Good is a thing that they the great can do,
> But puny little states can only be.
>
> (*CPPP* 361)

Just as the fourth line relies on the third to make its meaning, so, too, do these "puny little states" rely on the good will of others, incapable of exerting any influence on the world's stage. As the speaker goes on to point up the shortcomings of these nations, much bolder enjambment and a caesura dot the map:

> nations like the Cuban and the Swiss
> Can never hope to wage a Global Mission.
> No Holy Wars for them. The most the small
> Can ever give us is a nuisance brawl.

The suspension of syntax in the middle of the third line of this passage enacts the annihilation (the suspension of human life) that the atom bomb will wreak; moreover, the caesura points up the feebleness of the little nations, which cannot muster enough strength to "wage a Global Mission" any more than the sentence can muster enough strength to make it to the end of the line. The two instances of hard enjambment (the Swiss / Can never hope"; "the small / Can ever give") further suggest that these countries are not self-sufficient, as the splitting of syntax here denotes not an abundance, but a lack, of power. Frost describes a similar gamesmanship in the preamble to "The Gift Outright," where he harks back to the European race to claim America, expressing the culmination of political dominance through one-sentence noncaesural lines and the failure to attain such dominance through a mid-line sentence end:

> The French, the Spanish, and the Dutch were downed
> And counted out. Heroic deeds were done.
> Elizabeth the First and England won.
>
> (*CPPP* 435)

Elizabeth and England stand proud as winners of America, self-realized and self-possessed; the other nations fall short of the prize, their incompleteness pictured by enjambment and the only sentence in the seventy-seven-line poem that fizzles out before the goal of the line end is achieved.

In his Cold War sonnets "Why Wait for Science" and "Bursting Rapture," Frost again addresses contemporary political events and the terrifying

world that has been brought into being by the atom bomb. The only caesura in "Why Wait for Science" coincides with a forecast of oblivion:

> Sarcastic Science would like to know,
> In her complacent ministry of fear,
> How we propose to get away from here
> When she has made things so we have to go
> Or be wiped out.
>
> (CPPP 359)

The prosodic rupture on the page stands for the rupture between the world
and mankind in nuclear holocaust, the finality of the sentence marking our
own final moment. In "Bursting Rapture," Frost also takes up the threat
posed by a newly militarized science. The conclusion of the poem is shaped
not only around a politically coded enjambment, which I discussed earlier
in the chapter, but also around an ideologically potent caesura, as a doctor
tells his patient that international strife "Will find relief in one burst. You
shall see" (*CPPP* 362). Here, as in "Why Wait for Science," we experience a
break that signifies the end of human existence and are told that, ironically,
relief from encroaching science will come straight from science "in one
burst"—an atom bomb sent to seal our doom. The prosodic silence is not
only mimetic but expressive, signifying our mental pause in the face of such
overwhelming power; as Frost observed in 1962 in reference to the Cold
War: "We are given pause from the dread of the terribleness we feel capable
of" (*CPPP* 901).

Verse depends on visual and aural reading modes to convey its meaning,
despite the fact that Frost focuses exclusively on an aural semiotics in his
theory of poetic form. Our processing of line breaks and grammatical
lapses with the eye tells us much not only about the world of the poem but
about the world outside the poem. Whether line-sentence counterpointing
is mimetic or expressive or both, Frost's deliberate use of it articulates a political position, to which, as we will see in the next chapter, the figures of his
theory of poetic form contribute.

CHAPTER FOUR

Figures of Form, or Poetry and Power

Human life is made up of the two elements, power and form, and the proportion
must be invariably kept if we would have it sweet and sound.

—EMERSON, "EXPERIENCE" (1844)

We see how seriously the races swarm
In their attempts at sovereignty and form.
They are our wards we think to some extent
For the time being and with their consent,
To teach them how Democracy is meant.

—FROST, "DEDICATION" (1961)

Now that other races and other causes in the babel of the republic have been given
permission to speak in the very language that ruled and defined them, must everything be revised by the new order? Does Frost's ironic, jocular accent not apply to
them?

—DEREK WALCOTT, "THE ROAD TAKEN" (1995)

In previous chapters I have examined the relationship between Frost's
theory of "the sound of sense" and his prosodic practice, seeking to
show that some of his most significant patterns are not accounted for by
that theory. In this chapter I will consider more fully the figurative force of
both "the sound of sense" and meter, that other requisite element of Frost's
poetics, and show how Frost constructs what Stephen Cushman terms a
"fiction of form," that is, "an imaginative creation that imbues aesthetic
ideology with a sense of national significance."[1] If Frost's formalism at its
inception expresses a liberal *Weltanshauung*, aspects of it shift under the
pressure of domestic and international circumstances following his return

to America in 1915, as increasingly his poetics is shot through with conservative political strains. Even after Frost's death, the terms of his prosodic theory continue to figure (in) political discourse, as, quite recently, Frost's formalism has been reinscribed by a new generation of postcolonial and transnational poets, returned by them to its oppositional roots in their struggle to give voice to their cultural hybridity.

Frost makes clear the mind's requirement of metrical form, or "measure," in art and the symbolic importance of that item in social and political spheres in a commencement address he gave at Sarah Lawrence College in 1956: "I am always pleased when I see someone making motions like this [gesture of conducting a chorus]—like a metronome. Seeing the music measured. Measure always reassures me. Measure in love, in government, measure in selfishness, measure in unselfishness" (*RFPP* 437). I will return to the political formulation of "Measure . . . in government" later in this chapter; for now, I want to take up his citations "Measure in love" and "measure in selfishness, measure in unselfishness," which run on a politics of their own. As Frost believes, one must carefully monitor social engagement, since any affective stinginess or superfluousness is unhealthy. His earlier "'Letter' to *The Amherst Student*" (1935) makes this view particularly clear, as he insists that any point of order we can project on a chaotic world—even if only for a moment—can allay our fears and keep us sane: "When in doubt there is always form for us to go on with. Anyone who has achieved the least form to be sure of it, is lost to the larger excruciations" (*CPPP* 740). In *Atlantic Monthly* in 1951, amidst the growing emotional and political turmoil of the nuclear age, Frost encapsulates his faith in the staying power of form: "Practice of an art is more salutary than talk about it. There is nothing more composing than composition" (*CPPP* 808). As Mark Richardson has observed, "measure," for Frost, "signifies . . . sanity itself," thus acquiring moral significance.[2] In addition, that term accrues political significance, as Frost uses it to condemn the erratic social performance of other modernist artists and to allude to his own equanimity and sociability.

As Frost believes, the decision to write in or out of meter is inextricably linked to the habitudes of the poet: if he writes metrical verse, he symbolizes his normalcy; if he writes free verse, he symbolizes his aberrance, his refusal to submit to socially approved standards of conduct. As Frost's fiction goes, since meter is "very regular," so is the person writing in it, and he takes pains to fashion himself as just such a "regular" person (*SL* 128). Referring to himself in an interview as "Just ordinary, you see," he yokes that remark to his concept of verse form, immediately turning to disparage poets who, he says, "tear up forms and rhythms and measures" (*RFPP* 296–97):

I can't see that a man needs have his feet plowing through unhealthy mud in order to appreciate more fully the glowing splendor of the clouds. I can't see that a man must fill his soul with sick and miserable experiences, self-imposed and self-inflicted, and greatly enjoyed, before he can sit down and write a lyric of strange and compelling beauty. Inspiration doesn't lie in the mud; it lies in the clean and wholesome life of the ordinary man. . . . Men have told me, and perhaps they are right, that I have no "straddle". . . . That means that I cannot spread out far enough to live in filth and write in treetops. I can't. Perhaps it is because I am so ordinary. I like the middle way, as I like to talk to the man who walks the middle way with me. (*RFPP* 291–92)

Frost asserts here that one need not be strange to write lyrics of "strange" beauty, rejecting the idea that the poet must suffer for his art, that he must martyr himself or otherwise mark himself off from the world, making a badge of his abnormality. On "this business of straddling" he goes on to say that "It isn't the natural way, the normal way, the powerful way to ride. It's a trick" (*RFPP* 292). As we soon discover, those doing the "straddling" are free verse poets: "Today almost every man who writes poetry confesses his debt to Whitman. Many have gone very much further than Whitman would have traveled with them. They are the people who believe in wide straddling" (*RFPP* 296). The expression "the middle way" recalls "the measured way," a phrase Frost uses to designate metrical composition, and it is deployed here to distinguish Frost from his alienated peers.

In another slap at his free verse contemporaries, Frost again makes the link between social behavior and prosodic attachment, painting his competitors as deranged: "That is where the extreme modernists are defeating themselves. They do not care whether their communication is intelligible to others. It suffices that it has significance only to its creator. They desire, also, to play always on the insane fringe of things. Their interest is only in the abnormal. In painting and music, too, the same theory is now in vogue" (*I* 80). Frost's use of a pathological vocabulary to describe the aesthetic ideology of "the extreme modernists" is meant to suggest their social disengagement. As we have seen, his belief that "They do not care whether their communication is intelligible to others" informs his extreme statements that "the sounds of sense" in his poetry are unambiguous. As he also suggests, these poets who play only to themselves signify in the act of doing so their mental illness; unlike them, Frost takes pleasure in social interaction: "I like to talk to the man who walks the middle way with me."

Frost's smearing of free verse poets based on their use of enjambment also factors in his politics of form: "[O]nce you are in with the lawless in verse rum or dope you cant get out and live. I know too many of their secrets about breaking lines where they break them not to be dangerous running at large" (*SL* 375). Here Frost associates the rejection of the "law" of meter with a rejection of propriety and the laws of the state. On the "fringe of things," the *vers libre* poets are figured as social renegades, whose "breaking" of lines is seen as consistent with the breaking of extraliterary rules and regulations.

In 1932, Frost wrote to his daughter Lesley to inform her of his difference from the "extreme modernists" on the basis of his formalism, using the literary critic Herbert Read's book *Form in Modern Poetry* (1948) to highlight the distinction:

I assume you'll find in Reed [*sic*] his [Pound's] latest descendant a full statement of the doctrine of Inner Form, that is to say the form the subject itself takes if left to itself without any considerations of outer form. Everything else is to have two compulsions, an inner and an outer, a spiritual and a social, an individual and a racial. I want to be good, but that is not enough the state says I have got to be good. Everything has not only formity but conformity. Everything but poetry according to the Pound-Eliot-Richards-Reed school of art. For my part I should be as satisfied to play tennis with the net down as to write verse with no verse form set to stay me. (*CPPP* 735)

As Frost stated in his notebook a few years earlier, "inner" and "outer" discipline are not the same: "No one has really tasted discipline who is only self-disciplined" ("Notebook" 159). His conformity to literary tradition, including the rule of meter, sets him at odds, or so he claims, with the high modernists, who ignore "the harsher discipline from without" (*CPPP* 789). The contrary "compulsions" of which Frost speaks point to the politics embedded in his aesthetic, as a poet's use of fixed forms becomes a sign of his submission to the claims of culture. As Frost sees, to take up such forms is to express a readiness to connect to an audience, to make oneself intelligible to others—the very things he accuses high modernists of refusing to do.

Despite his stated dissatisfaction with the New Critical juggernaut of "Pound-Eliot-Richards-Reed," Frost's sense of form is not so different from theirs, as Mark Richardson has shown with respect to Eliot's "impersonal" theory of poetry; indeed, Richardson reminds us of the classical standards behind Frost's poetics—standards that he shares in large part with Eliot.[3] It was Hulme, under the tutelage of French conservatives

Charles Maurras and Pierre Lasserre, who brought classicism to Frost, finally persuaded as Hulme was that Bergson's philosophy was simply an end-stage romanticism, insofar as it is rooted in the concept of the individual free from social constraints. Whereas, in 1909, Hulme emphasized the individual and railed against tradition, arguing for "the complete destruction of all verse more than twenty years old," in 1912, he finds that the romantic attitude "shows a certain impatience of tradition, for it thinks that tradition is only a hampering restriction which prevents the greater possibilities of man appearing."[4] He derides the romantic as one who "imagines everything is accomplished by the breaking of rules"; the classical artist, on the other hand, feels "that there are certain rules which one must obey."[5]

Beginning in 1917 (with the classical attitude in ascendance), both Eliot and Pound begin ringing the virtues of "outer form," including metrical form. In his essay "Reflections on *Vers Libre*" (1917) Eliot distances himself from the free-for-all of free verse, arguing that complete prosodic freedom produces nothing but sloppy writing:

But the most interesting verse which has yet been written in our language has been done either by taking a very simple form, like the iambic pentameter, and constantly withdrawing from it, or taking no form at all, and constantly approximating to a very simple one. It is this contrast between fixity and flux, this unperceived evasion of monotony, which is the very life of verse.

We may therefore formulate as follows: the ghost of some simple metre should lurk behind the arras in even the "freest" verse; to advance menacingly as we doze, and withdraw as we rouse. Or, freedom is only truly freedom when it appears against the background of an artificial limitation.[6]

Frost does not approach and withdraw from metrical patterns the way that Eliot does, but he would agree with the spirit behind Eliot's statement in the same essay that "There is no escape from metre; there is only mastery." Frost's "evasion of monotony"—his avoidance of what he calls "the deadly singsong" of meter—is achieved through variegated "sounds of sense" (*PJ* 117). In fact, the paradox that Eliot spells out ("freedom is only truly freedom when it appears against the background of an artificial limitation") coincides quite neatly with Frost's thinking about prosodic performance: "The greatest freedom poetry can attain is having form, a frame, to work in."[7]

Eliot's discussion of Pound's metric and poetry in 1917 in connection with the American edition of Pound's *Lustra* reveals that Pound, too, cared deeply about the discipline of versification. Calling attention to the formalist background of Pound's book—"Pound's ver libre is such as is only possible for a poet who has worked tirelessly with rigid forms and different systems of metric"—Eliot reminds readers of "the great variety of rhythm which Pound manages to introduce into the ordinary iambic pentameter"—a remark that cannot help but remind us of Frost's own loosening of that pattern.[8] Insisting on Pound's emphasis on "discipline and form," Eliot builds on his own statement in "Reflections on *Vers Libre*" about the artistic counterpointing of fixity and flux: "The freedom of Pound's verse is rather a state of tension due to constant opposition between free and strict. There are not, as a matter of fact, two kinds of verse, the strict and the free; there is only a mastery which comes of being so well trained that form is an instinct and can be adapted to the particular purpose in hand."[9] In retrospect, Pound explained the renewed attention to traditional forms (as of about 1917) as an antidote to the present degenerate state of free verse:

At a particular date in a particular room, two authors, neither engaged in picking the other's pocket, decided that the dilutation of vers libre, Amygism, Lee Masterism, general floppiness had gone too far and that some counter-current must be set going. Parallel situation centuries ago in China. Remedy prescribed "Emaux et Camees" (or the Bay State Hymn Book). Rhyme and regular strophes.

  Results: Poems in Mr. Eliot's *second* volume, not contained in his first . . . also "H. S. Mauberley." (*EPPP* 5:363)

As Pound testifies, *Émaux et Camées,* a book of verse in quatrains of octosyllabic lines by the French poet Théophile Gautier, catalyzed the "counter-current." Eliot also tells of the advantages of "metrical servitude": "We studied Gautier's poems and then we thought, 'Have I anything to say in which this form will be useful?' And we experimented. The form gave the impetus to the content."[10] Even Herbert Read (another of that hated quartet) in *The Meaning of Art* (1931) speaks of the pleasure of form, in particular the practice of metrical substitution that Frost mastered: "It is well known that a perfectly regular metre in verse is so monotonous as to become intolerable. Poets have therefore taken liberties with their measure, feet are reversed within the metre, and the whole rhythm may be counterpointed. The result is incomparably more beautiful."[11]

  Frost's formalism may resemble Pound's and Eliot's, but it is rooted in Emerson, who taught Frost much not only about prosody but about the dialectical struggle of freedom and form in the universe. In his essay "Experience" (1844) Emerson observes that "Human life is made up of the two elements, power and form, and the proportion must be invariably kept if we would have it sweet and sound."[12] In his later essay "Fate" (1860) these two elements are known as freedom and fate or limitation, and Emerson imagines each imposing a check on the other ("if Fate follows and limits Power, Power attends and antagonizes fate"); ultimately, "fate slides into freedom and freedom into fate": one cannot know one without knowing the other, or, as Eliot puts it, "freedom is only truly freedom when it appears against the background of an artificial limitation."[13] Finding that, paradoxically, "limitation is power," Emerson predicts Frost's dialectic between freedom and limitation as expressed in the terms of his poetics, and when Emerson uses the word "meter" in the same essay to name fate ("We can afford to allow the limitation, if we know that it is the meter of the growing man"), we are assured of the connection between Emerson's "fate" and Frost's "form."[14]

If Frost's emphasis on the measure of rhythm by meter in poetry reflects new terms of praise in high modernist literary circles, it also has hidden within it a gender politics in line with the conservative and often misogynistic modernism of such poets as Pound and Eliot.[15] Frost's aesthetic exalts discipline, control, and "sense," as opposed to hormonal surge and emotional flow, the latter of which he codes feminine when he complains in 1915 about "the gushing and undisciplined verse of so many modern lady-poets."[16] Indeed, when, in 1920, he says of Amy Lowell's prosodic term "the periodic sentence" that it is "Nonsense and charlatanry," he cannot resist tying that notion of rhythm to the fact that she is female: "She knew ladies were periodic because they recurred monthly. She's loony—and so periodic by the moon herself" (LU 107). As opposed to what he sees as female emotional instability and unrestraint, Frost declares his commitment to "measure": "Poetry is measure in two senses. It is measured tread[,] but it is also a carefully measured amount of all you have to say" (PJ 65). In a lecture on Shakespeare's blank verse, Frost again distinguishes his formal practice from that of the run of women poets; explaining why he, like Shakespeare, writes blank verse, he notes: "One reason—because, like chewing tobacco, it's something girls can't do. There they come, always chirping after you with little lyrics."[17] Of course, Frost writes his share of rhymed poetry, but the rough-hewn cadences of "the sound of sense" are, he insists, a far cry from women poets' mincing forms ("always chirping after you"). In a letter to Edward Garnett in 1915, Frost further signifies the masculinist force behind his aesthetic, voicing his concern that the *Atlantic Monthly*'s Ellery Sedgwick would not publish Garnett's essay praising Frost because "he had already handed me over for review to some single-bed she professor with a known preference for the beautiful in poetry" (SL 178). As Frost insinuates, this reviewer is incapable of appreciating his manly measures because she is a woman, unmarried (de-sexed), and an Ivory Tower academic—someone who knows nothing of the messiness of the world and so presumably favors prim rhymes and straight-laced meters.

If female poets (like Lowell) have no control over their minds and bodies, good male poets do, according to Frost, and their prosody testifies to that fact. In a letter Frost wrote in 1921 to Grace Walcott (Hazard) Conkling, he speaks of his encouragement of Edward Thomas to turn from prose to poetry, and expresses his view of self-discipline as a precondition for metrical composition:

> I dragged him [Thomas] out from under the heap of his own work in prose he was buried alive under. . . . I made him see that he owed it to himself and the poetry to have it out by itself in poetic form where it must suffer itself to be admired. I had about given him up, he had turned his thoughts to enlistment and I mine to sailing for home when he wrote his first poem. The decision he made in going into the army helped him make the other decision to be a poet in form. And a very fine poet. And a poet all in his own right.[18]

Frost believes that Thomas's decision to enter the army—his self-discipline—conditions his becoming a "poet in form," as does Thomas's actual submission to the harsh discipline of military service. Imagining Thomas as both a self-disciplined *and* disciplined "soldier-poet" (the epithet he assigns him in his elegy "To E. T."), he implicitly alludes to his difference from women and free verse poets, the former of whom (he claims) do not know bodily or emotional discipline and the latter of whom, as he notes in his introduction to Robinson's *King Jasper,* "ran wild in the quest of new ways to be new," their comportment an indicator of their wild (unmetered) verse (*CPPP* 741). In her discussion of "To E. T.," Karen Kilcup reminds us that "the military provided a location for the elaboration of an exclusionary (and sometimes misogynous, inasmuch as it was formed as a rebuttal to the charge of effeminacy) masculinity," and my point here is that Frost's framing of Thomas's "decision to be a poet in form" in terms of his decision to enter the military represents an attempt to secure his and Thomas's masculinity as lyric poets.[19]

The misogynist framework of Frost's theory of form is meant to constitute proof of his masculinity, to stand as a defense against his culture's sense that poetry writing is an effeminate pursuit. As his popularity grows in the years after his repatriation, that framework becomes more obtrusive, as it is intimately related to issues of popularity and canonicity. Kilcup has observed that at that time literary popularity still was residually affiliated with women sentimentalist and regionalist writers of the nineteenth century, and, as I argue, that situation leads Frost to gender further his aesthetic with particular attention to the political control of meter—an attention that coincides with the increasingly masculinist voice of authority and control on which his poetic discourse turns.[20]

The evolving politics of form that I have been charting is portrayed not only in Frost's various prose writings but also in some of his most accomplished poems—poems that usually are not linked to his aesthetic and the ideologies embodied in it. Frost's dramatic dialogue "The Generations of Men," published in *North of Boston* in 1914, is one of his first poems to depict the imagination and control of "the sound of sense" by the "poet in form," and in it we watch as a sexualized power struggle between a boy and a girl at a family reunion unfolds. At one point, the two peer into a cellar hole—the sacred and haunted spot of their family's origin and one symbolic of "the cave of the mouth" in which Frost says "sentence tones" reside—and invoke a hereditary past just as the poet must conjure previously heard tones of voice. Indeed, Frost alludes to the mediumistic quality of poetic performance in his critical prose, finding that "One has it [the texture of tone of voice] as a visitation."[21] The boy, who warns the girl that "I mustn't feel too hurried, / Or I can't give myself to hear the voices," lays out his method to her:

> "I wanted to try something with the noise
> That the brook raises in the empty valley.
> We have seen visions—now consult the voices.
> Something I must have learned riding in trains
> When I was young. I used to use the roar
> To set the voices speaking out of it,
> Speaking or singing, and the band-music playing.
> Perhaps you have the art of what I mean.
> I've never listened in among the sounds
> That a brook makes in such a wild descent.
> It ought to give a purer oracle."
>
> (*CPPP* 78)

Although Robert Faggen, reading the poem in Darwinian terms, regards the brook's "wild descent" as "a metaphor for the entropic chaos of the natural world," it also can be seen as a metaphor for meter out of which voices are released (and against which they stand out in relief).[22] Indeed, such musical counterpoint is reminiscent of Spenser's notion of "undersong" in "Daphnaïda," a term that "suggests that, at bottom, the sound of moving water is the ground—musically as a bass," which "go[es] on underneath discourse" at a lower pitch.[23] Although Frost does not use the term "undersong," the boy obviously is interested in layered sound—discourse and ground—and we cannot help but think here of Frost's description of "the tone-of-voice element" as carried along on a "continuous flow," which meter must conduct.

"The Generations of Men" is not only a "meditation on poetic authority" by virtue of questions raised about the extent to which our imaginative renderings of the past are a projection of ourselves, but also, and more specifically, a meditation on the authority of metrical form.[24] In a trance the boy is instructed by his ancestor to

> take a timber
> That you shall find lies in the cellar charred
> Among the raspberries, and hew and shape it
> For a door-sill or other corner piece
> In a new cottage on the ancient spot.
> The life is not yet all gone out of it.
>   (*CPPP* 80)

The command to "hew and shape" the timber represents the work of meter, which converts raw materials in nature (including tones of voice) into artifact, and the final sentence of the passage hints at Frost's belief that metrical form in poetry is not outmoded. Notably, it is the boy who is charged with measuring the wood, but it is a female forebear that directs him. As Faggen finds, the poem stages "[u]ncertainty about sexual authority and power," with the girl a fit sparring partner, and this condition suggests that Frost has not yet gendered meter and, thus, denigrated the female through it.[25] In the poem Frost wryly comments on another stylistic concern, as the girl teases the boy about the voices that he hears: "I wonder where your oracle is tending. / You can see that there's something wrong with it, / Or it would speak in dialect." Frost's allusion to his own rejection of dialect—he explains to Amy Lowell that he does not "put dialect into the mouths of his people because not one of them, not one, spoke dialect"—further establishes this poem as at one level about the nature and function of poetic technique and the politics of vocal representation (*SL* 220).

The speaker of "The Oven Bird," a sonnet that Frost wrote early in his career (in 1906 or 1907) but did not publish until *Mountain Interval* (1916), likewise is attuned to the dramatic interplay of meter and "the sound of sense" in poetic song and its political charge, though not obviously:[26]

> There is a singer everyone has heard,
> Loud, a mid-summer and a mid-wood bird,
> Who makes the solid tree trunks sound again.
> He says that leaves are old and that for flowers
> Mid-summer is to spring as one to ten.
> He says the early petal-fall is past

When pear and cherry bloom went down in showers
On sunny days a moment overcast;
And comes that other fall we name the fall.
He says the highway dust is over all.
The bird would cease and be as other birds
But that he knows in singing not to sing.
The question that he frames in all but words
Is what to make of a diminished thing.

(*CPPP* 116)

The bird, who "knows in singing not to sing," talks instead ("He says" appears in the poem three times), refusing the melodies of old. When one "frames in all but words," one is performing as Frost does (or as he claims to do) with emphasis off lexical units. In his critical prose Frost even uses the term "frame" to denote the practice of plotting rhythms on the grid of meter: "[T]he metric frame . . . measure[s] the rhythm." Here the poet projects onto the bird an acute sense of belatedness, as in the modern world he must negotiate a relationship with literary tradition at a time when everything seems to have been used up already. In his early lyric "Pan with Us" Frost first meditates on this artistic dilemma and sounds his literary nationalism: Pan emerges from the woods and "tosse[s] his pipes, too hard to teach / A new-world song," finding that "Times were changed from what they were: / Such pipes kept less of power to stir" (*CPPP* 32). He ends by wondering: "Play? Play?—What should he play?" In the poem, Pan contents himself with natural sound: "the blue jay's screech / And the whimper of hawks beside the sun / Were music enough for him for one." But ultimately that is not enough for Frost, who makes a poem out of Pan's (and his own) plight. When the oven bird asks what to "make" of his situation, he calls up the etymological roots of that word in "poetry." How does one make something of a world that is past its prime? By retuning poetry through the imagination of "sounds of sense" within a context of meter. In subtle ways, too, Frost reflects in the poem his belief that this retuning is a virile project, with the bird's "Loud" muscular melodies at odds with the "chirping" sounds of feminine lyric tradition (itself "a diminished thing"). The middle way of the bird-poet ("mid-summer," "mid-wood") also resonates with Frost's formalist politics, as it establishes him as one who, unlike the "extreme modernists," cares to communicate to others and has been successful at it ("There is a singer everyone has heard").

Appropriately, in the magazine *The Measure* in 1921, Frost published for the first time his *ars poetica* "The Aim Was Song," a poem perfectly unambiguous about the fact that it is about his formalism, and in it he twice uses the word "measure" to relate the artist's restructuring of the wind, the raw sounds of (human) nature. Although at first glance there would seem to be no politics in the poem, Karen Kilcup has argued convincingly that it features a "masculine speaker" and signifies Frost's transformation from "the hospitable and affective access of his more sentimental lyrics to a harder, more intellectual challenge."[27] "Man" is shown harnessing the wind's power and producing a pleasing melody:

> He took a little in his mouth,
>   And held it long enough for north
> To be converted into south
>   And then by measure blew it forth.
>
> By measure. It was word and note,
>   The wind the wind had meant to be —
> A little through the lips and throat.
>   The aim was song — the wind could see.
>   (*CPPP* 207)

Here we note the radical historic change from the romantic conception of the Aeolian harp, the inspired but passive imagination, to the pragmatist conception of the mind as actively making the world of consciousness out of the stream of sensation. Taking a "little" in his mouth, the man carefully measures, holding the wind long enough for the north wind of adversity to "be converted" into the south wind of gentleness and warmth. When the poet blows forth a "song," meter shapes it, disciplining the wind's wild energies. It is at the moment when the conversion of brute sound to "song" takes place that the word "measure" appears: "And then by measure blew it forth. / By measure." The recurrence of the term at the head of the line calls attention to the metrical regularity of the poem, which is in unwavering iambic tetrameter. In a poem about the restraining of speech rhythm (the wind) by meter (man's imposed unit), the latter asserts its dominance. The indentation of rhymed lines, an unusual arrangement in Frost's poetry outside of *A Boy's Will*, symbolizes poetic artifice, and in the company of a masculine voice that inscriptional feature emphasizes the subject of the poem: the artist's manly remodeling of raw sounds into carefully modulated lyric utterance.

In another poem in *New Hampshire* (1923), "The Ax-Helve," Frost again tackles the issue of the formal measuring of poetry, but this time his discussion takes shape around gender and racial politics. The Yankee narrator harbors suspicions throughout the poem about the character of his neighbor Baptiste, a French-Canadian woodchopper, not least because he is ethnically other, his difference emphasized by dialect. As he recalls, he was caught off-guard one day when Baptiste came "Behind me on the snow in my own yard / Where I was working at the chopping-block" (*CPPP* 173). The narrator does not know how to take this intrusion "in my own yard," the word "own" intensifying his claim on the plot of land and marking the neighbor's entrance as trespass. Immediately, he finds himself locked in a power struggle with Baptiste, who has come to point out the inferiority of his ax-handle and offer to make him a sturdier one; as Robert Faggen rightly sees, "displays of material power . . . [are] the basis for cultural acceptance" in the poem, as are displays of formal power, with Baptiste wielding his handiwork in order to prove himself and his argument against "laid-on education."[28] The narrator soon sizes up the situation and his neighbor once inside Baptiste's house:

> Baptiste knew best why I was where I was.
> So long as he would leave enough unsaid,
> I shouldn't mind his being overjoyed
> (If overjoyed he was) at having got me
> Where I must judge if what he knew about an ax
> That not everybody else knew was to count
> For nothing in the measure of a neighbor.
> (*CPPP* 174)

The word "measure" stands out here, expressing the narrator's mental task of appraisal and letting in a prosodic meaning. Frost's use of the word "count" in the line above the one in which "measure" appears further hints at an accentual-syllabic system; as he once remarked, "What marks verse off from prose is that it talks letters in numbers" (*CPPP* 809). Moreover, Frost's observation that "Poetry is . . . measured tread[,] but it is also a carefully measured amount of all you have to say" applies to this passage, since the narrator maintains that Baptiste must weigh his words carefully if he does not want to insult him.

In this way, "The Ax-Helve" is a poem about "measure" in two senses: Baptiste is judged by the delicacy of his feeling of where to stop short, and, as an artist, he is charged with bringing raw materials to form. As we learn from Baptiste, his neighbor's helve is "bad," because

> "Made on machine," he said, plowing the grain
> With a thick thumbnail to show how it ran
> Across the handle's long-drawn serpentine,
> Like the two strokes across a dollar sign.

Notably, these lines are not strict iambic. The first contains two trochees. The second and fourth include frequent metrical substitutions, including pyrrhics and spondees. Only the third line, which points up the natural grain of the wood, is metrically regular. In the narrator's description of his neighbor's aesthetic, Frost continues to make use of the play between metrical regularity and irregularity:

> He liked to have it slender as a whipstock,
> Free from the least knot, equal to the strain
> Of bending like a sword across the knee.
> He showed me that the lines of a good helve
> Were native to the grain before the knife
> Expressed them, and its curves were no false curves
> Put on it from without.
>
> (*CPPP* 175)

Here the line "Of bending like a sword across the knee" is metrically regular, a sign that the rhythm has been bent like a sword across the knee of meter in much the same way as nature has been bent to human design. Of course, a "good helve" is true to the lines of nature, a fulfillment of them, not some act of violence against them: it is the wood the wood had meant to be. Or as Frost put it in a letter dated 1919: "Free rhythms are as disorderly as nature; meters are as orderly as human nature and take their rise in rhythms just as human nature rises out of nature" (*SL* 242).

The figure of the ax-helve represents the balance in a poem between meter and rhythm and is reminiscent of "the straight crookedness of a good walking stick," Frost's oxymoronic image of the harmonious blending of "the sounds of sense" and meter (*CPPP* 175). In addition, it expresses Frost's view that the making of art is a masculine affair, and it is telling that in the 1916 interview in which Frost complains about the undisciplined verse of modern female poets, he also claims that the "poetry" of "the ax-handle of a French Canadian woodchopper" teaches us that "Art should follow lines in nature, like the grain of an axe-handle. False art puts curves on things that haven't any curves" (*I* 19). As Frost believes, whereas female poets put artificial frills on poetry (especially in the guise of rhyme), male poets venture forth and by brute strength hew poems to form.

Although the title poem of *West-Running Brook* (1928) also is metapoetical in nature, few have recognized its reflection of Frost's sense of the politics of poetry either. In the poem a husband and wife locate in a brook whose waves run counter to its current a dynamic figure of their relationship to each other—a relationship that runs on difference—and, by extension, of form in poetry:

> "It must be the brook
> Can trust itself to go by contraries
> The way I can trust with you—and you with me—
> Because we're—we're—I don't know what we are.
> What are we?"

> "Young or new?"
>   "We must be something.
> We've said we two. Let's change that to we three.
> As you and I are married to each other,
> We'll both be married to the brook."

(CPPP 236)

The movement in and out of metrical regularity in these lines signifies the balance of rhythm and meter that the poem is in part about. The triadic structure in the middle of the passage is also striking. Rarely does Frost split a line in three; more usually, he divides a line into two parts, designating two different speakers. Here that division serves as an emblem of the love triangle that the wedding of husband, wife, and brook creates. But the wife and husband do not always see eye to eye, or speak the same language, as the following verbal jousting makes plain. The husband begins by contradicting his wife's exuberant claim that the brook "is waving to us with a wave," alleging that she has "take[n] it off to lady-land, / As't were the country of the Amazons," a country that rules men out. In their exchange husband and wife stand opposed, her fancy set against his reason, and Donald Sheehy has argued based on such passages that in the poem there exists a "hierarchical distinction between man's and woman's voice," that the husband's "philosophical-poetic discourse" subsumes the woman's speech.[29] Extending these remarks to the prosodic realm, I would say that the husband's attempt to reign in her female extravagance symbolizes the restraining of "the sound of sense" by meter, and when he declares "I have no more to say," he stops short, carefully measuring all he has to say, just as Frost claims that masculine meter in poetry is there to monitor passionate feeling.

However, by viewing the poem simply as a drama of feminine subordination to the masculine, Sheehy does not credit the mutual affection that radiates from their words to each other. After all, it is mostly raillery here, and when Frost told a friend that the poet "should let the spoken word and the verse pattern fight out the issue; the best poetry results from the nicest compromise between them," he reflects on the pleasurable resolution of that formal antagonism. In the husband's analogy between the movement of the brook and his and his wife's own gentle conflict, the contained clash of prosodic elements is the unspoken third:

> "Speaking of contraries, see how the brook
> In that white wave runs counter to itself.
> It is from that in water we were from
> Long, long before we were from any creature."

(CPPP 237)

The first line of this statement is highly irregular, including in it two trochees, which symbolize the reversal of the water, its backward motion to
the source. The second and third lines are regular iambic pentameter, a
condition that highlights the deviations from that pattern in surrounding
lines. However, Frost's switching from metrical regularity to irregularity
does more than mime the counter-currents of the brook; it also expresses
the emotional ebb and flow of the couple in marriage and the marriage of
rhythm and meter in the structure of the poem itself. Indeed, the husband
includes "tone" in his list of abstract impulses in the symbolic course of the
brook: "it is time, strength, tone, light, life, and love." Here Frost spiritu-
alizes tone by tracing it back to the stream of consciousness, that is, our unmediated emotional existence. The brook's "strange resistance in itself" reveals the dialectic of his poetics and echoes Emerson's poem "Two Rivers,"
which includes the lines "Through light, through life, it forward flows" and
"I hear the spending of the stream."[30] But whereas Emerson's two rivers
are joined as one, with the forward flow of the brook counteracted by a
natural desire to resist the "spending," or gradual running down, Frost's
brook contains within itself that counterforce (as "sentence sounds" inhabit nature) in recognition of our resistance to decline.

The measure of the brook, the measure of marriage, the measure of
poetry—all of these hinge on the incorporation and containment of conflict, its tuneful resolution. "West-Running Brook" closes not in argument,
then, but in mutual recognition and accreditation, as the husband and wife
recognize themselves in the movement of the water:

> "It is from this in nature we are from.
> It is most us."
> > "Today will be the day
> You said so."
> > "No, today will be the day
> You said the brook was called West-running Brook."
> "Today will be the day of what we both said."

A high degree of metrical regularity marks these lines, as if to signify the
overcoming of contrariness. Richard Poirier sums up Frost's performance
nicely: "The reference [at the end of the poem] is not to the day 'when' but
to 'the day of what we both said.' The poem thus suggests that speaking or
saying is a true measure of time, that human exchange, like poetry, is a
manifestation of life resisting any unimpeded movement toward death."[31]
His use of the word "measure" is apt, too, since the poem, and the others at
which we have been looking, is about precisely that—our measure of our
world and of poetry in it. Poirier also finds that "West-Running Brook" is "a

celebration of metaphor and of its tensions," and it is, but it is also a celebration of the tension between meter and rhythm, two units that for Frost also symbolize distinct political positions; as he once said, the poem represents "my position between socialism and individualism," which I take to mean the "middle way" forged by the accommodation of rhythm (individualism) to meter (socialism or, rather, sociality).[32]

In a later lyric entitled "Never Again Would Birds' Song Be the Same," which was published in *A Witness Tree* in 1942, Frost similarly highlights interpersonal ties and, in doing so, further reveals the politics of his formalism. In the sonnet, we are returned to Biblical time and issued a new myth of our common mother that cannot help but resonate with the terms of his poetics:

> He would declare and could himself believe
> That the birds there in all the garden round
> From having heard the daylong voice of Eve
> Had added to their own an oversound,
> Her tone of meaning but without the words.

Here Frost commemorates the tonal vibrancy of Kay Morrison, his secretary who saw him through his deepest grief after his wife Elinor's death and to whom he was deeply grateful.[33] We know that Frost regarded the poem as a showcase of "sentence sounds," since he read it on occasion with a running commentary on the various tones of voice to be found in it, but it is also *about* "sentence sounds" and their affective power.[34] Less obviously, Frost calls attention to the Western cultural tradition in the poem; indeed, we might say that "Never Again" is a poem about echo that contains a "figure of echo"—what John Hollander terms "the poetic device of revising a word or phrase or trope from a precursor text."[35] The first line revises one of Frost's favorite lines from *Hamlet,* a line that he cites elsewhere to exemplify "the sound of sense": "So have I heard and do in part believe it." When, later in the lyric, the speaker claims that Eve's voice "Had now persisted in the woods so long / That probably it never would be lost," Frost pays homage to the venerable artistic uses of "the sound of sense"; he recognizes that by virtue of intonation contours being entrenched in literary tradition, which is to say metrical poetry, they have been exalted as vital traces.

Notably, the allusive network does not stop with Shakespeare. In the poem Frost also engages another Renaissance poet concerned with layered voice; as Hollander contends, in "Never Again" the word "oversound," "playing against the modern figurative sense of 'overtone,' is returning [Spenser's] 'undersong' in a strangely inverted way."[36] Spenser uses the

word "undersong" to describe the refrain of his *Prothalamion,* "that mag-
nificent spousal verse that Spenser wrote on the occasion of the announced
marriage of the two daughters of the earl of Somerset in the fall of 1596."[37]
That Frost would be open to Spenser's poem makes sense, since he is celebrating his new attachment to Kay and, at the same time, his vigorous heterosexuality. In addition, in the fourth poem of *Eupheme* (a cycle in praise
of Lady Venetia Digby), Ben Jonson mythologizes his heroine in a way
strikingly similar to Frost's mythologizing of Kay:

> The voice so sweet, the words so fair,
> As some soft chime had stroked the air;
> And though the sound were parted thence,
> Still left an echo in the sense.[38]

Kay's voice, like Lady Digby's, is described as "soft," and Jonson's statement that the sound of her voice "Still left an echo in the sense" parallels
perfectly Frost's "tone of meaning but without the words." Through the
literary echo chamber of the poem, Frost figures the vibrancy of the metrical tradition, which, he reminds us, is not politically neutral, expressing as
it does the values of the dominant culture. The sonnet, which operates
most often as a vehicle for the expression of heterosexual affection, codifies
these values most effectively. Although Hollander has observed that once
Eve's voice is implicated in the birds' song the poem says that "nature
would exist as a meaningful communicant . . . to be listened to because
human meaning would always be in it," if we read that song as emblematic
of the formal tradition, we can see Frost generating a myth about the
meaningful communication that takes place in his brand of lyric, where the
happy subordination of rhythm to meter symbolizes a network of political
and cultural affiliations.[39]

II

In addition to reflecting the cultural attitudes just described, Frost's poetics
serves as a powerful expression of and figure for his nationalist politics—a
politics sharpened in response to two world wars and an incipient cold war.
His "Fourth of July" 1913 letter in which he issues the phrase "the sound of
sense" indicates his patriotic fervor even before this international turmoil,
as he frames his struggle to break free from outmoded (British) aesthetic
procedures (while in England) as an act of American independence. Immediately upon his return home in 1915, Frost points up the indigeneity of
his concept of "the sound of sense": "I have even read that our American

Indians possessed, besides a picture-language, a means of communication (though it was not said how far it was developed) by the sound of sense" (*RFPP* 262). Frost is led to this correspondence not only by his early literary political interest in the "primitive," but also by his nationalism, and he seeks to remind us that meaningful tones of voice are nothing new to the American landscape, conveniently collapsing racial distinctions in an effort to claim these American Indian rhythms as his legacy. Notably, though, Frost does not assign American Indian poetry a place in the dominant cultural tradition; as Louis Untermeyer explains:

Mary Austin, Natalie Curtis, and others were causing a stir with books purporting to prove that the basic American rhythm was that of the Indian and that our indigenous poetry was in what they called the Amerindian song. Robert was one of those who maintained that, stirring as the Indian songs may be to the Indians, they were not, and could not be, part of our cultural heritage. He proved this by reading three different versions of one Indian chant which, according to the three translators, incorporated three differing symbols and meant three different things. (*LU* 81)

Thus, Frost rejects the idea that American Indian poetry can be meaningful to white Americans but at the same time suggests that his notion of "the sound of sense" constitutes a national rhythm by virtue of its ties to that poetry; in effect, then, he expresses the superiority of the Anglo-American voice over the "primitive" voice while drawing from it in his quest for artistic renewal and in order to forge for his poetry an American cultural identity, just as other modernist poets did.[40] In *The American Rhythm* (1923) Mary Austin even cites Frost as a poet who partakes of these "native rhythms," as she notes the "stream of rhythmic stimuli proceeding from the environment" that work upon early and late American poets.[41]

Not content to link rhythm alone to American aboriginal expression, Frost suggests that meter, too, corresponds to an aspect of the American Indian performance aesthetic. In a lecture on Shakespeare where he hails the "genius" of blank verse, Frost is recorded as saying, "If one writes verse that doesn't rhyme is there really much else to write except this iambic pentameter? Carl Sandburg, talking a 'naïve' view of America, democracy, etc. 'lacks the beat of the tom-tom.'"[42] Faulting Sandburg's prosodic and political commitments, Frost links meter to Native American drumming and, indirectly, to his conception of modern American democracy (as opposed to Sandburg's jejune populism). His politicizing of the terms of his prosodic theory expands dramatically as the U.S. becomes increasingly roiled by domestic disputes and world wars. For instance, in a 1942 preface to "The Death of the Hired Man" that he wrote for a textbook in which the poem was to be reprinted, he draws a much clearer connection between blank verse and ideological conservatism:

In asking me to preface my poem, Mr. Burnett's idea is no doubt to have me bring it up to date by connecting it with some such thing as National Labor Relations. I am always glad to give my poems every extraneous help possible. The employee here depicted is no longer numerous enough to be dealt with statistically by the Departments of Economics and Sociology. Nevertheless I should like to flatter myself that it is at least partly for his sake that the revolution is being brought on. In conclusion I beg to protest that it was with any such thoughts as these that the poem was written. By the way, it's in blank verse, not free verse. (*CPPP* 785)

Here Frost jokingly tries to float his poem in the prevailing political winds, referring to the New Deal National Labor Relations Board meant to secure collective bargaining rights for workers, but he ends up discounting any relationship. The last sentence echoes earlier statements (as of 1915) that he writes blank verse, not free verse, as some critics had failed to see. But his correction is not politically neutral, as he teases that those who mistake the prosody of the poem do so because they adhere to a leftist political philosophy: in Frost's fiction of form, blank verse stands for self-reliance and democracy, and free verse for self-surrender and socialism.

Earlier in the chapter I noted the salutary effects that Frost attributes to metrical composition ("Measure always reassures me"), but passed over his political formulation "Measure . . . in government." It is time now to take that up and consider it in light of his politicizing of poetic form. Later in the speech in which he invokes "Measure . . . in government" Frost interprets the ideological message of one of the framers of the Constitution:

Now I know—I think I know, as of today—what Madison's dream was. It was a dream of a new land to fulfill with people in self-control. In self-control. That is all through his thinking. And let me say that again to you. To fulfill this land—a new land—with people in self-control. And do I think that dream has failed? Has come to nothing, or has materialized too much? It is always the fear. We live in constant fear, of course. To cross the road, we live in fear of cars. But we can live in fear, if we want to, of too much education, too little education, too much of this, too little of that. But the thing is, the measure. (*RFPP* 437)

In these remarks Frost hammers home his belief that Madison, a staunch federalist and vigorous proponent of limited government, understood the importance of self-discipline to American democracy. He winds up hailing the virtue of "measure," the balancing of extremes that signifies not only psychic and social, but political, health.

As important as Madison's thinking is to Frost on the subject of limited freedom, Emerson's meant more to him, and it is in his reflections on Emerson that we sense the full force of Frost's American myth of form. Indeed, Frost identifies Emerson as a distinctly national figure, including him in his pantheon of those who blueprinted American democracy and sought its fulfillment. In "On Emerson" (1959), a speech to the American Academy of Arts and Sciences, Frost remarked: "I suppose I have always thought I'd like to name in verse some day my four greatest Americans: George Washington, the general and statesman; Thomas Jefferson, the political thinker; Abraham Lincoln, the martyr and savior; and fourth, Ralph Waldo Emerson, the poet" (*CPPP* 860). Although Frost refers to Emerson as "the poet," and to Jefferson as "the political thinker," all of the men cited are ingrained in the American political landscape. Indeed, in his essay "Politics" (1844) Emerson restates what Frost identifies as Madison's dream: "The tendencies of the times favor the idea of self-government, and leave the individual, for all code, to the rewards and penalties of his own constitution, which work with more energy than we believe, whilst we depend on artificial restraints."[43] Explaining that the individual should not be imposed on from without, Emerson uses the same term ("self-control") that Frost does in his discourse on Madison: "This undertaking for another, is the blunder which stands in colossal ugliness in the governments of the world. . . . I can see well enough a great difference between my setting myself down to a self-control, and my going to make somebody else act after my views."[44] By virtue of such statements, Emerson serves Frost as an important political model and even prefigures Frost's hostility to New Deal ideology in the most succinct of terms: "[T]he less government we have the better."[45]

But it is not just the content of Emerson's political theories that whips up Frost's nationalism; it is also Emerson's prosody, which Frost explicitly links to his notion of America. In comments scrawled in the margins of a copy of *Poetry and Drama* (December 1913) that he sent to his friend John Bartlett, Frost responds to an ungenerous review of recent American poetry by John Alford published in it—one that includes the following sentence: "Now it is just as well to state at the beginning that I can find no support to the belief that there is any such thing as American poetry; just as an examination of the Metropolitan Museum of Art finally destroyed my idea that there was any such thing as American art." Frost asserts his Americanness in the face of Alford's chauvinistic remark: "This is what makes it impossible that I should live long under a criss-cross flag. Me for the three colors the bluebird wears. This cub [Alford] doesn't know how to find his way around among American writers. No one he mentions is thought anything of on the other side—no one of recent date. Emerson is so American, so original, especially in form. I'll bet you five he couldn't read him if he tried" (*SL* 105–06). As I noted in the first chapter, Frost points to Emerson as a poet who worked according to "the sound of sense," so presumably what establishes his form as American is in large part his crossing of meter with speech rhythms. This prosodic technique is intensely national, Frost claims, so much so that a person living under the Union Jack could not possibly understand it. As we will see, Frost's antagonism toward the British only grows—along with his fiction of form—as America becomes more involved in world affairs.

In the play of rhythm and meter, then, Frost finds a figure for the political condition of limited freedom, and about this condition Emerson has much to say. Indeed, it is important to remember that Emerson's notion of "balance," which he expresses in his essay "Fate," represents a specific political ideal as well. In "Politics" he observes: "The fact of two poles, of two forces, centripetal and centrifugal, is universal, and each force by its own activity develops the other. Wild liberty develops iron conscience. Want of liberty, by strengthening law and decorum."[46] Claiming that in the political realm, freedom calls forth law, and law freedom, he points to the need for ideological equilibrium, or "measure": "There is a middle measure which satisfies all parties, be they never so many, or so resolute for their own."[47] In politics, "a middle measure" is a compromise in which the rights of one party are weighed against those of another, and personal freedom against the rule of law; in prosody, "a middle measure" would correspond to Frost's phrase "the measured way," which stands for "regular," or metrical, writing.

The emergence of fascism in Nazi Germany provided Frost with an opportunity to discuss his notion of "balance" in Emersonian terms. In 1939, Frost, about to begin his appointment as Harvard's Emerson Fellow, gave an interview to the Associated Press in the course of which he reflects on the recent German invasion of Poland:

The world is swaying to the left and to the right. It is a drunken world, going home we know not where, but the important thing to realize is that it is not swaying too far to the left or too far to the right. . . . My life has been all holidays, whether it has been work or play. The secret? I say it is this: Never allow yourself to become a "case" if you can help it; and never froth at the mouth about things. That's the trouble with too many people. They froth at the mouth because they're reading the same newspaper too much. They get all scared about what they think Germany's going to do. They get all worried about "reds" in the country. They get frothed up about what's going to become of democracy. And all the time they forget that there are limitations to all things; that there always is a balance to everything.[48]

Lawrance Thompson suggests that these remarks are influenced by Emerson's essay "Compensation," which Frost, as Emerson Fellow, might have reread, as in that essay Emerson sets forth his view of the counterpoise of forces that makes for a moral universe: "Polarity, or action and reaction, we meet in every part of nature; in darkness and light; in heat and cold; in the ebb and flow of waters; in male and female."[49] When Frost says that "there are limitations to all things," he means not only that the natural world entails such balance, but also that politics is a binary business, that ideologies mediate. Although his dismissal of those worried about what the Germans are going to do is troubling, suggesting as it does an unconcern about those affected by the extremes (particularly in light of what Germany actually does), his point is that no extreme ideology can wreck the world for democracy, which is itself a model of limited freedom. Indeed, when Frost asserts the need for "balance" and "form" in poetry, he declares his opposition to what he calls "unchartered freedom," deftly alluding to the political charter of the Constitution, which establishes a system of checks and balances in government in order to safeguard personal liberties (*I* 159).

In 1962, Frost again suggests the correspondence between U.S. political form and the form of his poetry, using the prosodically charged term "tone" in evoking the Emersonian force of "Wild liberty": "The tone is freedom to the point of destruction. Democracy means all the risks taken—conflict of opinion, conflict of personality, eccentricity" (*I* 194). Expanding on this figure of antagonism, Frost writes in his notebook: "A nation should be just as full of conflict as it can contain, physically[,] mentally, financially. But of course *it must contain*. The strain must be short of the bursting point—*just short*."[50] The noun "strain" resonates with his description of the "strained relation" that must exist between meter and rhythm, and he further links national and poetic structure when he says that "All a man's art is a bursting unity of opposites" (*IMO* 226). It is telling that Frost describes Emerson's writing in related terms, since he ties that writer's form to America: "The form should be there, but the poet should hit it so hard as to shake it, to make it tremble, to make the reader feel it may be broken—as sometimes indeed in Emerson it is broken."[51] For Frost, the challenge to form that Emerson poses is analogous to the forces that tear at the seams of American democracy, as "conflict[s] of opinion, conflict[s] of personality, eccentricity" threaten to "burst" the nation wide open. If, as Richard Poirier states, "Emersonian pragmatism is formalist in spirit in the sense that, as [Emerson's essay] 'Circles' makes clear, the making of form is the necessary prelude of the effort to escape its limitations," it is also, Frost believes, quintessentially American.[52]

In his political poem "To a Thinker," written in 1933, Frost constructs a figure of ideological extremism, invoking two well-worn words, "sound" and "sense," in his contemptuous characterization of those politicians who elude the "middle measure" of American democracy by bobbing left to right "like a stabled horse":

> From force to matter and back to force,
> From form to content and back to form,
> From norm to crazy and back to norm,
> From bound and free and back to bound,
> From sound to sense and back to sound.
> So back and forth. It almost scares
> A man the ways things come in pairs.
> Just now you're off democracy
> (With a polite regret to be),
> And leaning on dictatorship;
> But if you will accept the tip,
> In less than no time, tongue and pen,
> You'll be a democrat again.
>
> (*CPPP* 298)

By opposing "sound" and "sense" in this litany of binaries, Frost suggests the moderation of his own poetics, tidily summed up by "the sound of sense," an expression that binds the two. As Frost explained, the poem "was aimed at the heads of our easy despairers of the republic and of parliamentary forms of government," that is, knee-jerk liberals in the communist camp (*I* 88). Calling attention to the consistency between political and aesthetic ideology, he positions "the sound of sense" as a metonym of the compromise between itself and meter in a poem and, at the same time, as a symbol of the poet's democratic values.

While a true believer in American democracy, however, Frost was not always ready to rush to the defense of "parliamentary forms of government." In the wake of World War I, he begins to bristle at America's major ally, Great Britain, decrying the threat to America's freedom—indeed, to its very sovereignty—that he felt that country posed. In an interview in 1923, Frost expresses his sense of national difference and again appeals to Emerson as a symbol of democratic American values, setting him in the midst of an impressive array of national political icons. Discussing an immigrant's gradual incorporation into America, he observes:

America means certain things to the people who come here. It means the Declaration of Independence, it means Washington, it means Lincoln, it means Emerson—never forget Emerson—it means the English language, which is not the language that is spoken in England or her provinces. Just as soon as the alien gets all that—and it may take two or three generations—he is as much an American as is the man who can boast of nine generations of American forebears. He gets the tone of America, and as soon as there is tone there is poetry. (*I* 50)

Overlooking Frost's rather far-fetched notion that immigrants associate Emerson with America just as he does, we can see that Frost's move from politics to poetry in this passage, a move that culminates in his final statement ("He gets the tone of America, and as soon as there is tone there is poetry"), asserts a connection between prosody and nationality. The phrase "as soon as there is tone there is poetry" would be at home in Frost's early discourses on the element of "the sound of sense," but his nationalizing of it constitutes a new wrinkle in the evolution of his theory of form.

Frost owned Thomas Pyles's *Words and Ways of American English* (1952) and *Webster's New World Dictionary of the American Language* (1952), both of which record differences between American and British locution, as well as H. L. Mencken's *The American Language* (1919), a book that helped shape his tonal nationalism and earned Mencken the moniker "Linguistic Patriot."[53] Despite the caution of a recent editor of *The American Language* that that book "did not spring from anti-British and pro-German sentiment during World War I," as some thought it had, its nationalist sentiment is quite clear: "The 1919 version had emphasized the increasing divergence of American and British speechways; that of 1936 proclaimed that the march of events had so shifted the balance of the English-speaking world that future scholars might well study 'English' as a dialect of 'American.'"[54] Mencken's suggestion of a reverse (linguistic) colonialism no doubt attracted Frost, whose nationalism was fueled by it. In the first chapter of *The American Language* Mencken outlines the history of British stated opinion of America, Americans, and American English; as he finds, the English attitude is profoundly affected by political conditions: "In times of peace and security the British critics of American speech seldom pull their punches; they lay about them in a berserk and all-out manner, and commonly couple flings at the American character with their revilings of the American language"; however, "in wartime this forthright attitude is considerably ameliorated in all the great organs of British opinion."[55] But it is not just the American idiom that is subject to these vagaries; it is American speech rhythm as well: "When Commander Reginald Fletcher, M.P., private secretary to the

First Lord of the Admiralty, undertook in 1941 to confute and confuse 'the people who say that Germany will be out of oil next week or will crack next month' by hurling at them a derisive 'Oh, yeah!' a [British] columnist applauded," citing the distinctive American tone.[56]

In 1925 in the *Nation* Frost's friend John Erskine, a professor at Columbia University, published an article entitled "Do Americans Speak English?" about the linguistic distance that separates the U.S. and Great Britain. Erskine's answer to the question that he poses in his title is remarkable for its closeness to Frost's rhetoric. He begins by noting that, although the language that Americans and the British speak is the same, the way they speak it is not: "When we are learning to talk, as babies in our own language or as adults in a foreign tongue, we have to work our way syllable by syllable, but when we have a mastery of speech, we express ourselves and understand others largely through the tune, the accent, the rising and falling of the voice. When we call out a question to someone in another room, we can tell the answer if we can hear the tune of it; the words don't matter."[57] Frost's linguistic skepticism ("The best place to get the abstract sound of sense is from voices behind a door that cuts off the words") shines through Erskine's statement, which recycles the trope of a speaker behind a closed door. Erskine's sense of American rhythm leads him to the concept of "the sound of sense," although he does not use Frost's phrase: "In so far as the American accent moves in a logical direction, we may be reconciled to our ignorance of the English tune," which, he claims, "often brings the accent of the sentence into conflict with the logic of it."[58] In other words, in American English the pitch of the sentence indicates semantic content, and he is not surprised to find that "thoughtful American poets should be consciously trying to write in the American tune, in the shorter cadences most of us use."[59] Although he does not mention Frost by name, Erskine clearly has Frost's literary example in mind.

In "A Romantic Chasm" (1948), the preface to the British edition of his play *A Masque of Reason,* Frost credits the impact of this emergent linguistic nationalism, particularly of *The American Language,* on his thinking: "It took an American, a friend, Henry L. Mencken, to rouse me to a sense of national differences. My pedantry would be poor and my desert small if I could pretend to look unscared into the gulf his great book has made to yawn between the American and English languages" (*CPPP* 802). Frost celebrates "the separation of the parts," but at the same time claims that he "would go to any length short of idolatry to keep Great Britain within speaking, or at least shouting, distance of America in the trying times seen ahead." The title phrase "the romantic chasm" alludes to Coleridge's poem

"Kubla Khan," where from a "deep romantic chasm"—a "savage place"—issue "ancestral voices prophesying war."[60] His phrase "the trying times seen ahead" prophesies the Cold War, which will demand international solidarity, but his desire to preserve national particularity leads him at the end of the preface to claim that his poetry is written "in American" (*CPPP* 803). Objecting to U.S. involvement in World War II in 1941, Frost paints political affiliation in terms of a familiar prosodic term: "Our seaboard sentimentalists think of nothing but saving England. Some of them would go so far as to sacrifice America to save England. They are the Anglophiles with the English accent."[61] These nationalist prejudices find their way into a figurative reworking of that "romantic chasm," a poem entitled "Does No One at All Ever Feel This Way in the Least?" (1952):

> O ocean sea for all your being vast,
> Your separation of us from the Old
> That should have made the New World newly great
> Would only disappoint us at the last
> If it should not do anything foretold
> To make us different in a single trait.
>
> This though we took the Indian name for maize
> And changed it to the English name for wheat.
> It seemed to comfort us to call it corn.
> And so with homesickness in many ways
> We sought however crudely to defeat
> Our chance of being people newly born.
>
> And now, O sea, you're lost by aeroplane.
> Our sailors ride a bullet for a boat.
> Our coverage of distance is so facile
> It makes us to have had a sea in vain.
> Our moat around us is no more a moat,
> Our continent no more a moated castle.
>
> (*CPPP* 456)

Lamenting the erosion of nationality as a result of the closing of the gap between England and America in the twentieth century, Frost looks to language as a marker of the degree to which the settlers of the New World remained dependent on British culture and custom ("we took the Indian name for maize / And changed it to the English name for wheat"). In the poem he takes an isolationist stance, and in the final stanza (note the strict endstopping symbolic of his isolationism) expresses his worry that modern technology will erase altogether the wholesome distinctions between the two countries.

Frost registers his wariness of international enterprise in other remarks during this same period. In the *New York Times* (October 27, 1957) he is quoted as saying: "The question for every man and every nation is to be clear about where the first answerability lies. Are we as individuals to be answerable only to others or to ourselves and some ideal beyond ourselves? Is the United States to be answerable first to the United Nations or to its own concept of what is right?" (*RFPP* 438). His use of the word "answerability," resonates with his use of that same word in "The Constant Symbol," where he imagines a statesman "closed in on with obligations and answerabilities" in terms of the formalist poet: "He might as well have got himself into a sestina royal" (*CPPP* 787). Indeed, in the four-line poem "Beyond Words" in *Steeple Bush* (1947) the prosodic unit of "the sound of sense" seems to serve as an emblem of Frost's isolationism, with the speaker, fenced in by an "armory" of icicles hanging off his gutter, venting through charged tones his vengeful fury over America's forced engagement in world affairs: "And you, you . . . you, you utter . . . / You wait!" (*CPPP* 356).

When Frost traveled to England in 1957 as "a distinguished representative of the American cultural scene" and self-described "national American poet," he used his theory of form to dig deeper the chasm between the United States and the mother country.[62] As Thompson describes, in a reading of his poetry at the Senate House of the University of London, Frost "demonstrat[ed] through his poems [including 'The Witch of Coös'] and otherwise various 'voice ways' of American speech, so different from the British in inflection." In another illustration of tonal difference he alluded to the culture of the Cold War: "After the world had been destroyed by the atomic bomb he said (as he often did at home), there would be an interesting 'tone of voice' in the survivor's remark, '*Wasn't* that *some*pin!'"[63] The survivor of the nuclear holocaust is an American rustic whose simple wonder is more immense than the bomb's burst. By way of this grim joke and his emphasis on a distinctive American intonation contour, Frost revises his earlier view that "the sound of sense" could be found in poetry in English on both sides of the Atlantic and gives vent to his deep-seated nationalist sentiments. Frost's jabs at T. S. Eliot, who was in the audience at the Senate House, further reveal Frost's intense chauvinism and return us to his deep concern for literary politics. In a letter to Eliot a few weeks before his arrival, Frost claimed common ground with him even as he drew out national differences between them: "You and I shot off at different tangents from the same pin wheel. We had America in common and we had Ezra [Pound] in common though you had much more of him than I. If I was ever cross with you it was for leaving America behind too far and Ezra not far enough."[64] At the reading, Frost had fun at Eliot's expense, again making the point that the poet had given up American citizenship to become a

British subject: "I can understand," he said, "how someone of another nationality might wish to become an American. But I could never see how an American chose to become, for instance—a Canadian."[65] Clearly, Frost's patriotism—his sense of American exceptionality—was strong upon him at this time.

At his performance in the Senate House at Cambridge University during the same tour of England, Frost's thoughts continued to run to tone in poetry: "Expanding the remarks he had made at London University, he said that a dead language was one in which perhaps everything survived except the sound of sense—the tone of voice, or speech-way, of that language. Translation failed, he said, because speech-ways could not be translated."[66] This time he used as his example "The Gift Outright," which he identifies elsewhere as a poem "about the Revolutionary War," promoting through it both his formal theory and his Americanism:[67]

> The land was ours before we were the land's.
> She was our land more than a hundred years
> Before we were her people. She was ours
> In Massachusetts, in Virginia,
> Possessing what we still were unpossessed by,
> Possessed by what we now no more possessed.
> Something we were withholding made us weak
> Until we found out that it was ourselves
> We were withholding from our land of living,
> And forthwith found salvation in surrender.
> Such as we were we gave ourselves outright
> (The deed of gift was many deeds of war)
> To the land vaguely realizing westward,
> But still unstoried, unenhanced,
> Such as she was, such as she would become.
>
> (*CPPP* 316)

The chiastic statement at the beginning of the poem ("The land was ours before we were the land's") encapsulates the paradox at the heart of the American colonial experience: we had taken physical possession of the land, but in spirit were elsewhere, still British subjects ("We were possessed by Parliament and all that, you know").[68] Our "salvation in surrender" to the land signifies our refusal to surrender to imperial forces, our determination to slip the yoke of British rule. The choice of blank verse here would seem to stress the theme of political freedom, with rhyme dismissed as a relic of the colonial system and a traditional meter sufficiently subverted by American speech rhythms; Frost's politics of form harks back to Milton, whose headnote to *Paradise Lost* frames blank verse as "liberty" and rhymed verse as "bondage."[69] In 1955, Frost made clear the ideological charge of the poem for him at a time of heightened global tension: "This is what I was talking about—our Revolutionary War, you know. Was it an escape or a pursuit? Pursuit of nationality—as simple as could be. Not an escape at all. One person understood it one way, one another. Tom Paine understood it as the beginning of a world revolution. That's wrong. It wasn't that; it was a pursuit of nationality. Wanting to be, feeling that we were, something" (*CPPP* 822). The Revolutionary War represents a "pursuit of nationality," a purchase on our integrity as Americans, Frost contends, not the start of internationalism ("a world revolution"), and so the poem, as activated in the 1950s, stands as a rebuke to "reds" in his own country and so-called "One-worlders."[70] His Cambridge reading of "The Gift Outright" broadcast his nationalism in both form and theme.

But if "the sound of sense" takes on national political meaning in response to international events, so, too, does metrical form in Frost's late poetry. In the proem to "The Gift Outright" (titled "Dedication") that Frost was unable to finish reading at Kennedy's inauguration because of the glare of the sun on his page, he hails American democracy, which serves as a beacon to the world's infant nations:

> We see how seriously the races swarm
> In their attempts at sovereignty and form.
> They are our wards we think to some extent
> For the time being and with their consent,
> To teach them how Democracy is meant.
> (*CPPP* 436)

Here the word "form" stands for the rule of law that brings nations to order and guarantees their freedom, but it applies equally to politics and verse. Frost highlights that double sense when he remarks that America is on the brink of a "golden age of poetry and power," thus tying together the glory attainable "in life and art." In his three-line poem entitled "Pertinax" (1936), he first pairs "swarm" and "form," with the "discipline" of "rhyme and meter" symbolized by the strict iambic dimeter pattern and bold bondage of the triple rhyme (*I* 270):

> Let chaos storm!
> Let cloud shapes swarm!
> I wait for form.
> (*CPPP* 281)

Just as he waits for the cool hand of formal convention in poetic composition, so, too, he waits for newly decolonized nations to embrace the discipline of democratic government under America's tutelage and of their own free will. Written in heroic couplets that skip in and out of metrical regularity, Frost's inauguration poem allegorizes the interplay of freedom and constraint in democracy. The triplet in the passage quoted above (*extent / consent / meant*), like the one in "Pertinax," is intended to depict the pressure of civic form, but the irregular rhythms of some of the lines suggest the political liberties available within a democratic system.

Frost figures the correspondence between prosodic and political form on a grander scale in his poem "How Hard It Is to Keep from Being King When It's in You and in the Situation," which was first published in 1951. He alludes to the ideological dimensions of that poem at Dartmouth College a little over ten years later: "It's kind of, in a way, political and invidious—but you wouldn't know who I was driving at, maybe—maybe you would" (*CPPP* 920). In it, a king and his son run away from their kingdom to find release from the duties of governance. The king proposes that his son sell him as a slave to get the money he needs to start a business or "make a poet of himself," and so he does. Sold to King Darius, the king-turned-slave distinguishes himself through his intellect and becomes Darius's chief counselor. When Darius tells him that "Another word that bothers me is Freedom," the king-turned-slave gestures to his son:

> He'll tell you about Freedom.
> He writes free verse, I'm told, and he is thought
> To be the author of The Seven Freedoms:
> Free Will, Trade, Verse, Thought, Love, Speech, Coinage.
> (*CPPP* 468)

Here the father makes the humorous assumption that because his son writes "free" verse, he is an expert on the subject of "Freedom." After making the joke, the king-turned-slave addresses more seriously the issue that troubles Darius:

> Freedom is slavery some poets tell us.
> Enslave yourself to the right leader's truth,
> Christ's or Karl Marx' and it will set you free.
> Don't listen to their play of paradoxes.
> The only certain freedom's in departure.

In this passage Frost represents his own political views, his determination to blend "liberty" and "law" in his poetry, just as the speaker of these lines says they must be blended "in school and state." In his critical prose he credits Emerson for instilling in him his "troubled thoughts about freedom," for "disabus[ing] me of my notion I may have been brought up to that the truth would make me free. My truth will bind you slave to me"

(*CPPP* 863). Frost's admiration of this formula leads him to write a taunting poem entitled "The Prophet" in 1936 at the height of anti-democratic feeling in the U.S.:

> They say the truth will make you free.
> My truth will bind you slave to me —
> Which may be what you want to be.
> (*CPPP* 559)

It is not in "truth" that we find freedom; "truth" is always of someone's making, and, therefore, always makes the person who embraces it a follower. Although one may escape political institutions and find unfettered freedom ("The only certain freedom's in departure"), there is another, more desirable freedom attainable within the parameters of the state ("chartered" freedom).

"How Hard It Is to Keep from Being King" echoes Frost's remarks in his speech "On Emerson," where he looks ahead to a time when freedom and law are in a Kantian dialectical relationship: "I am on record as saying that freedom is nothing but departure—setting forth—leaving things behind, brave origination of the courage to be new. We may not want freedom. But let us not deceive ourselves about what we don't want. Freedom is one jump ahead of formal laws, as in planes and even automobiles right now. Let's see the law catch up with us very soon" (*CPPP* 863). In the same talk, Frost credits Emerson for shaping his tolerance of "radicals," but it is a tolerance with limits: "No subversive myself, I think it very Emersonian of me that I am so sympathetic with subversives, rebels, runners out, runners out ahead, eccentrics and radicals. I don't care how extreme their enthusiasm so long as it doesn't land them in the Russian camp" (*CPPP* 865). The balance of freedom and discipline in democracy is, for Frost, a salutary one, and any disloyalty to democracy in the American ranks threatens that precious political order: "There is such a thing as getting too transcended. There are limits. Let's not talk socialism" (*CPPP* 863).

The poet-son who sells his father into slavery in "How Hard It Is to Keep from Being King" points up the link between the "formal laws" of poetic and political composition. His rebuttal also reveals a link between his biography and that of Frost:

> I'm not a free-verse singer. He was wrong there.
> I claim to be no better than I am.
> I write real verse in numbers, as they say.
> I'm talking not free verse but blank verse now.
> Regular verse springs from the strain of rhythm
> Upon a meter, strict or loose iambic.

From that strain comes the expression *strains of music.*
The tune is not that meter, not that rhythm,
But a resultant that arises from them.
Tell them Iamb, Jehovah said, and meant it.

(*CPPP* 469)

Just as Frost was thought erroneously by some to be a free verse poet at the start of his career, the king-turned-slave confuses his son as one. The son's rejection of that mantle sounds a lot like Frost's and, as we have seen, is politically charged. Indeed, much of this passage is cribbed from Frost's poetics. The poet-son's jab at Whitman and Sandburg a little later on echoes Frost's evaluations of them in his prose jottings. The pun on "I AM," which appears as the prosodic term "Iamb," figures Frost's effort to separate himself from nonmetrical poets and insinuates that metrical composition is divinely ordained. However, Frost is not as free from error as "Jehovah," misreading etymology through the persona of the poet-son: "Regular verse springs from the strain of rhythm / Upon a meter, strict or loose iambic. / From that strain comes the expression *strains of music.*" The word "strain" in *"strains of music"* derives from the Middle English "stren," which means "stock" or "race," not "streinen," which means to "wring hard" or "draw tight" (*OED*). However, this mistake is consistent with the meaning that Frost assigns the word in theorizing "the sound of sense" ("strained relation"); as he makes clear, what he is interested in is "a tune arising from the stress on those [the rhythm and the meter]—same as your fingers on the strings, you know. The twang!" (*I* 203). Finally, the son's insistence that a poet in English only has "strict or loose iambic" from which to choose mirrors Frost's claim in "The Figure a Poem Makes": "All that can be done with words is soon told. So also with meters—particularly in our language where there are virtually but two, strict iambic and loose iambic. The ancients with many were still poor if they depended on meters for all tune" (*CPPP* 776).

Of course, Frost's choice not to write free verse does not stop him from "holding forth on" freedom, and the same is true of the poet-son in the poem. After he has made clear exactly what kind of writer he is, he turns in his final speech to the subject of "freedom" in democracy, pleading indifference to "public freedom" and reproducing nearly verbatim another credo in "The Figure a Poem Makes": "Political freedom is nothing to me. I bestow it right and left. All I would keep for myself is the freedom of my material—the condition of body and mind now and then to summons aptly from the vast chaos of all I have lived through" (*CPPP* 778). Despite his rather casual claim that "Political freedom is nothing to me," Frost spends a great deal of time after World War I promoting America and the political system of democracy—a system that he believes provides people with the best chance for freedom and the best kind at that. In "How Hard It Is to Keep from Being King" his characters refer often to "public freedom," and the king-turned-slave even invokes Madison ("If we could only stop the Progress somewhere, / At a good point for pliant permanence, / Where Madison attempted to arrest it"). Far from expressing "little interest" in political freedom, Frost shows through his aesthetic his preoccupation with that issue. As a fiction of form, then, his prosodic theory, fashioned in self-defense early in his career, later is brandished to defend his country in the face of what he sees as threats rampant at home and abroad, to figure a world that will satisfy his psychological needs and, in turn, his political preferences—a world that is orderly, lawful, democratic, American.

III

If Frost's theory of form grows into an instrument of his conservatism, its legacy is far different: in the wake of Frost's death, his theory has influenced a range of contemporary artists, perhaps most interestingly subaltern and transnational poets struggling with the legacies of colonialism and the problems (and promise) of intercultural inheritance. In *Homage to Robert Frost* (1996) three Nobel Laureates—Joseph Brodsky, Seamus Heaney, and Derek Walcott—address the issue of Frost's prosody, and in speaking of his method negotiate their unique political situations: Brodsky as an exiled Russian poet living in America; Heaney as a postcolonial Irish poet; and Walcott as a postcolonial Caribbean poet. As all three find, Frost's concepts of rhythm and meter bear directly on issues of place and identity that are central to their concerns, and their tropes of his theory constitute powerful fictions of form in their own right. To see what these poets are up to in their reflections on (and inflections of) Frost's poetics, I will explore their poetry and critical prose through the lens of postcolonial theory. As my investigations prove, Frost's prosodic theory continues to intervene in important ways in some of the most stirring political and cultural debates of our time.

Although the theory of "the sound of sense" originally is shaped in opposition to the dominant culture and its imperialistic designs, Frost voices an ambivalence about colonialism later in his career, as his own theory of form turns increasingly nationalistic. A lack of concern about the racist politics of colonialism is on display in letters he wrote to friends and family in the early 1940s when colonialism was in crisis. As he tells Earle J. Bern-heimer in 1943, "I never have failed for a moment to appreciate their (En-gland's) greatness, their imperial greatness. Not once in the present emer-gency have I joined in the easy talk of our liberals disposing of their dispossessions in the break up of the Empire so fondly predicted" (*SL* 512). To his daughter Lesley in March 1942, he again comes to the defense of En-gland, but his feelings are more mixed:

You mustnt be too hard on the British in their day of adversity. I hate to hear them starting to free India under fire. If one were fanciful he might venture the figure that it sounds like the Empires death bed repentance. Neither do I quite like their fawning on us at such a time. Still it ill becomes a Frost not to sympathise with a na-tion that has done so much for our family. Possibly you calculate it has not been all good—good only for me and not for the rest of the family. I have no answer for that. Any way I am on their side. But what would Rudyard Kipling say—Had he lived to see this day—of having his poems edited by worlds-end-whimper T. S. El-liot [*sic*]—to rouse the spirit of the British to the Natzi [*sic*] level to meet the Natzi-greatness?[71]

Here he makes a joke out of England's dismantling of colonialism in India under signs of revolt, showing no great compassion for the rights of the subject people and yet suggesting that perhaps "repentance" for the crimes committed in the name of "civilization" is not unwarranted. He also laughs at the political use to which Kipling is put, as colonial art becomes a moti-vator of nationalist sentiment during World War II.

In his equivocal "Dedication," the prefatory piece to "The Gift Out-right," Frost welcomes the postcolonial moment and the hope of a demo-cratic world it offers but refuses to censure the politics of the past:

> Colonial had been the thing to be
> As long as the great issue was to see
> What country'd be the one to dominate
> By character, by tongue, by native trait,
> The new world Christopher Columbus found.
> . . . .
> Now came on a new order of the ages
> That in the Latin of our founding sages
> (Is it not written on the dollar bill
> We carry in our purse and pocket still?)
> God nodded his approval of as good.
> So much those heroes knew and understood,
> I mean the great four, Washington,
> John Adams, Jefferson, and Madison,—
> So much they knew as consecrated seers
> They must have seen ahead what now appears,

> They would bring empires down about our ears
> And by the example of our Declaration
> Make everybody want to be a nation.
>
> (*CPPP* 435)

A similar ambivalence—that is, a refusal to condemn colonial power coupled with a cheery optimism about subaltern agency—marks Frost's statements in the 1960s about "The Gift Outright" itself, in particular as he considers in its light the breakdown of colonialism around the world:

> I gave it ["The Gift Outright"] to him [Kennedy] for his inauguration, and it's just
> a history of—a little piece of history—about the Revolutionary War. Isnt it funny
> about how politics comes into poetry somewhat, you know? The Revolutionary
> War! I often say that most tragedy is like that great tragedy—a conflict of good and
> good. Colonialism is good. Something else has come to the world now; we don't
> know how good and bad it is. Colonialism is gone; it's out. Today's papers [have]
> some more of it. We [U.S.] led off in that way . . . and for very slight reasons. . . . It
> worked well with us. I hope it works well for everybody.[72]

Needless to say, Frost's statement that "Colonialism is good" would not
please most of those who have been colonized; indeed, his sense that nothing sinister lies behind such expansionism, that imperialism has benefited
the Third World in its way, suggests a blindness on Frost's part to the
abuses and systematic oppression of native peoples presumed not to be
able to govern themselves. However, Frost's wish that decolonizing efforts
in the world in the second half of the twentieth century will prove as successful as America's ("It worked well with us. I hope it works well for
everybody") signifies his blessing of the "new order" of national self-
determination.

   It is seemingly ironic, then, that postcolonial writers have shown such
interest in Frost's theory of form, since he seems so far removed from their
political situation and expresses little sympathy for their suffering. But certain comments Frost makes about the rhetoric of "The Gift Outright" are
in fact intimately related to postcolonial concerns. As we have seen, Frost
refers to that poem as figuring Americans' "Pursuit of nationality," and in it
he lays emphasis on "the meaning of the land," what he calls "the doctrine
of belonging [to] the ground."[73] Borrowing a term from Frederick Jackson Turner, who referred to the American West as "the richest gift ever
spread out before civilized man," Frost hails that "gift" of territory and the
doctrine of Manifest Destiny that brings it under white control—a control
only fully realized after the American Revolution.[74] The postcolonial literary
critic Edward Said has argued that "the imagination of anti-imperialism" is

distinguished by "the primacy of the geographical in it," and he expresses concern about the role of nationalism in the struggle for liberation by non-elite or subordinated social groups: "Nationalism is a word that has been used in all sorts of sloppy and undifferentiated ways, but it still serves quite adequately to identify the mobilizing force that coalesced into resistance against an alien and occupying empire on the part of peoples possessing a common history, religion, and language. Yet for all its success in ridding many countries and territories of colonial overlords, nationalism has remained, in my opinion, a deeply problematic ideological, as well as socio-political, enterprise."[75] Postcolonial poets with an eye to these dangers nonetheless are able to identify Frost with a territorial grounding fundamental to their own aim of self-legitimation.

In his essay "Poetry and Power: Robert Frost," given as a paper at a conference on "The Nation and its Cultural Borders" at the University of Southampton in July 1990, the Irish writer Tom Paulin critiques Frost's representations of colonialism and the colonial subject in his poetry. Claiming that "Frost's status as national poet must in part be based on this tactic of acknowledging and then propitiating that North American unease about property and land ownership," a tactic he sees at work in his poem "Trespass," Paulin examines Frost's dismissal of American Indian culture in "The Gift Outright," calling to account "the poem's triumphal invocation to the land" ("vaguely realizing westward, / But still unstoried, artless, unenhanced, / Such as she was, such as she would become"); as Paulin finds, "This version of Manifest Destiny wipes out Indian culture," but "Frost can't confront directly [the process of displacement]; instead he shunts it into a parenthesis": "(The deed of gift was many deeds of war)."[76] In fact, Frost said at a reading in 1956 that those "deeds of war" are meant to invoke the skirmishes between American and British soldiers during the Revolutionary War.[77] The American Indian genocide is suppressed, then, even more fully than Paulin realizes. Paulin further believes that "The Gift Outright" is of a piece with the unsettling racism of Frost's poem "New Hampshire," which has the colonist John Smith imagining that he sees on America's banks not "Red Indians," but "veritable / Pre-primitives of the white race, dawn people, / Like those who furnished Adam's sons with wives" (*CPPP* 153). As Paulin notes, Frost invokes Smith, the principal founder of the Jamestown settlement, "as a witness to the absolute right of all White Anglo-Saxon Protestants to be in North America."[78]

It is in his analysis of "The Vanishing Red," however, that Paulin gets at the matter of poetic form as it relates to the colonial condition. In Frost's poem a white miller pushes an American Indian man to his death in a wheel-pit, although we do not see it happen, and laughs about it to his friends. Speaking out against Reuben Brower's accession to the racism of the poem, Paulin argues that in it "Frost is justifying both the American industrial revolution and the early colonists' violent seizure of the land. Pain, he implies, is historically necessary. . . . The poem upholds that idea [of white civilizers and Indian savages] by identifying a historical process—those many deeds of war—with the sounds made by white technology. The great big thumping shuffling grindstone is the active memory of war, and it substitutes for all that Frost dismisses as 'too long a story to go into now.'"[79] That metronomic grindstone—symbolic of the sounds made by the Anglo-American poetic tradition as well—looks forward to Paulin's discussion of Frost's poem "The Wood-Pile" in the same essay, with that title figure pitched as a "classical monument": "It was a cord of maple, cut and split / And piled—and measured, four by four by eight" (*CPPP* 101).[80] The strict metrical regularity of these two lines allegorizes what Paulin regards as Frost's insistence "on formal constraints and closed symmetry."[81] Alluding to poems by Shelley and Hardy on classical Rome, "The Wood-Pile," Paulin argues, constitutes "the expression of a long cultural tradition that begins in ancient Rome and finds renewal in a New England swamp"; it represents the voice and values of the white race: "New World neoclassicism overlooks Indian culture in order to reassure American readers that even in a swamp may be found traces of the Old World their ancestors left."[82]

But if in Paulin's political construction meter represents the conservative claims of the republic, speech rhythm represents the claims of the individual against the state, that is, liberty as opposed to authority. In "The Vanishing Red" he recognizes as "the real core of the poem" the following lines in which the Indian vocalizes his presence:[83]

> Some guttural exclamation of surprise
> The Red Man gave in poking about the mill
> Over the great big thumping shuffling millstone
> Disgusted the Miller physically as coming
> From one who had no right to be heard from.
> (*CPPP* 136)

Paulin believes in the subversive force of "the sound of sense," which he argues mounts in the poem an "acoustically coded criticism of pragmatic puritan values": "This may seem decisively biased until we realize that the poem's actual vocalization, its subtle sentence-sound, plays against the traditional attitude it offers those lazy 'eye-readers,' as Frost termed them. That vocal counterpoint is created by a cunning series of natural internal rhymes which allows John's [the Indian's] single utterance to reverberate through the lines that follow. Thus the uh-sound in 'gutteral' and 'surprise' is picked up by those same sounds in 'thumping shuffling' and 'disgusted.' It's as if the Indian reacts to the grindstone with an instinctive *ugh!*"[84] For a moment, a native tone of voice is let into the poem, and in it the colonized speaks out against the genocidal practices of the white man. In a footnote Paulin suggests that "The Vanishing Red" might have had some influence on Heaney's poem "Churning Day," where "the churning process becomes subtly symbolic of historical suffering":

> The staff, like a great whisky muddler fashioned
> in deal wood, was plunged in, the lid fitted.
> My mother took first turn, set up rhythms
> that slugged and thumped for hours. Arms ached.
> Hands blistered. Cheeks and clothes were spattered
> with flabby milk.[15]

Into these menial "rhythms" we can read Frost's interest in expressive, democratic "sounds of sense," which stand for the lives overrun in the course of empire, lives like this Irish mother's.

Paulin's interpretation of "the sound of sense" as a form of political resistance comes into focus if we look at it in the light of postcolonial theories of language. Homi Bhabha maintains that the hybrid cultural space "outside the sentence," the "enunciatory present" that is "disjunctive and multi-accentual," amounts to a liberatory discursive strategy; indeed, his statement that "the nonsentence is contiguous with the sentence, near but different, not simply its anarchic disruption . . . both spatially and temporally ex-centric, interruptive, in between, on the borderlines, turning inside outside" has affinities with Frost's concept of tone and its relation to formal sentence structure.[86] As Frost asserts, "the sound of sense" is not expressed by the grammatical code; rather, it lies on the margins of the sentence—a suprasegmental phonological entity that is somehow implicated in syntax but at the same time outside its logic. In viewing the relation between postcolonial or migrant experience and the dominant culture as not simply antagonistic, Bhabha elaborates on Roland Barthes's conception in *The Pleasure of the Text* (1973) of the relation between the "nonsentence" and the "sentence":

One evening, half asleep on a banquette in a bar, just for fun I tried to enumerate all the languages within earshot: music, conversations, the sounds of chairs, glasses, a whole stereophony of which a square in Tangiers (as described by Severo Sarduy) is the exemplary site. That too spoke within me, and this so-called "interior" speech was very like the noise of the square, like that amassing of minor voices coming to me from the outside: I myself was a public square, a *sook;* through me passed words, tiny syntagms, nits of formulae, and *no sentence formed,* as though that were the law of such a language. This speech, at once very cultural and very savage, was above all lexical, sporadic; it set up in me, through its apparent flow, a definitive discontinuity: this *non-sentence* was in no way something that could not have acceded to the sentence, that might have been *before* the sentence; it was: what is eternally, splendidly, *outside the sentence.*[87]

For Barthes, the distinction between the "non-sentence" and the "sentence" is absolute; for Bhabha, though, a relation of contiguity exists between the two. In other words, Bhabha disarticulates the "non-sentence" from "outside the sentence" and thus makes it a third term or space "in between" the sentence and non-sentence. Frost's notion that "the sound of sense" is implicated in, but lies on the border of, the sentence is in accord with Bhabha's views, and, thus, allows itself to be read as a resistant force nonetheless involved in the identity of the dominant culture. Moreover, like Barthes and Bhabha, Frost feels the insufficiency of traditional grammar (a "linguistics which . . . has always attributed an exorbitant dignity to predicative syntax as the form of a logic, of a rationality"), and his celebration of "the vital sentence" at the expense of "the grammatical sentence" answers Barthes's charge that as yet "there exists no locutive grammar (a grammar of what is spoken and not of what is written . . .)."[88]

Barthes's subsequent definition of the sentence in *The Pleasure of the Text,* which Bhabha invokes, clarifies the subaltern politics of Frost's theory of tone in poetry: "The Sentence is hierarchical: it implies subjections, subordinations, internal reactions. Whence its completion: how can a hierarchy remain open?"[89] Opposed to such linguistic closure and the political subordinations for which it stands, Barthes promotes "the definitive discontinuity of the text," a form of writing he calls "writing aloud" or "vocal writing."[90] Admittedly, Barthes's focus on "the pulsional incidents, the language lined with flesh, a text where we can hear the grain of the throat, the patina of consonants, the voluptuousness of vowels, a whole carnal stereophony: the articulation of the body, of the tongue, not that of meaning, of language" is not identical to Frost's tonal concerns; indeed, Frost theorizes against a prosody of "harmonised vowels and consonants."[91] However, Frost *is* devoted to the grain of the voice as constituted by human intonation contours, and prominent exilic poets have found in his formal theory—and in the tonal interstices of his texts—a symbolic performative space in which to locate their own cultural identities.

One such poet is Joseph Brodsky, who contributes the lead essay to *Homage to Robert Frost,* "On Grief and Reason" (first published in 1994), where he analyzes two of Frost's poems and their formal designs in terms of his own political experience. Brodsky, a Russian-American poet, begins the essay by taking up the issue of Frost's nationality—one far less complicated than his own: "He was indeed a quintessential American poet; it is up to us, however, to find out what that quintessence is made of, and what the term 'American' means as applied to poetry and, perhaps, in general."[92] As Brodsky finds, Frost's poetry of "terror"—to be distinguished from a poetry of tragedy ("the Continental tradition of the poet as tragic hero")—marks him (and his lyric utterance) as American (*HRF* 7). But Brodsky acknowledges that his "dark" view of Frost's poems is partially a projection on his part (he is unconcerned, he says, with "academic objectivity"), and he describes himself as a reader as "paranoid" and "suspicio[us]," his mental habits presumably shaped by his subjection to the Soviet state (*HRF* 8, 11). In conversation with Solomon Volkov, Brodsky relates Frost's conception of horror to his own political circumstances more directly, saying that during his exile in the Russian North, it "was easier for me to identify with Frost. I spent basically three years in the Soviet Union under the mark of Frost. First came Sergeyev's translations, then getting to know Sergeyev, then Frost's book in Russian. Then I was imprisoned. Evidently I was more susceptible than I am today. Frost made an incredible impression on me."[93] In fact, Brodsky even speaks momentarily of Frost as if he, too, were an émigré, noting that Frost "senses the utter isolation of his own existence."[94]

In his extended analysis of "Home Burial," Brodsky finds a symbol for his exilic condition—the clash of languages and cultures he experiences—in the clash of husband and wife in the poem. Meditating on interrogation tactics, Brodsky contends that the poem should not be read "as a tragedy of incommunicability, a poem about the failure of language," but rather as "a tragedy of communication, for communication's logical end is the violation of your interlocutor's mental imperative. This is a poem about language's terrifying success, for language, in the final analysis, is alien to the sentiments it articulates. No one is more aware of that than a poet" (*HRF* 39). The poet knows that words cannot express adequately our deepest thoughts and feelings, and yet we are forced to language—and language is forced upon us. Indeed, the dissident transnational poet is most aware of that, and Brodsky's understanding of the confrontation in "Home Burial" cannot help but resonate on a political level; as he says of husband and wife: "Thus you've got a clash not just of two sensibilities but of two languages. Sensibilities may merge—say, in the act of love; languages can't.

Sensibilities may result in a child; languages won't. And, now that the child is dead, what's left is two totally overlapping systems of verbalization. In short: words. His versus hers, and hers are fewer. . . . His job, or, more exactly, the job of his language, is, therefore, the explication of her language, or, more exactly, her reticence" (*HRF* 40). As Brodsky observes of his own status in another essay: "For one in our profession the condition we call exile is, first of all, a linguistic event: he is thrust from, he retreats into his mother tongue."[95] He also depicts this double movement in his Nobel lecture, where he cites Frost as one of five crucial poetic precursors (along with several Russian poets), by referring to "the two cultures to which fate has willed me to belong."[96]

When Brodsky compares the husband's linguistic assaults on his wife and the expansion of her reticence in the face of those assaults to "Napoleon invading Russia and finding it goes beyond the Urals," he sees the poem in terms of his own urgencies, linking together the politics of empire-building and of utterance (*HRF* 40). Indeed, when he says of the wife's desperate intonation in response to her husband's digging of the grave, "This is the voice of a very foreign territory indeed: a foreign language," he could just as well be speaking of his own alienation, which requires him to come to terms with native and foreign voices (*HRF* 42). Commenting on Frost's dual role as both husband and wife in the poem, Brodsky builds out this metaphor of imperialism, stating that "the poet's mind plays both the invading army and the territory; in the end, he can't take sides" (*HRF* 40, 41). At once colonist and colonized, Frost refuses to have the wife succumb to the husband's rhetorical force; as the Russian-born poet finds, "A language invading reticence gets no trophy here, save the echo of its own words" (*HRF* 41). In this echo, Brodsky suggests the apparently solidly constituted subjective identity of the colonizer fragmenting and splitting in the face of mimicry, repetition, and parody by the colonized.

Ineluctably, Brodsky is drawn to Frost's fiction of "the sound of sense," which, he says, "had to do with his observation that the sound, the tonality, of human locution is as semantic as actual words. For instance, you overhear two people conversing behind a closed door, in a room. You don't hear the words, yet you know the general drift of their dialogue; in fact, you may pretty accurately figure out its substance. In other words, the tune matters more than the lyrics, which are, so to speak, replaceable or redundant" (*HRF* 26). For Brodsky, "nonsemantic sounds" represent the root of human colloquy, and conversation our life's blood (*HRF* 27). That he chooses to examine so closely the tonal detail in "Home Burial," as opposed to some other poem, is apt, since he must confront the burial of his own home (that is, his mother land) as an exile. Finding that in the poem "The character and the narrator are, as it were, pushing the author out of any humanly palatable context: he stands outside, denied re-entry, perhaps not coveting it at all," Brodsky reflects on his own condition, as he stands outside Russia, denied re-entry, perhaps not coveting it at all (*HRF* 55). Indeed, as Walcott attests, Brodsky's love of both the English and Russian language constitutes "the happiness he has learned from exile."[97] Ultimately, Brodsky finds an image for the "utter autonomy" of Frost (this "utterly American" poet) in his "monotone, his pentametric drawl: a signal from a far-distant station" (*HRF* 31, 55). For Brodsky, metrical cadence serves as a symbol of the poet's stateliness, his national distinction, and his use of the locational linguistic term "drawl" points back to Frost's own nationalizing of tone. Earlier in the essay Brodsky hails "the pentametrically triumphant" lines of another poem and notes that the "pentametric" is "congenial" to the job of Frost's "formulaic, quasi-proverbial one-liners," which are meant to carry the weight of cultural authority (*HRF* 36, 33). If rhythm is "disjunctive and multi-accentual," the "monotone" of meter in Brodsky's fiction stands for its opposite—the imperious and monolithic state whose authority is challenged by it.

Brodsky ends his essay with a potent figure—one that relates to the issues of identity and nationality on which his reading of Frost's poems centers: "One may liken him [Frost] to a spacecraft that, as the downward pull of gravity weakens, finds itself nonetheless in the grip of a different gravitational force: outward. The fuel, though, is still the same: grief and reason. The only thing that conspires against this metaphor of mine is that American spacecraft usually return" (*HRF* 56). Here he alludes to the Cold War rivalry between the United States and the Soviet Union, which in 1957 launched Sputnik and with it the space race. His point finally is that Frost is bound to his native soil in a way that he cannot be, since he cannot go home again.

In Heaney's contribution to *Homage*, an essay entitled "Above the Brim" (1990), he, too, is led to reflect on Frost's mythologizing of his formalism and its political value for a poet caught between two worlds. In an essay in *The Government of the Tongue* (1989) Heaney points out his mixed cultural inheritance, noting his affinity with Eastern bloc writers: "I keep returning to them because there is something in their situation that makes them attractive to a reader whose formative experience has been largely Irish. There is an unsettled aspect to the different worlds they inhabit."[98] For his part, he experiences the pull of two cultures—Irish and English—and in the autobiographical essay "Belfast" he attests, "I speak and write in English, but do not altogether share the preoccupations and perspectives of an Englishman. I teach English literature, I publish in London, but the English tradition is not ultimately home. I live off another hump as well."[99] Heaney's sense of place (a complex interaction of language, history, and environment) and his displacement as a postcolonial poet shape his view of Frost's poetic method:

> Inevitably, a discussion like this, which concentrates on the poem's musical life, must lead us to take cognizance of Frost's theory of "the sound of sense." This theory, as Frost expressed it in interviews and letters over the years, does fit and complement our experience of what is distinctive about the run of his verse, its posture in the mouth and in the ear, its constant drama of tone and tune. . . . To summon such sounds, therefore, is to recapitulate and refresh a latent resource of our nature. . . . And so it follows that a poetry embodying the lineaments of pristine speech will fulfill, at a level below theme and intention, a definite social function. (*HRF* 72)

Heaney's imputation of a "social function" to vocal contour reveals his belief that that prosodic element is able to bind people together, to conjoin at the cultural level; as he relates, "Such cadences, Frost is at pains to insist, re-establish a connection with the original springs of our human being," and, therefore, draw us to others and others to us. He agrees with the critic Margery Sabin that "'Frost in 1914 wanted to believe—and wrote poems out of the belief—that human vitality takes on a supra-personal existence in the established intonations of speech. . . . What Frost calls "the abstract vitality of our speech" . . . participates in the verbal forms through which other people also enact their lives'" (*HRF* 72, 73). In this shared tonality, and in the figure of tonality itself, Heaney finds a cure for the wound of colonialism, a way to surmount the trauma of the Northern Irish experience, which entails "being in two places at once, needing to accommodate two opposed conditions of truthfulness simultaneously."[100]

In the title essay of *The Government of the Tongue* (1989) Heaney alludes to Frost's theory of "the sound of sense" and its sense of place, or nativist force, when he says that several lines of a poem by Elizabeth Bishop "possess the *sine qua non* of all lyric utterance, a completely persuasive inner cadence. . . . The lines are inhabited by certain profoundly true tones, which as Robert Frost put it, 'were before words were, living in the caves of the mouth.'"[101] For Heaney, the truth of these tones depends on their placement in—their inhabitation of—a homeland. In "Above the Brim" he similarly notes of Frost's poem "Desert Places" that its first two lines ("Snow falling and night falling fast, oh, fast / In a field I looked into going past") are "native to living speech, without any tonal falsity" (*HRF* 67). As Heaney reveals in discussing the importance of place in the work of the Irish poet Thomas Kinsella, "Tone is the inner life of a language, a secret spirit at play behind or at odds with what is being said and how it is being structured in syntax and figures of speech. It has subtly to do with the deepest value system that the group speaking the language is possessed by."[102] As he finds, then, tone (in his case the South Derry intonation, which he says has been lodged "at the back of my throat for a long time") expresses a person's true self, which is perforce an expression of the immediate cultural conditions that make up that self.[103] In the end, he identifies "the living speech of the landscape" with the poem itself, the single, adequate "vocable," which, for Frost, is "the sound of sense."[104]

Dennis Lee, a postcolonial Canadian poet who has narrated his struggle in and with the English language, sheds light on the problem of writing in colonial territory—in particular the need to cultivate native tones of voice in order to reclaim the language and land—that occupies Heaney. In his essay originally entitled "Cadence, Country, Silence," Lee states:

I have been writing of cadence as though one had merely to hear its words and set them down. But that is not true, at least not in my experience. There is a check on one's pen which seems to take hold at the very moment the cadence declares itself. Words arrive, but words have also gone dead. . . . To get at this complex experience we must begin from the hereness, the local nature of cadence. We never encounter cadence in the abstract; it is insistently here and now. Any man aspires to be at home where he lives, to celebrate communion with men on earth around him, under the sky where he actually lives. And to speak from his own dwelling—however light or strong the inflections of that place—he will make his words intelligible to men elsewhere, because authentic. In my case, cadence seeks the gestures of being a Canadian human: *mutatis mutandi,* the same is true for anyone here—an Israeli, an American, a Quebecker. . . . To explore the obstructions of cadence is, for a Canadian, to explore the nature of colonial space.[105]

Like Lee, Heaney believes that cadence must contradict and reinscribe the language of the oppressor, that tone is a matter of the survival of the mother tongue and native traditions. In his poem "The Other Side" Heaney insists:

> But now our river tongues must rise
> From licking deep in native haunts
> To flood, with vowelling embrace,
> Demesnes staked out in consonants.[106]

In his politicizing of the terrain, Heaney demonstrates the extent to which language and place are intertwined, and here he calls on a local (and vocal) disruption of English linguistic and literary tradition—the latter of which he imagines in another poem in *North* as "Iambic drums / Of English beat."[107] Notably, though, meter is not dismissed in "The Other Side," whose lines hold to iambic tetrameter, or in Heaney's other poems; instead, speech rhythms insinuate themselves in and revise colonial cadences, a prosodic condition that signifies Heaney's own cultural hybridity.

Not only in his own verse, but also in his readings of Frost's verse and the figures of tone in it, Heaney locates allegorical figures for the postcolonial condition, although, like Brodsky, he is oblique. Noting "the upsurge of language" at the close of "Home Burial," a poem that rings in Brodsky's ears as well, Heaney observes that "The husband seeks to clear the emotional air too soon and too proprietorially, in a move to suppress the wildness of the wife's sorrow; but when the sound of *her* sense rises in the perfectly pitched anger, he can no longer restrain the note of tyranny" (*HRF* 76). Here he imagines the husband (rather reductively, but in light of his concerns) as a colonial power, with "the mixture of anger, panic, and tyranny in the husband's voice at the end of the poem" a sign of England's disposition toward Ireland (*HRF* 76). The "tormented home" pictured in "Home Burial" is an emblem, then, of Heaney's own tortured homeland, and when he notes that the poem's "buoyancy is achieved in direct proportion to its pressure upon the ground of the actual," we are reminded of the crucial feature of place ("ground") in postcolonial politics (*HRF* 76, 75). If we read between the lines of Heaney's discussion of another Frost poem, we again can hear his reflections on his own intercultural inheritance. Of the penultimate line "Never again would birds' song be the same" in the poem of that title, he observes that "The Adam figure, the 'he' of the poem, has suffered exile from his prelapsarian bliss, so there is a counterweight of heartbreak in the statement of what seemed in the beginning a heart-lifting truth" (*HRF* 80). As Heaney says elsewhere in the essay, "the counterweight, the oversound, the sweetest dream within the fact—these things are poetically more rewarding than a record, however faithful, of the data," and it is "the sound of sense"—in particular the "note of repining"—in that penultimate line that expresses the colonial subject's sense of exile (*HRF* 86).

The West Indian poet Derek Walcott's "The Road Taken" (1995) also dwells at length on the ideological dimensions of Frost's formalism and its cultural power as he seeks to reinscribe that formalism in terms of his own mixed heritage. The piece begins by acknowledging more openly than either

Brodsky (whom Walcott identifies as basically "in a colonized situation") or Heaney do the imperial aspect of Frost as national poet, crystallized by his oration of "The Gift Outright" on January 20, 1961: "On that gusting day of the inauguration of the young emperor [John F. Kennedy], the sublime Augustan moment of a country that was not just a republic but an empire, no more a homespun vision of pioneer values but a world power, no figure was more suited to the ceremony than Robert Frost" (*HRF* 93). However, as Walcott observes, the poem is not historically honest, hiding as it does the brutality of the oppressor regime: "This was the calm reassurance of American destiny that provoked Tonto's response to the Lone Ranger. No slavery, no colonization of Native Americans, a process of dispossession and then possession, but nothing about the dispossession of others that this destiny demanded. The choice of poem was not visionary so much as defensive" (*HRF* 93–94). For Walcott, Frost at the end of his career stands as "an emblem of the republic," an imperialist in his justification of the westward course of empire (*HRF* 94).

Walcott comes to Frost as a colonized subject (his father is English, his mother black West Indian), as one whose history he imagines Frost seeks to erase from the record, and he has reflected, as Brodsky and Heaney have, on his interethnic identity as it relates to voice: "I have not only a dual racial personality but a dual linguistic personality. My real language, and tonally my basic language, is patois. Even though I do speak English, it may be that deep down inside me the instinct that I have is to speak in that tongue."[108] Just as Frost insists that "the sound of sense" is an instinctive part of our being, so Walcott understands unwritten regional dialect (St. Lucian French-lexicon Creole) as native, his mother('s) tongue. In his Nobel lecture (1992) Walcott reflects on the postcolonial "remaking" of poetry, what he calls the "gathering of broken pieces," and the place of speech rhythm in that project: "There is the buried language and there is the individual vocabulary, and the process of poetry is one of excavation and of self-discovery. Tonally, the individual voice is a dialect; it shapes its own accent, its own vocabulary and melody in defiance of an imperial concept of language."[109] Imagining native tone as a feature resistant to the forces of colonization—"an ecstatic rhythm in the blood that cannot be subdued by slavery or indenture"—Walcott racializes tonal performance, investing it with subversive political significance.[110] In Walcott's anti-imperialist poem "Forest of Europe," which figures his relationship to Brodsky and which Heaney observes is "aimed at the center of Walcott's themes—language, exile, art," he calls this contrary rhythm the "exile's tongue."[111]

But Walcott does not advocate that the poet use only indigenous rhythms; he calls attention to the cross-cultural fabric of postcolonial poetry by insisting as well on the need for meter, a symbol of the English tradition. His advocacy of meter suggests his openness to the West, his view that poets must come to terms with the fact that originality is, and always has been, an impossibility, that imitation is both a burden and creative resource for the artist. Like Frost and Eliot, Walcott mythologizes meter as tradition, noting that free verse "is sort of an expression of unrestrained free will, as opposed to subjugation to a kind of order superior to the idea of the individual artist."[112] In addition, it is the ability of meter to lodge a poem in the consciousness of a culture—to build community—that signifies its importance for a new generation of poets: "Most free verse does not write from memory. It writes for reading, it writes for the appreciation of its design on the page. It writes as if it chooses to evaporate the moment it is finished. . . . Poetry is communication and communication is memory. There is a lot of waste in contemporary poetry. It is not intended for memory; it is not intended to last beyond the book that comes out, the page it is on, or the magazine it is in. If that continues, memory can decay."[113] In his essay on Frost, Walcott similarly states that "In formal verse, tension creates memory," and in reflecting on the power of Frost's performance of "The Gift Outright" he says it is a poem that "many [Americans] had heard and learned by heart," a fact that helps explain its tremendous (conservative) cultural power (*HRF* 105, 93).

Ironically, if, for Walcott, Frost in his old age stands for the colonial violence of the U.S., Frost at the beginning of his career appears in the guise of postcolonial poet. In Frost's incorporation of "sounds of sense" into his verse, Walcott marks that precursor poet's resistance to hegemonic forces: "But something wonderful, revolutionary within the convention, happened to Frost's ear between *A Boy's Will* and *North of Boston*. He wrote American, without vehement challenge. He wrote free or syllabic verse within the deceptive margins of the pentameter. He played tennis, to use his famous description, but you couldn't see the net. . . . [His verse] dislocates the pivot of traditional scansion; and the consequence is seismic but inimitable, because it is first of all Frost's voice, which in meter is first regional, then generic, eventually American" (*HRF* 103). Here Walcott asserts that Frost's tones signify his place (both local and national), just as his own "individual voice" identifies him as St. Lucian. Frost does not jettison the tradition, Walcott argues, but profitably contends with it ("To fight against a predictable tone of incantation was a great task for the American"), revising "within the . . . margins." Similarly, Walcott refuses a separatist poetics, creolizing (and, thus, dislocating) the canonical (English) language that is part of his inheritance with a Caribbean accent. When Walcott remarks that Frost's prosodic achievement is "inimitable," he further comments on his own political situation, hinting at the double-edged postcolonial practice of mimicry that Brodsky does in his critique of Frost. As Bhabha points out, mimicry is "one of the most elusive and effective strategies of colonial power and knowledge," as it expresses "the desire for a reformed, recognisable Other."[114] At the same time, however, mimicry destabilizes colonial authority in "the strategic reversal of the process of domination . . . that turns the gaze of the discriminated back upon the eye of power."[115] To say that Frost's voice is "inimitable" is to say that in a new temporality or "time-lag" (Frost is coming onto the poetic scene belatedly) he is in a position to subvert and transform the tradition he inherits (he is "revolutionary within the convention").[116] In other words, and as Walcott fictionalizes it, the "melody" of dialect defies and defeats "an imperial concept of language." Walcott again comments on the politics of mimicry when he mentions in his essay Frost's mentoring of Edward Thomas: "Thomas's poems are not minor Frost, and Frost would not have encouraged Thomas to write verse that was only an English rendition of his voice. He could not make an echo of the Englishman because their accents were different, and accent is scansion" (*HRF* 107–08). Accent is inimitable because specific to location and cultural identity, and that is why Frost is unable to subjugate Thomas (here cast as resistant colonial subject) to him. Walcott's sonnet "Homage to Edward Thomas" represents the relationship between landscape and language, in particular vocal contour, for the poet:

> Formal, informal, by a country's cast
> topography delineates its verse,
> erects the classic bulk, for rigid contrast
> of sonnet, rectory or this manor-house
> dourly timbered against these sinuous
> Downs[117]

In the adjective "timbered" we hear "timbre," or tone of voice, which soaks up the surrounding English countryside ("these sinuous Downs"). It is in this local inhabitation of tone, what Walcott in his poem "Names" calls "our natural inflections," that the promise of postcolonial poetry finds its fulfillment.[118]

Finally, Walcott's assessment of Frost echoes remarks in his essay "The Muse of History" (1974) about the need of colonized writers to free themselves from that title figure, that is, a linear sense of history that upholds the notion of "language as enslavement" and produces nothing more than "a literature of recrimination and despair, a literature of revenge written by the descendants of slaves."[119] Finding a new creativity in hybridity, Walcott insists on the need for subaltern poets to remain open to Frost's prosodic legacy: "Now that other races and other causes in the babel of the republic have been given permission to speak in the very language that ruled and defined them, must everything be revised by the new order? Does Frost's ironic, jocular accent not apply to them? But it does, because the new order would be repeating the old order if it made a policy of exclusion and an aesthetics of revenge" (*HRF* 113–14). Walcott, a self-described "mulatto of style," believes that in mimicry is not only repetition but change, that the "tone of the past" must be mastered by the victim and seen not "as servitude" but instead "as victory."[120]

Through both their mastery of form and their critical examination of the terms of Frost's poetics, Brodsky, Heaney, and Walcott are able to figure their transnational identities and unique aesthetic and political ideologies, to conjoin, as Frost did, poetry and power. By recasting Frost's formalism for a postcolonial world, they extend his reach and demonstrate the continued relevance of his prosodic theory in an evolving politics of culture.

Conclusion

Frost's politics are much more ambivalent and complex than most have imagined, and the evolution of his ideology of form clarifies that fact for us. Although Richard Poirier has charged that Frost was lacking in "historical vision" and "blind to social systems," Frost often calculates with great care in his poetry the effects of such systems.[1] Reginald Cook, a critic and friend of Frost's, similarly remarked that "Frost was oddly naive about politics. He had theories, lots of them, but they were often based on school yard dynamics; he was not a sophisticated political thinker, although he could offer startling insights, and occasionally strike a remarkably prophetic note."[2] This point is well taken insofar as some of Frost's political equations and assumptions are not especially well informed; however, it is also true that in many instances Frost is quite sophisticated in his political thinking, balancing competing political interests in the figures of his poetry and his theory of poetic form.

Despite this fact, Frost once warned a student at a reading "not to attach to his poems undue political . . . importance," licensing the misleading notion that his poems do not operate in a public political sphere.[3] Louis Untermeyer gave credence to that claim when in a review of Frost's politically charged book *A Further Range* he stated baldly that "there is little politics in most of his poetry" (*CR* 138). Indeed, the contrary is true: there is a whole lot of politics in and behind most of his poetry, whether overt or not. Although Frost (again misleadingly) claims in his introduction to Robinson's *King Jasper* that poetry should deal with "griefs," not "grievances," he gives voice to both in a range of poems in his effort to come to terms with—and weigh in on—contemporary social and political issues (*CPPP* 742). Correspondingly, the theory of poetic form that Frost expounded throughout his career has an ideological valence, intervening in cultural and literary politics in crucial, and idiosyncratic, ways.

Frost's politics has been debated hotly for a long time, but its true lineaments have never been made very clear. Some critics noted his conservatism in reviews of his late poems, with an anonymous reviewer of *Steeple Bush* in *Time* lamenting Frost's drift to the right: "Frost is the dean of living U.S. poets by virtue of both age and achievement. At 72, the four-time Pulitzer Prize-winner has lost little of his craftsmanship and none of his crackling vigor. But what was once only granitic Yankee individualism in his work has hardened into bitter and often uninspired Tory social commentary."[4] In fact, as Jay Parini has argued, Frost's politics are highly ambivalent: "Frost is hardly a typical conservative; he is not, in fact, a conservative in the contemporary sense. He is an agrarian freethinker, a democrat with a small 'd,' with isolationist and libertarian tendencies."[5] This correction is an important one, as Frost's reviewers and critics too often and too easily slip him, his poetry, and his formalism into late twentieth- and early twenty-first-century political rubrics. Returning to a political movement of Frost's day, I would argue that his personal politics and politics of form (both early and late) are progressive, notwithstanding what Karen Kilcup rightly sees as "criticism [of Frost] by the cultural elite for his regressive, anti-modern formality."[6] Richard Hofstadter explains that the typical progressive in America (from 1890 through World War I) resisted socialist thinking, believing that the grievances of the people were remediable under capitalism by limiting or regulating monopoly, and feared any concentration of power in a single organization: "The Progressive sympathized with the problems of labor, but was troubled about the lengths to which union power might go if labor-unionism became the sole counterpoise to the power of business."[7] Frost's poem "Good Relief," written in the age of reform, reveals his closeness to progressivism on this point (I discuss it in the first chapter). Furthermore, the "persistent individualism" of progressives, who saw business monopoly as robbing average Americans of political and economic freedom and, thus, of personal responsibility, is in line with "Yankee values of individualism and enterprise"—values that Frost shared.[8]

One might step in here and argue that Frost does not advocate reform in the manner of progressives in the political sphere, and it is true that we should be cautious in ascribing to Frost an activist political agenda. Indeed, time and again Frost puts forth his view that as a poet he is not interested in the plight of the dispossessed. In one letter he explains that "The Need of Being Versed in Country Things" (1920) stands as a rebuke to "the welfare-minded," who with their "damned [liberal] party politics" believe that his subject ought to be "the sadness of the poor" (*LU* 304–05). In other words, as Frost contends, one needs to know "people of simplicity" (as he does) not to believe those people wept. However, if he lets loose such poems to distance himself from those who would put all faith in the welfare state, he suppresses others that give off very different sympathies. For example, in the unpublished poem "On the Inflation of the Currency 1919" Frost meditates on the drastic halving of monetary value as it affects the standard of living of working-class Americans:

> The pain of seeing ten cents turned to five!
> We clutch with both hands fiercely at the part
> We think we feel it in—the head, the heart.
> Is someone cutting us in two alive?
>
> Is someone at us cutting us in half?
> We cast a dangerous look from where we lie
> Up to the enthroned kings of earth and sky.
> They know what's best for them too well to laugh.
> (CPPP 535)

As the speaker asserts, the nation's monetary policy is determined by a privileged few without concern for the loss of purchasing power suffered by the majority of Americans. (The "enthroned kings" of the Wilson administration expanded the money supply by 75 percent between 1916 and 1920, which meant that war contracts could be paid in devalued dollars and the real costs of war disguised, at least for the time being, by inflation.) The marked class antagonism and bitter tone of the poem suggest quite clearly whose side Frost is on, even if he does not want to make such sentiments public for fear of being lumped with those on the left.

Frost's poem "The Parlor Joke," which he wrote about ten years earlier, expresses a similar anger at the exploitation of the working class and specifically figures the labor conditions in Lawrence, Massachusetts, in the years leading up to the 1912 textile strike in that city. Although the poem is not included in any of Frost's books, it was published in Louis Untermeyer's *A Miscellany of American Poetry* in 1920. Originally, Frost sent the poem to Untermeyer in a letter (March 21, 1920) with the following note indicating its date of composition: "Patented 1910 by R. (L.) Frost" (*CPPP* 991). Here he jokingly suggests to his anthologist friend—and committed socialist—that he has protected his poem against imitation by competitors, marking it as a commodity in a capitalist culture, despite the fact that the poem mounts a critique of capitalism. Frost's speaker begins by asserting that what he has to say is a well-kept (and dirty little) secret of that economic system:

You won't hear unless I tell you
How the few to turn a penny
Built complete a modern city
Where there shouldn't have been any,
And then conspired to fill it
With the miserable many.

They drew on Ellis Island.
They had but to raise a hand
To let the living deluge
On the basin of the land.
They did it just like nothing
In smiling self-command.

If you asked them *their* opinion,
They declared the job as good
As when, to fill the sluices,
They turned the river flood;
Only then they dealt with water
And now with human blood.

(*CPPP* 516)

The moralism of this passage is hard to miss: Frost is exposing the arrogance of the corporate elite by showing with what callousness they treat immigrant laborers, and at the same time he is pointing up the unnaturalness of their designs. As the polluted city grows, the mill owners cynically retreat with their families to live in the "hillside suburb," but to their consternation the strongholds that they erect cannot keep the poor at bay:

As their tenements crept nearer,
It pleased the rich to assume,
In humorous self-pity,
The mockery of gloom
Because the poor insisted
On wanting all the room.

This expression of the rich constitutes the "feeble parlor joke" of the title, and the speaker goes on to imagine that the compassionless words of "the gentlefolk" will dawn on them and serve as a self-administered "gentle retribution," thus encouraging them to change their contemptuous attitudes and ways.

However, the situation does not resolve itself so simply, as the speaker notes an alternative form of retribution taking shape:

some beheld a vision:
Out of stench and steam and smoke,

Out of vapor of sweat and breathing,
They saw materialize
Above the darkened city

Where the murmur never dies,
A shape that had to cower
Not to knock against the skies.

They could see it through a curtain,
They could see it through a wall,
A lambent swaying presence
In wind and rain and all,
With its arms abroad in heaven
Like a scarecrow in a shawl.

The ghostly presence is interested in overturning the hierarchical order, as it is heard to say

Something about rebellion
And blood a die for wool,
And how you may pull the world down
If you know the prop to pull.

Frost defined this vision more clearly in a letter to Untermeyer in 1919: "Sometime I must copy you out a poem I did on Bolshevism in 1911 as I saw it spectral over Lawrence at the time of the strike. It will show you where I was" (*LU* 80). The "lambent swaying presence" represents, then, the communist spirit energized by unfair labor practices, but it cannot help but resonate with political cartoons of the period that exposed police brutality in Lawrence. In one such cartoon that ran in *Collier's* (February 24, 1912), a giant policeman with club in hand—a figure that must "cower / Not to knock against the skies"—bears down on the strikers and their huddled families; the caption points to the social disparities that have instigated the trouble: "Dividends for mill owners / Starvation wages for workers."

That the ambivalent image in the poem suggests the strong-arm tactics of the mill owners and state agents as well as the ominous force of communism attests to where Frost was politically when he wrote the poem. In the same 1919 letter to Untermeyer he vents his anger at the greedy industrialists but hesitates to align himself fully with the working class: "If the poor promised themselves no more than vengeance in the oncoming revolution I'd be with them. It's all their nonsense about making a better or even a different world that I can't stand. The damned fools!—only less damned than the God damned fools over them who have made and made such a mess of industrialism." The poem ends by harshly criticizing the capitalists who have provoked the workers' outrage and driven them into the communist camp in their effort to ensure greater profits for themselves:

What to say to the wisdom
That could tempt a nation's fate

> By invoking such a spirit
> To reduce the labor-rate!
> Some people don't mind trouble
> If it's trouble up-to-date.

Frost expresses the same concern in a notebook that he kept during this period, highlighting the xenophobic strain that also marks the poem: "A great many more than half the industrial class [i.e., working class] are where by a wise stroke of concession they can be detached from the party of dissatisfaction that threatens the state. We are of little faith not to see the simple way to save ourselves from the Russian contagion" ("Notebook" 159). As a result of his condemnation of the mercenary zeal of American industrialists in "The Parlor Joke," Frost was wary of how the poem would be received, telling Untermeyer that "as a friend you are going to be delighted with anything I give you no matter how damaging it may prove to me as an author and to you as an editor" (*LU* 104). Obviously, Frost believed in 1920 that his popular reputation might be jeopardized by any show of sympathy for the working class—a sympathy that could be read as an endorsement of socialism—and in later years he expressed his dislike of the poem, in effect distancing himself from it.[9] Despite this fact, his concern for social and economic justice comes through in such poems, as it does in the political formulation of his poetics, where the reformist energy of "the sound of sense" in counterpoise with meter symbolizes his progressivism.

With the New Deal as backdrop, Frost actually is moved to distinguish his progressivism from that of others in a 1935 notebook entry: "I heard a false progressive say that self-discipline was the only discipline, and I was tempted to say that he who has had only self-discipline knows no discipline at all."[10] Of course, this statement is closely connected to his statements about poetic form, in particular his insistence on the disciplinary force of meter, or "outer form," and it is important to note that Frost's negative reaction to New Deal liberalism (in this entry and in some of his poems) does not controvert his progressivism; indeed, as Hofstadter has shown, the New Deal "was itself a product of that overorganized world which had so troubled the Progressives. The trend toward management, toward bureaucracy, toward bigness everywhere had gone so far that even the efforts of reform itself had to be consistent with it."[11] One development in particular worried Frost: "The demands of a large and powerful labor movement, coupled with the interests of the unemployed, gave that later New Deal a social-democratic tinge that had never before been present in American reform movements."[12] If Frost took exception with the new politics of labor in America in the 1930s, interested as he was in saving personal entrepreneurship and individual opportunity, he was perfectly in line with the populist-progressive tradition. In addition, like the characteristic progressive (as Hofstadter limns him), Frost was "often of two minds on many issues," including on the issue of industrialism: just as the progressives "did not seriously propose to dismantle" the new industrial society and "return to a more primitive technology," but instead tried "to keep the benefits of the emerging organization of life and yet . . . retain the scheme of individualistic values that this organization was destroying," so, too, did Frost.[13]

Indeed, as we have seen, Frost is explicit about his desire not to dismantle industrialism in his 1933 poem "A Lone Striker" (with its subtitle *"Without Prejudice to Industry"*), and in other poems of the period he expresses his concern for individualistic values in his focus on the yeoman farmer whose welfare (he feels) is threatened by rampant industrialism. When populism merged with progressivism after 1900, agrarian values and interests became an important part of early twentieth-century reformism, and Frost's agrarian attitudes further align him with that radical political tradition. Wanting to hold on to some of the values of agrarian life, Frost comes to the defense of the yeoman farmer at the same time as he derides New Deal farm policy, harking back to the notion of loosely confederated farmers' cooperatives that the progressives had put forth. Irving Bernstein has shown that "by 1933 the family farm was in decay in many sectors of American agriculture and was being rapidly displaced by industrial agriculture—cash crops raised on large holdings with professional management, scientific methods, and heavy investments in machinery—by what Carey McWilliams called 'factories in the field.'"[14] The rise of this system of agriculture, and the wide-scale displacement of family farmers that it engenders, deeply disturbs Frost, who states that "Government's chief end [should be] to propagate small farmers" ("Notebook" 159). In his notebook Frost explains that such a situation immediately bears on one's class sympathies: "You can't favor the industrial class as against the capitalist without doing it as against the agricultural, and so turning the agricultural industrial. . . . Abolishing the capitalist would mean abolishing the farmer included" ("Notebook" 148, 150). As much as he suggests that he might like to side with the "industrial class" (i.e., city workers) in opposition to "the capitalist," he does not feel free to do so, because, to his thinking, he then would be endorsing socialism and, thus, be complicit in the extinction of the small farmer. What Frost fails to acknowledge is that "the capitalist" is responsible for the growth of corporate farms that by 1933 already endangered Frost's ideal of the husbandman tending his soil.

In "Build Soil," a "political pastoral" that he delivered at Columbia University on May 31, 1932, before the political party conventions of that year and later published in *A Further Range,* Frost airs his opinions about the farm problem through the personae of Tityrus, the farmer-poet who voices Frost's personal politics, and Meliboeus, his farmer friend who has been dispossessed of his land. That he borrows his characters from Virgil's first eclogue is apposite, too, since Virgil's ideal landscape is put at risk by an alien world encroaching from without (in Virgil's case, the government in Rome). In "Build Soil" the forces of industrialism that impinge on the farm threaten the bucolic environment on which Frost stakes so much. In conversation with Tityrus, Meliboeus wonders why things should not be "Made good for everyone—things like inventions—/ Made so we all should get the good of them—/ All, not just great exploiting businesses" (*CPPP* 291). His concern about the effects of untempered capitalism on the small farmer leads him to ask, "But don't you think more should be socialized than is?" to which Tityrus makes ironic reply:

> None shall be as ambitious as he can.
> None should be as ingenious as he could,
> Not if I had my say. Bounds should be set
> To ingenuity for being so cruel
> In bringing change unheralded on the unready.

Tityrus does not advocate socializing ingenuity, even if he does see that new technologies will mean the end of a livelihood for some (he remarks that a hypothetical new wool substitute when "let loose upon the grazing world / Will put ten thousand farmers out of sheep"). He mocks the notion that such a force could be bounded—that our ambition could or should be held in check so as to protect those who would be adversely affected. Refuting Meliboeus's distrust of big business and wariness of commerce, Tityrus claims: "To market 'tis our destiny to go. / But much as in the end we bring for sale there / There is still more we never bring or should bring." He urges Meliboeus to adopt not a five-year plan like the one "That Soviet Russia has made fashionable," but his own plan of self-enrichment:

> You shall go to your run-out mountain farm,
> Poor castaway of commerce, and so live
> That none shall ever see you come to market—
> Not for a long, long time.

The embargo that Tityrus proposes does not depend for its efficacy on collective political action (what he calls "general revolution"), but on action undertaken by a lone farmer: "I bid you to a one-man revolution—/ The only revolution that is coming."

In a letter to Frost, Ferner Nuhn, a family friend who worked for a time in Franklin Roosevelt's administration, challenges that political vision, and Frost's response sheds more light on his struggle with the issues raised by industrialism—namely, his opposition to New Deal liberalism and guarded sympathy for the proletariat. Nuhn tries to explain to Frost the inadequacy of Tityrus's prescriptions:

[A]s once we changed modes from monarchy to democracy, so now we are changing modes from individual to corporate economics. . . . If any large proportion of farmers took the advice given Moloebeus [*sic*] and "dug in" and ate and wore their own products and didn't go to market to buy and sell more than a little dribble of excess, city people and easterners including poets and homilizers would pretty quickly be starved out, by the millions. . . . You'll excuse this finger-counting arithmetic, but you know, a westerner, a corn-belter, some times has to stand up and talk western farm arithmetic to Vermonters with their hankering for self-sustaining mountain farms which, however excellent as a way of life, are not sustaining the United States at present. . . . Farmers and poets and machine-tenders, we've all got beyond self-containment economically; the mode has passed; the emphasis is misplaced. . . .[15]

Nuhn finds that Frost "give[s] comfort to . . . the real surplus-grabbers, who want to see all the Moelebeuses [*sic*] stay contented and quiet," that by defending the times Tityrus in effect aids and abets the "fat boys, the cashers-in on the system as it works now." In a letter to Untermeyer, Frost expresses his distaste for Nuhn's position; however, in a letter of reply to Nuhn that he never sent, Frost seeks to moderate his hard-line stance, informing him that "Both those people in the dialogue are me."[16] Our ability to see Frost in Meliboeus is hampered somewhat by Frost's remarks outside his poetry, which suggest a clearer ideological connection with Tityrus. And yet Meliboeus's opinion that "great exploiting businesses" have deprived individual Americans of economic and political freedom does correspond with Frost's (often suppressed) sense that greedy capitalists (like those in "The Parlor Joke") have made a mess of things, a sense that he shared with progressive politicans like Theodore Roosevelt who "were often furious with the plutocrats because their luxury, their arrogance, and the open, naked exercise of their power constituted a continual provocation to the people and always increased the likelihood that social resentments would find expression in radical or even 'socialistic' programs."[17]

Frost's assault on federal government policies that would industrialize agriculture and, as he believed, defuse the polarity of city and country parallels his construction of a dialectical progressive poetics. In an interview published in the magazine *Rural America* in 1931, Frost asserts the need for measure in our lives—a measure that requires the existence of both urban and rural modes: "I should expect life to be back and forward—now more individual on the farm, now more social in the city—striving to get the balance" (*I* 76). When the boundaries between farm and city are blurred, the ability to strike that healthy balance is imperiled:

We are now at a moment when we are getting too far out into the social-industrial and are at the point of drawing back—drawing in to renew ourselves. The country life we are going back to I can't describe in advance, but I am pretty sure it will not be the country life we came out of years ago. Farming, what survives of it, has demeaned itself in an attempt to imitate industrialism. It has lost its self-respect. It has wished itself something other than what it is. That is the only unpardonable sin: to wish you were something you are not, something other people are. It is so in the arts and in everything else. . . . The farmer has industrialized to his own hurt right on the farm. He has entered into the competitive outside life. The strength of his position is that he's got so many things that he doesn't need to go outside for. The country's advantage is that it gives many pleasures and supplies many needs for nothing. The tendency of our day is to throw away all of these things and count them worthless. (*I* 76)

Frost finds that the farmer has compromised his self-sufficiency by submitting to the forces of industrialism, and fails to give credence to Nuhn's accurate statement that "we've all got beyond self-containment economically; the mode has passed." In the *Denver Post* (October 11, 1932) an article entitled "Robert Frost, Famous Poet, Praises Farm Strike Idea" quotes Frost as saying "We Americans are doing everything in our power to narrow, industrialize and mechanize this [agricultural] base." Exhorting midwestern farmers to decrease productivity, Frost claims that "If the farmers would go Robinson Crusoe and dole out just enough of their produce to keep the cities alive for purposes of visiting and recreation, the agricultural problem might be settled, without benefit of politics, politicians or congress, for the good of all." Here he crosses the line between "a one-man revolution" and "general revolution," asserting his interest in the latter, provided that the action is not tainted by "politics." Of course, the action is inevitably political, but, because it is the idea of farmers, and not of "politicians or congress," Frost sees these cooperatives in a positive light.

Such conservative impulses do not nullify Frost's progressivism; on the contrary, they reveal his alignment with the ambiguous character of that political movement, which is mirrored in his ambivalently coded formalism.

As Richard Hofstadter (writing in the 1950s) has explained, after 1917 progressivism began "very strongly to foreshadow some aspects of the cranky pseudo-conservatism of our time," and in the "coexistence of reformism and reaction" we can locate Frost and his aesthetic and make sense of the biases of both. "Such tendencies in American life as isolationism and the extreme nationalism that usually goes with it, hatred of Europe and Europeans, racial, religious, and nativist phobias, resentment of big business, trade-unionism, intellectuals, the Eastern seaboard and its culture—all these have been found not only in opposition to reform but also at times oddly combined with it," Hofstadter finds, and it is noteworthy that one of the "gangs" in which Tityrus permits membership is "the United States."18 As of about 1917, Frost's progressive formalism also has mixed within it, and comes to figure, some of these reactionary traits (in particular the tendencies toward isolationism and extreme nationalism and resentment toward big business and trade-unionism).

Notwithstanding this ideological shift, the contest between authority and liberty, or meter and rhythm, at the heart of Frost's poetics was ongoing throughout his career, and at different points in that career he felt compelled to highlight one or the other. Frost remarked in his 1936 epigram "Precaution," "I never dared be radical when young / For fear it would make me conservative when old," but the slogan does not apply very well to Frost, whose early political affiliations are radical in their way and whose later conservatism is nevertheless not as pat as it may at first appear ("They think I'm no New Dealer. But really and truly I'm not, you know, all that clear on it") (*CPPP* 281). His ambivalence is perhaps most clearly indicated by the transformation of the political weight of a phrase in two different works at two different points in his career. In his 1912 poem "Good Relief" (discussed in the first chapter), he laments that striking workers must be "partizan and grim" (*CPPP* 523). In his 1936 preface to the liberal poet Sarah Cleghorn's autobiography *Threescore*, he identifies with her brand of reformism ("Some of us have developed a habit of saying we can't stand a reformer. But we don't mean it except where the reformer is at the same time a raw convert to the latest scheme for saving the soul or the state"), commending her for being "partisan and even a trifle grim" (*CPPP* 749). Clearly, Frost was of two minds, and by devising a theory of form that symbolically negotiates the competing demands of self and state—that strives to strike a "balance . . . between our being members of each other and being individuals"—he assures us of his deep involvement in the politics of poetry and the enduring, if not uncomplicated, reformism of his aesthetic (*I* 208).

Notes

Abbreviations

CPPP	*Robert Frost: Collected Poems, Prose, and Plays.*
CR	*Robert Frost: The Critical Reception.*
EPPP	*Ezra Pound's Poetry and Prose: Contributions to Periodicals.*
HRF	*Homage to Robert Frost.*
I	*Interviews with Robert Frost.*
IMO	*Into My Own: The English Years of Robert Frost, 1912–1915.*
LU	*The Letters of Robert Frost to Louis Untermeyer.*
"Notebook"	"Notebook: After England."
PJ	*Prose Jottings of Robert Frost: Selections from His Notebooks and Miscellaneous Manuscripts.*
RFPP	*Robert Frost: Poetry and Prose.*
RFW	*Robert Frost on Writing.*
SL	*The Selected Letters of Robert Frost.*

Introduction (pp. 1–11)

1. *Family Letters of Robert and Elinor Frost,* ed. Arnold Grade (Albany: State University of New York Press, 1972), 61–62. Frost's theory of verse form was a common subject of his early notebook writings, some of which also are published in *Prose Jottings of Robert Frost: Selections from His Notebooks and Miscellaneous Manuscripts,* eds. Edward Connery Lathem and Hyde Cox (Lunenberg, Vermont: Northeast-Kingdom, 1982). Subsequent references to this edition will appear in the text as *PJ*.

2. T. S. Eliot, "Reflections on *Vers Libre,*" in *To Criticize the Critic* (New York: Farrar, 1965), 184. Frost imagined himself in a state of siege as a result of his advocacy of colloquial speech cadences in poetry, writing frequently of his "enemies" to critic-friends; see especially *The Letters of Robert Frost to Louis Untermeyer,* ed. Louis Untermeyer (New York: Holt, 1963), 4, 5, 11, 19. Subsequent references to this edition will appear in the text as *LU*.

3. Vernon Shetley, *After the Death of Poetry: Poet and Audience in Contemporary America* (Durham: Duke University Press, 1993), 2.

4. *The Poetry of Robert Frost,* ed. Edward Connery Lathem (New York: Holt, 1969), 610.

5. *Robert Frost: Collected Poems, Prose, and Plays,* eds. Mark Richardson and Richard Poirier (New York: Library of America, 1995), 26. Subsequent references to this edition will appear in the text as *CPPP*.

6. Richard Poirier, *The Renewal of Literature: Emersonian Reflections* (New Haven: Yale University Press, 1987), 130.

7. *Selected Letters of Robert Frost,* ed. Lawrance Thompson (New York: Holt, 1964), 98. Subsequent references to this edition will appear in the text as *SL*.

8. Randall Jarrell, *Poetry and the Age* (New York: Vintage, 1955), 26–27.

9. Frank Lentricchia, *Modernist Quartet* (Cambridge: Cambridge University Press, 1994), 186.

10. Ibid., xiii.

11. Richard Poirier, *Robert Frost: The Work of Knowing* (Stanford: Stanford University Press, 1977), 38.

12. See Maud Ellman, *The Poetics of Impersonality: T. S. Eliot and Ezra Pound* (Cambridge: Harvard University Press, 1987).

13. *Family Letters* 233.

14. Mark Richardson, *The Ordeal of Robert Frost: The Poet and His Poetics* (Urbana: University of Illinois Press, 1997), 99.

15. Katherine Kearns, *Robert Frost and a Poetics of Appetite* (Cambridge: Cambridge University Press, 1994), 168.

16. Ibid., 138.

17. Karen Kilcup, *Robert Frost and Feminine Literary Tradition* (Ann Arbor: University of Michigan Press, 1998), 107.

18. Robert Faggen, *Robert Frost and the Challenge of Darwin* (Ann Arbor: University of Michigan Press, 1997), 40.

19. Stanley Burnshaw in his corrective biography *Robert Frost Himself* (New York: Braziller, 1986) reminds us of Frost's sometimes left-leaning political convictions. In *Robert Frost and Feminine Literary Tradition* Karen Kilcup further remarks on Frost's liberalism—"his consistent empathy for working-class people (usually agrarian)" (304)—and in doing so she recovers Randall Jarrell's early view that Frost was "radical when young—he was a very odd and very radical radical, a much more interesting sort than the standard *New Republic* brand," that his poetry contains "a final identifying knowledge of the deprived and dispossessed, the insulted and injured" (*Poetry and the Age* 30).

1. The Sound of Sense and the Ethics of Early Modernism (pp. 12–63)

1. John Evangelist Walsh, *Into My Own: The English Years of Robert Frost, 1912–1915* (New York: Grove, 1988), 225. The appendix contains selected entries from two of the notebooks that Frost kept while in England. Subsequent references to this edition will appear in the text as *IMO*.

2. *Selected Letters of Ezra Pound, 1907–1941,* ed. D. D. Paige (New York: New Directions, 1971), 14.

3. Peter Ackroyd notes of Eliot's hand in George Williamson's book-length study *The Talent of T. S. Eliot* (1929) that "A process was beginning here which is unique in twentieth-century poetry: of a poet setting the context and the principles for the description and critical evaluation of his own work" (*T. S. Eliot: A Life* [New York: Simon and Schuster, 1984], 176–77). In *Discovering Modernism* (Oxford: Oxford University Press, 1987), Louis Menand states that "Pound, always a great clipper of his own notices, gave Ford's review [of *Cathay*] to Eliot, who dutifully quoted from it in his promotional pamphlet, *Ezra Pound: His Metric and Poetry* (1917)" (135). Of course, one can go back to Whitman to see this ghostwriting in full swing.

4. Elaine Barry, *Robert Frost on Writing* (New Brunswick, New Jersey: Rutgers

University Press, 1973), 88. Subsequent references to this edition will appear in the text as *RFW*.

5. *Poets at Work: The Paris Review Interviews,* Second Series, ed. George Plimpton (New York: Viking, 1963), 54.

6. In *Robert Frost: A Biography* (New York: Houghton, 1996), Jeffrey Meyers reports that "Frost attended the Tuesday 'at homes' of . . . T. E. Hulme, in the house of his patron at 67 Frith Street in Soho" (94).

7. Quoted in John Sears, "Robert Frost and the Imagists: The Background of Frost's 'Sentence Sounds,'" *New England Quarterly Review* 54 (1981): 468.

8. *Interviews with Robert Frost,* ed. Edward Connery Lathem (New York: Holt, 1966), 77. Subsequent references to this edition will appear in the text as *I*.

9. *The Gender of Modernism: A Critical Anthology,* ed. Bonnie Kime Scott (Bloomington: Indiana University Press, 1990), 58–59.

10. Ezra Pound to Robert Frost (6 December 1915), ms., Robert Frost Collection, Dartmouth College Library.

11. *Robert Frost: The Critical Reception,* ed. Linda W. Wagner (N.p.: Burt Franklin, 1977), 1. Subsequent references to this edition will appear in the text as *CR*.

12. Elie Halévy, *The Rule of Democracy, 1905–1914,* trans. E. I. Watkin, vol. 6 of *A History of the English People in the Nineteenth Century* (London: Ernest Benn, 1934), 441.

13. Sally Peters, *Bernard Shaw: The Ascent of the Superman* (New Haven: Yale University Press, 1996), 93. In *The Frost Family's Adventure in Poetry: Sheer Morning Gladness at the Brim* (Columbia: University of Missouri Press, 1994), Lesley Lee Francis asserts that Frost "came to view the Fabian freethinker [Shaw] as something of a plutocrat with arrogant manners, who offended his sense of social equality" (75).

14. Jay Parini, *Robert Frost: A Life* (New York: Holt, 1999), 8. In a letter to Amy Lowell in 1917, Frost reported that he "[k]new Henry George well" in his attempt to impress upon her his worldliness (*SL* 226).

15. Lawrance Thompson, *Robert Frost: The Early Years, 1874–1915* (New York: Holt, 1966), 431.

16. Wilfrid Wilson Gibson, *Poems (1904–1917)* (New York: Macmillan, 1917), 136. In *The Frost Family's Adventure in Poetry* Lesley Lee Francis suggests Gibson's politics as one reason for Frost's attraction to him; however, she wrongly agrees with another critic who believes that Abercrombie and Gibson were "shallow in their knowledge" and that Frost was "horrified" by their lack of indignation over treatment of the poor (153).

17. Ibid., 300.

18. See Karen Kilcup's *Robert Frost and Feminine Literary Tradition* for a detailed account of Frost's calculated response to the nineteenth-century American sentimental tradition.

19. Eleanor Farjeon, *Edward Thomas: The Last Four Years* (Oxford: Oxford University Press, 1958), 90.

20. See Robert Newdick, *Newdick's Season of Frost: An Interrupted Biography of Robert Frost,* ed. William A. Sutton (Albany: State University of New York Press, 1976), 268.

21. Thompson, *The Early Years,* 155.

22. Ibid., 379.

23. *A Roger Fry Reader,* ed. Christopher Reed (Chicago: University of Chicago Press, 1996), 57.

24. Ibid., 56. My discussion also is informed by Christopher Reed's article "Through Formalism: Feminism and Virginia Woolf's Relation to Bloomsbury Aesthetics" (*Twentieth Century Literature* 38 [1992]: 20–43).

25. See Meyers, *Robert Frost: A Biography,* 109.

26. Virginia Woolf, *The Voyage Out* (1915; New York: Harcourt, 1948), 326.

27. Elizabeth Shepley Sergeant, *Robert Frost: The Trial by Existence* (New York: Holt, 1960), 86.

28. Virginia Woolf, *Collected Essays* (New York: Harcourt, 1925), 2:106.

29. Ibid., 2:54.

30. Ibid., 2:155.

31. *The Collected Writings of T. E. Hulme,* ed. Karen Csengeri (Oxford: Clarendon Press, 1994), 166.

32. Ibid., 85.

33. In the most extensive study of Frost's debts to Bergson, Ronald Bieganowski relates Frost's annotations of *Creative Evolution* to his later statements about poetic method, particularly his 1939 essay "The Figure a Poem Makes," but he does not look at the connection between these annotations and Frost's theory of "the sound of sense" ("Sense of Time in Robert Frost's Poetics: A Particular Influence of Henri Bergson," *Resources for American Literary Study* XIII [Autumn 1983]: 184–93).

34. Richard Poirier, *Poetry and Pragmatism* (Cambridge: Harvard University Press, 1992), 138.

35. Quoted in Thompson, *The Early Years,* 536.

36. New York University Library has Frost's annotated copy of *Creative Evolution* as well as the 1920 edition of *Mind-Energy* that he owned.

37. *The Selected Letters of William James,* ed. Elizabeth Hardwick (New York: Doubleday, 1960), 236.

38. Henri Bergson, *Time and Free Will,* trans. F. L. Pogson (New York: Macmillan, 1910), 134.

39. William James, *Psychology: Briefer Course,* in *William James: Writings, 1878–1899,* ed. Gerald E. Myers (New York: Library of America, 1992), 156. When passages appear in both *Psychology: Briefer Course* and *The Principles of Psychology,* my reference is to *Briefer Course,* since Frost used that edition as both a student and teacher.

40. Ibid., 159.

41. Ibid., 159–60.

42. Ibid., 161–62.

43. In a remark in *The Principles of Psychology* (Cambridge: Harvard University Press, 1981) not included in *Briefer Course,* James asserts baldly that "language works against our perception of the truth," representing as it does an intellectual construct that bars direct access to our mental stream (234). It is this belief that lies at the heart of James's *Pragmatism:* "The common-sense categories one and all cease to represent anything in the way of *being;* they are all but sublime tricks of human thought, our ways of escaping bewilderment in the midst of sensation's irremediable flow" (*William James: Writings, 1902–1910,* ed. Bruce Kuklick [New York: Library of America, 1987], 567).

44. *Robert Frost: Poetry and Prose,* ed. Edward Connery Lathem and Lawrance Thompson (New York: Holt, 1972), 261. Subsequent references to this edition will appear in the text as *RFPP.*

45. In *The Principles of Psychology* James explains the phenomenon of the kinesthetic image, or "after-image," that appeals to Frost: "But in addition to these impressions upon remote organs of sense, we have, whenever we perform a movement ourselves, another set of impressions, those, namely, which come up from the parts that are actually moved. These *kinaesthetic* impressions, as Dr. Bastian has called them, are so many *resident* effects of the motion. Not only are our muscles supplied with afferent as well as with efferent nerves, but the tendons, the ligaments, the ar-

ticular surfaces, and the skin about the joints are all sensitive, and being stretched and squeezed in ways characteristic of each particular movement, give us as many distinctive feelings as there are movements possible to perform" (1100). In his poem "After Apple-Picking" Frost writes about kinesthetic images and reveals his debt to James in conversation with Sidney Cox: "In 'After Apple Picking' are: the intoxication of extreme exhaustion, and 'after-images,' those of the apples 'stem end and blossom end' probably due to an injury to the retina (caused by constant fixing of the eyes upon them. The feeling of the ladder rung is another after-image.)" (quoted in William R. Evans, *Robert Frost and Sidney Cox: Forty Years of Friendship* [Hanover, New Hampshire: University Press of New England, 1981], 90).

46. Robert Kern, "Frost and Modernism," *American Literature* 60 (March 1988): 7.

47. This statement in *SL* includes the word "audial" in brackets, but it is a parenthetical term in Frost's letter, which is at Dartmouth College Library.

48. James, *Briefer Course*, 289.

49. Ibid., 289–90.

50. James, *The Principles of Psychology*, 698.

51. Ibid., 700.

52. Bergson, *Time and Free Will*, 199–200.

53. Ibid., 131–32.

54. Ibid., 132.

55. William James, *A Pluralistic Universe*, in *William James, Writings, 1902–1910*, ed. Bruce Kuklick (New York: Library of America, 1987), 741.

56. Henri Bergson, *Creative Evolution*, trans. Arthur Mitchell (New York: Holt, 1911), 17.

57. James, *A Pluralistic Universe*, 739.

58. James, *Pragmatism*, 508–09.

59. Quoted in Sergeant, *Trial by Existence*, 295.

60. Reginald L. Cook, *Robert Frost: A Living Voice* (Amherst: University of Massachusetts Press, 1974), 189.

61. James, *Briefer Course*, 159.

62. Bergson, *Creative Evolution*, 1–2, 3.

63. Ibid., 39.

64. Quoted in Bieganowski, "Sense of Time in Robert Frost's Poetics," 186.

65. James, *The Principles of Psychology*, 240.

66. Robert Frost, *Notebook: After England*, ed. Margot Feldman, *Antaeus* 61 (1988): 152. Subsequent references will appear in the text as "Notebook."

67. Bergson, *Creative Evolution*, 16.

68. James, *The Principles of Psychology*, 240.

69. Quoted in Alun R. Jones, *The Life and Opinions of T. E. Hulme* (Boston: Beacon, 1960), 51.

70. James, *The Principles of Psychology*, 245.

71. Henri Bergson, *Matter and Memory*, trans. Nancy Margaret Paul and W. Scott Palmer (New York: Macmillan, 1911), 124.

72. Ibid., 125.

73. Ibid., 118.

74. Henri Bergson, *Mind-Energy: Lectures and Essays*, trans. H. Wildon Carr (New York: Holt, 1920), 55–56.

75. Ibid., 56–57.

76. Bergson, *Matter and Memory*, 118.

77. Bergson, *Time and Free Will*, 18–19.

78. Ibid., 129.

79. Ibid., 27.

80. Bergson, *Creative Evolution*, 5.

81. James, *The Principles of Psychology*, 221.

82. Quoted in Newdick, *Newdick's Season of Frost*, 406.

83. James, *Briefer Course*, 164; Bergson, *Matter and Memory*, 210.

84. William James, *The Will to Believe*, in *William James: Writings, 1878–1899*, ed. Gerald E. Myers (New York: Library of America, 1987), 474.

85. James, *Pragmatism*, 498.

86. James, *The Principles of Psychology*, 244.

87. Ibid., 634.

88. Bergson, *Matter and Memory*, 82–83.

89. Charles Darwin, *The Expression of the Emotions in Man and Animals*, 3rd ed. (New York: Oxford University Press, 1998), 92. For a full discussion of James's interest in Darwinism and its role in his psychology and pragmatism, see Philip Wiener's *Evolution and the Founders of Pragmatism* (Cambridge: Harvard University Press, 1949). In 1889, Frost had access to the library of a high school friend, Carl Burrell, a returning student ten years Frost's senior; it contained key works on the science of evolution, including volumes by Darwin and Spencer (Thompson, *Early Years*, 89).

90. Herbert Spencer, *Essays: Scientific, Political, and Speculative* (New York: D. Appleton, 1910), 3:427.

91. Ibid., 359.

92. Ibid., 421–22.

93. Ibid., 357–58.

94. Ibid., 425.

95. Faggen, *Robert Frost and the Challenge of Darwin*, 61–62.

96. Patricia Rae, *The Practical Muse: Pragmatist Poetics in Hulme, Pound, and Stevens* (Lewisburg, Pennsylvania: Bucknell University Press, 1997), 38.

97. Ibid., 113.

98. In *Robert Frost and Feminine Literary Tradition* Karen Kilcup points out the "genderedness" of Frost's early conception of the poet responsible for gathering tones of voice (106).

99. Lentricchia, *Modernist Quartet*, 22.

100. *The Collected Writings of T. E. Hulme* 163. Frost owned a copy of *Speculations*, in which "Bergson's Theory of Art" appears, but its 1924 publication postdates his theorizing of "the sound of sense." No doubt, though, Frost and Hulme talked about the ideas expressed in it when they met in 1913.

101. Ibid., 197.

102. Sears, "Robert Frost and the Imagists," 469. Sears points up the similarities between Frost's practice and that of the imagists, stating that "If one defines Imagism in the terms the Imagists used themselves, Frost can be included in the revolution of which they were a part," but he believes that Frost's theory of "the sound of sense" is meant to distinguish him from them.

103. Kern, "Frost and Modernism," 8.

104. Kearns, *Poetics of Appetite*, 69.

105. Kern, "Frost and Modernism," 12.

106. David Dow Harvey, *Ford Madox Ford, 1873–1939: A Bibliography of Works and Criticism* (Princeton: Princeton University Press, 1962), 879.

107. For Frost's view of Flint, see J. Isaacs, "Best Loved of American Poets," *The Listener* 51 (April 1954): 565.

108. Michael Levenson, *A Genealogy of Modernism: A Study of English Literary Doctrine, 1908–1922* (Cambridge: Cambridge University Press, 1984), 104, 126.

109. *Ezra Pound's Poetry and Prose: Contributions to Periodicals*, 10 vols., ed. Lea

Baechler, A. Walton Litz, and James Longenbach (New York: Garland, 1991), 1:248. Subsequent references to this edition will appear in the text as *EPPP*.

110. Ezra Pound to Robert Frost (6 December 1915), ms., Robert Frost Collection, Dartmouth College Library.

111. Kern, "Frost and Modernism," 11.

112. Harvey, *Bibliography*, 195.

113. Ford Madox Ford, *The Critical Attitude* (London: Duckworth, 1911), 175.

114. Reginald L. Cook, *The Dimensions of Robert Frost* (New York: Rinehart, 1958), 64.

115. Newdick, *Season of Frost*, 363.

116. *Literary Essays of Ezra Pound*, ed. T. S. Eliot (London: Faber, 1954), 5.

117. Ford, *The Critical Attitude*, 174.

118. *Selected Letters of Ezra Pound* 49. In 1918, Frost cites Yeats as one of his poetic models based on his insistence that the language of poetry coincide with that of passionate, normal speech: "I agree with the poet who visited this country not long ago when he said that all our literature has got to come down, sooner or later, to the talk of everyday life. William Butler Yeats says that all our words, phrases, and idioms to be effective must be in the manner of everyday speech" (*RFW* 145). Pound's view of Yeats, to whom he introduces Frost in 1913, is consistent with Frost's: "Mr Yeats has once and for all stripped English poetry of its predamnable rhetoric. He has boiled away all that is not poetic—and a good deal that is. . . . He has made our poetic idiom a thing pliable, a speech without inversion" (*EPPP* 1:62).

119. *Critical Writings of Ford Madox Ford*, ed. Frank MacShane (Lincoln: University of Nebraska Press, 1964), 154.

120. *Literary Essays of Ezra Pound* 7.

121. Amy Lowell, *Some Imagist Poets: An Anthology* (first volume, 1915; New York: Kraus, 1969), vii.

122. Ford Madox Ford, "Literary Portraits—XXXVI: Les jeunes and 'Des Imagistes,'" (Second Notice) *Outlook*, XXXIII (May 16, 1914): 683; Ford Madox Ford, "A jubilee," rev. of *Some Imagist Poets, Outlook*, XXXVI (July 10, 1915): 46.

123. Levenson, *A Genealogy of Modernism*, 119–20.

124. *Critical Writings of Ford Madox Ford* 143.

125. Edward Garnett, *Friday Nights: Literary Criticism and Appreciations* (New York: Knopf, 1922), 241, 237.

126. *Critical Writings of Ford Madox Ford* 36.

127. Levenson, *A Genealogy of Modernism*, 116.

128. *Literary Essays of Ezra Pound* 25.

129. Quoted in N. Christophe de Nagy, *Ezra Pound's Poetics and Literary Tradition* (Bern: Francke, 1966), 79.

130. Eric W. Carlson, "Robert Frost on 'Vocal Imagination, the Merger of Form and Content,'" *American Literature* 33 (1959): 521.

131. Ezra Pound to Robert Frost (10 April 1936), ms., Robert Frost Collection, Dartmouth College Library.

132. Cook, *Dimensions*, 59.

133. Ford, "Les jeunes and 'Des Imagistes,'" 683, 653.

134. Harvey, *Bibliography*, 195.

135. *Literary Essays of Ezra Pound* 12.

136. Quoted in Jean Gould, *Amy* (New York: Dodd, 1975), 170.

137. *The Collected Writings of T. E. Hulme* 89.

138. See Herbert N. Schneidau, *Ezra Pound: The Image and the Real* (Baton Rouge: Louisiana State University Press, 1969), 51–53.

139. *The Collected Writings of T. E. Hulme* 31–32.

140. Levenson, *A Genealogy of Modernism*, 99.

141. Ibid., 133.

142. Ibid., 104.

143. Quoted in Richard Cork, *David Bomberg* (New Haven: Yale University Press, 1987), 43. In part, Bomberg's statement of his aesthetic grows out of discussions with Hulme.

144. *The Collected Writings of T. E. Hulme* 297.

145. It is not until his essay "How to Read" (1929) that Pound relaxes his insistence on the "primary pigment" that each art has and shares with no other, specifying three different kinds of poetry: "melopoeia," "phanopoeia," and "logopoeia" (*Literary Essays of Ezra Pound* 25).

146. *Critical Essays on Gertrude Stein*, comp. Michael J. Hoffman (Boston: G. K. Hall, 1986), 30.

147. Amy Lowell, *Some Imagist Poets: An Anthology* (second volume, 1916; New York: Kraus, 1969), vii.

148. Levenson, *A Genealogy of Modernism*, 127–28.

149. Poirier, *Poetry and Pragmatism*, 25.

150. Levenson, *A Genealogy of Modernism*, 77, 229.

151. Schneidau, *The Image and the Real*, 148.

152. Albert Gelpi, *A Coherent Splendor: The American Poetic Renaissance, 1910–1950* (Cambridge: Cambridge University Press, 1987), 20.

153. Sergeant, *Trial by Existence*, 423.

154. Evans, *Forty Years of Friendship*, 103.

155. Newdick, *Season of Frost*, 61.

156. Thomas Carlyle, *On Heroes, Hero-Worship, and the Heroic in History* (Boston: Ginn, 1901), 95.

157. William C. Wees, *Vorticism and the English Avant-Garde* (Toronto: University of Toronto Press, 1972), 177, 191.

158. Ernest Fenollosa, *The Chinese Written Character as a Medium for Poetry* (1936; San Francisco: City Lights, 1968), 23.

159. Ibid., 12.

160. Ibid., 11.

161. Emerson, *Essays and Lectures*, ed. Joel Porte (New York: Library of America, 1983), 449–50.

162. Quoted in Sergeant, *Trial by Existence*, 325.

163. See Lentricchia, *Modernist Quartet*, 190–99.

164. Richardson, *The Ordeal of Robert Frost*, 151, 4.

2. The Sense of Sound and the Silent Text (pp. 64–121)

1. T. E. Hulme, "Bax on Bergson," *New Age* 9 (August 3, 1911): 328. Martin A. Kayman argues that the tendency to apply uncritically the terms that poets establish to describe their work is true of Pound criticism as well: "Hugh Kenner's use of Buckminster Fuller's 'knot' theory and Donald Davie's 'forma' or 'ontwerp' (adapted from Pound himself and Allen Upward, respectively) may both paraphrase principles of Poundian technique (in this case, the 'vortex'), but they are not instruments for its analysis" (*The Modernism of Ezra Pound: The Science of Poetry* [New York: St. Martin's, 1986], viii).

2. Frank Lentricchia, "Robert Frost: The Aesthetics of Voice and the Theory of Poetry," *Criticism* 15 (Winter 1973): 40.

3. For a discussion of Williams's flawed descriptions of his own prosodic practice, see Stephen Cushman's *William Carlos Williams and the Meanings of Measure* (New Haven: Yale University Press, 1985).

4. Lewis Carroll, *Alice's Adventures in Wonderland* (New York: Random House, 1946), 105.

5. I am indebted to John Hollander for these insights into the Carroll text.

6. Mohan Singh Karki, *Robert Frost: Theory and Practice of the Colloquial and Sound of Sense* (Aligarh: Granthaayaan, 1979), 54.

7. Thompson, *Early Years*, 419. Others, too, have noted Frost's "exaggerated claims" and "self-conscious extravagance" in the name of "the sound of sense" but do not pursue new readings of his poetry in light of that fact (see Sears, "Robert Frost and the Imagists," 480; Kern, "Frost and Modernism," 5).

8. Joseph M. Garrison, "'Our Singing Strength': The Texture of Voice in the Poetry of Robert Frost," in *Frost: Centennial Essays*, ed. Jac Tharpe (Jackson: University Press of Mississippi, 1974): 340–50.

9. Marie Borroff, "Sound Symbolism as Drama in the Poetry of Robert Frost," *PMLA* 107 (January 1992): 133.

10. Ibid., 134.

11. Ibid., 142–43.

12. John Hollander, *Vision and Resonance: Two Senses of Poetic Form*, 2nd ed. (New Haven: Yale Univesity Press, 1985), 247.

13. Borroff, "Sound Symbolism," 139.

14. Roman Jakobson, *Language in Literature* (Cambridge: Belknap Press, 1987), 69.

15. See Richardson, *The Ordeal of Robert Frost*, 66–87.

16. Evans, *Forty Years of Friendship*, 26–27.

17. Lentricchia, *Modernist Quartet*, 92.

18. Jonathan N. Barron, "A Tale of Two Cottages: Frost and Wordsworth," in *Roads Not Taken: Rereading Robert Frost*, eds. Jonathan N. Barron and Earl J. Wilcox (Columbia: University of Missouri Press, 2000), 240.

19. John Hollander, *Melodious Guile: Fictive Pattern in Poetic Language* (New Haven: Yale University Press, 1988), 56.

20. *Robert Frost Reads* (New York: Caedmon, 1992). The recording was made in May 1956 at Frost's home in Cambridge.

21. Robert Frost, "Between Prose and Verse," *Atlantic Monthly* (January 1962), 51.

22. Quoted in Thompson, *Years of Triumph*, 116.

23. Frost's interest in etymology is not predicted by his theory of form, as indicated by his claim that "Words in themselves do not convey meaning." However, in *Language and the Poet: Verbal Artistry in Frost, Stevens, and Moore* (Chicago: University of Chicago Press, 1979), Marie Borroff shows that Frost's choice of words attains figurative significance, with Romance and Latinate elements of diction tending to point up in his poetry "an aesthetic or meditative turn in the speaker's train of thought," "a dramatized movement in which some saving grace of widening awareness at once builds on and transcends, in New Testament fashion, the limitations of an original point of view" (35–36).

24. Karen Kilcup, *Robert Frost and Feminine Literary Tradition*, 158.

25. Poirier, *The Work of Knowing*, 185.

26. Ibid., 184–85.

27. Reginald L. Cook, "Robert Frost's Asides on His Poetry," in *On Frost: The Best from American Literature*, eds. Edwin H. Cady and Louis J. Budd (Durham: Duke University Pess), 34.

28. *Princeton Encyclopedia of Poetry and Poetics*, ed. Alex Preminger, et al., 3rd ed. (Princeton: Princeton University Press, 1993), 37–38.

29. Louis Mertins, *Robert Frost: Life and Talks-Walking* (Norman, Oklahoma: University of Oklahoma Press, 1965), 198–99.

30. Robert Alter, *The Art of Biblical Narrative* (New York: Basic Books, 1981), 27.

31. This is Stephen Cushman's well-turned phrase in his discussion of anaphora in Elizabeth Bishop's verse in *Fictions of Form in American Poetry* (Princeton: Princeton University Press, 1993).

32. Richard Hofstadter and Beatrice Hofstadter, *Great Issues in American History*, rev. ed. (New York: Vintage, 1982), 140–41.

33. Quoted in Newdick, "Robert Frost and the Sound of Sense," *American Literature* 9 (1937–38): 299–300.

34. Lentricchia, *Modernist Poetics*, 15–16.

35. Antony Easthope, *Poetry as Discourse* (London: Routledge, 1983), 153–154.

36. Dwight Bolinger, *Intonation and Its Parts: Melody in Spoken English* (Stanford: Stanford University Press, 1986), 3, 68.

37. Hollander, *Vision and Resonance*, 138.

38. Louis Untermeyer, *The New Era in American Poetry* (New York: Holt, 1919), 30.

39. B. L. Packer, *Emerson's Fall: A New Interpretation of the Major Essays* (New York: Continuum, 1982), 7.

40. Ibid., 8.

41. Thompson, *Years of Triumph*, 427.

42. Evans, *Forty Years of Friendship*, 103.

43. Henry Fielding, *A Journey from This World to the Next*, in *Works* (London: John Bumpus, 1822), 5:39.

44. Thompson, *Years of Triumph*, 426–27.

45. Amy Lowell, *Some Imagist Poets* (1916), x.

46. Mark Morrisson, "Performing the Pure Voice: Elocution, Verse Recitation, and Modernist Poetry in Prewar London," *Modernism/Modernity* 3 (1996): 37, 27.

47. Ibid., 37.

48. Ibid., 38.

49. Richard Bradford, "Speech and Writing in Poetry and Its Criticism," *Visible Language* 22 (Spring 1988): 178, 179.

50. Michel Foucault, "What Is an Author?" *Textual Strategies*, ed. Josué Harari (Ithaca: Cornell University Press, 1979), 147.

51. Jacques Derrida, "Signature Event Context," *Margins of Philosophy*, trans. Alan Bass (Chicago: University of Chicago Press, 1982), 326.

52. See Jacques Derrida, "Plato's Pharmacy," *Dissemination*, trans. Barbara Johnson (Chicago: University of Chicago Press, 1981), 61–171.

53. Derrida, *Margins of Philosophy*, 319.

54. In *The Ordeal of Robert Frost* Mark Richardson has demonstrated ably that "Frost's analysis of the conditions of authorship anticipates later insights of Derrida and Michel Foucault," but also that his poetics affirms authorial power and integrity in a way unimagined by Foucault or Derrida (176). Frost's "impersonalist conception of authorship" (as expressed, say, in "The Constant Symbol") coexists with his efforts to "believe" himself into existence as author of his works (203, 215).

55. Eric Griffiths, *The Printed Voice of Victorian Poetry* (Oxford: Oxford University Press, 1989), 83.

56. Quoted in Mertins, *Life and Talks-Walking*, 133.

57. Quoted in Burnshaw, *Robert Frost Himself*, 238.

58. Quoted in Newdick, "Robert Frost and the Sound of Sense," 298.

59. Newdick, "Robert Frost and the Sound of Sense," 298–99. Frost's theory has led a number of his critics to submit his poetry to acoustic analysis. Linda Bradley Funkhouser conducts such an analysis of his lyric "Dust of Snow," believing that "what Frost accomplished is acoustically measurable with an audio spectrometer and level recorder," and justifies her investigation by citing the poet's position: "Frost

himself, of course, regarded his poetry as an act of speech" ("Acoustic Rhythm in Frost's 'Dust of Snow,'" *Language and Style* 14, no. 4 [Fall 1981]: 287–88).

60. Ibid., 299.

61. Ibid., 299.

62. Seymour Chatman, "Robert Frost's 'Mowing': An Inquiry into Prosodic Structure," *Kenyon Review* 18, no. 3 (Summer 1956): 423.

63. Ibid., 426.

64. Ibid., 431–32, 435.

65. Burnshaw, *Robert Frost Himself,* 237.

66. Thompson, *Years of Triumph,* 669.

67. Lawrance Thompson, *Fire and Ice* (New York: Holt, 1942), 46.

68. Samuel R. Levin, "Suprasegmentals and the Performance of Poetry," *The Quarterly Journal of Speech* 48 (1962): 367.

69. See Laura Riding and Robert Graves, *A Survey of Modernist American Poetry* (London: Heinemann, 1927).

70. William K. Wimsatt and Monroe C. Beardsley, "The Concept of Meter: An Exercise in Abstraction," *PMLA* 74 (December 1959): 587.

71. Jakobson, *Language in Literature,* 85.

72. David Crystal, *Prosodic Systems and Intonation in English* (Cambridge: Cambridge University Press, 1969), 116.

73. J. L. Austin, *How To Do Things with Words,* ed. J. O. Urmson (Oxford: Oxford University Press, 1962), 74.

74. Pound, *Selected Letters,* 322.

75. Quoted in Burnshaw, *Robert Frost Himself,* 238–39.

76. Frost, "Between Prose and Verse," 51.

77. Evans, *Forty Years of Friendship,* 103.

78. Joseph Blumenthal, *Robert Frost and His Printers* (Austin, Texas: W. T. Taylor, 1985), 29, 58. Although it is not clear that Frost engineered the layout of poems in his *Complete Poems* (1949), the positioning of some of the short lyrics on a page by themselves—that is, their graphic placement—sometimes enhances the meaning of the poem, as in the case of the two-line "An Answer" ("But islands of the Blessèd, bless you, son, / I never came upon a blessèd one"); in *A Literary Life Reconsidered* William Pritchard observes of the poem that "Surrounded by much white space, occupying one page of the old *Complete Poems,* the utterance took on an added point" (239).

79. *CPPP* reprints Frost's poems as they appeared in *Complete Poems.*

80. Donald Hall, "Robert Frost Corrupted," *The Weather for Poetry* (Ann Arbor: University of Michigan Press, 1982), 146.

81. Ibid., 155, 157.

82. Quoted in Hall, "Robert Frost Corrupted," 155.

83. Carlson, "Robert Frost on 'Vocal Imagination, the Merger of Form and Content,'" 520.

84. Sidney Lanier, *The Science of English Verse* (New York: Scribner's, 1880), 251–52.

85. Ibid., 28.

86. Ibid., 255–56.

87. Jed Rasula, "Understanding the Sound of Not Understanding," in *Close Listening: Poetry and the Performed Word,* ed. Charles Bernstein (New York: Oxford University Press, 1998), 239.

88. Ibid., 240.

89. William Pritchard, "Frost Revised," *Playing It by Ear: Literary Essays and Reviews* (Amherst: University of Massachusetts Press, 1994), 26.

90. Hall, "Robert Frost Corrupted," 149.

91. Ibid., 143.

92. Quoted in Hall, "Robert Frost Corrupted," 149.

93. Hollander, *Vision and Resonance*, 102.

94. Evans, *Forty Years of Friendship*, 216–17.

95. Ibid., 216.

96. *Robert Frost Reads* (New York: Caedmon, 1956), cassette 2.

97. Griffiths, *The Printed Voice*, 66.

98. Reuben Brower, *The Poetry of Robert Frost: Constellations of Intention* (Oxford: Oxford University Press, 1963), 1.

99. Evans, *Forty Years of Friendship*, 103.

100. Carlson, "Robert Frost on 'Vocal Imagination, the Merger of Form and Content,'" 520.

101. Griffiths, *The Printed Voice*, 205.

102. Richardson, *The Ordeal of Robert Frost*, 49–50.

103. Kilcup, *Robert Frost and Feminine Literary Tradition*, 83.

104. Poirier, *The Work of Knowing*, 108.

105. Brower, *Constellations of Intention*, 18.

106. Evans, *Forty Years of Friendship*, 89.

107. Kearns, *Poetics of Appetite*, 18.

108. Brower, *Constellations of Intention*, 160.

109. Ibid., 159.

110. Ibid., 159, 18, 158, 162.

111. Kearns, *Poetics of Appetite*, 19, 18.

112. Poirier, *The Work of Knowing*, 128.

113. Ibid., 198.

114. Evans, *Forty Years of Friendship*, 89.

115. I am drawing on Freud's terminology as set forth in his essay "Mourning and Melancholia" (1917), vol. 14 of *The Standard Edition of the Complete Psychological Works of Sigmund Freud*, ed. James Strachey (London: Hogarth, 1953–74).

116. Randall Jarrell, "To the Laodiceans," in *Robert Frost: A Collection of Critical Essays*, ed. James M. Cox (Englewood Cliffs: Prentice-Hall, 1962), 191.

117. Cook, *A Living Voice*, 136.

118. Cook, "Robert Frost's Asides on His Poetry," 35.

119. Burnshaw, *Robert Frost Himself*, 279.

120. Cook, *A Living Voice*, 82; *Family Letters* 267.

121. Borroff, *Language and the Poet*, 136.

122. Lionel Trilling, "A Speech on Robert Frost: A Cultural Episode," in *Robert Frost: A Collection of Critical Essays*, 156.

123. Lentricchia, *Modernist Quartet*, 121.

124. Meyers, *Robert Frost: A Biography*, 216.

125. Jarrell, "To the Laodiceans," 86–87.

126. Brower, *Constellations of Intention*, 106.

127. Ibid., 106.

128. Ibid., 107.

129. Cook, *A Living Voice*, 126.

130. Ibid., 112.

131. Pritchard, *A Literary Life Reconsidered*, 127.

132. See Yvor Winters, "Robert Frost: or, the Spiritual Drifter as Poet," in *Robert Frost: A Collection of Critical Essays*, 58–82.

133. William Empson, *The Structure of Complex Words* (Totowa, New Jersey: Rowman and Littlefield, 1979), 101.

134. Poirier, *The Work of Knowing*, 164–65.

135. Cook, *A Living Voice*, 123.

136. Meyers, *Robert Frost: A Biography*, 140.

137. Evans, *Forty Years of Friendship*, 113.

138. Ibid., 109.

139. Burnshaw, *Robert Frost Himself*, 66, 279.

140. Jarrell, *Poetry and the Age*, 41.

141. Thompson, *Years of Triumph*, 437.

142. Jarrell, *Poetry and the Age*, 42.

143. Meyers, *Robert Frost: A Biography*, 215–16.

144. For the elaboration of this metaphor, see Leo Marx, *The Machine in the Garden: Technology and the Pastoral Idea in America* (Oxford: Oxford University Press, 1964).

145. Ibid., 27.

146. *Rebel Voices: An I.W.W. Anthology*, ed. Joyce L. Kornbluh (Ann Arbor: University of Michigan Press, 1965).

147. Ibid., 66.

148. Winters, "Robert Frost: or, The Spiritual Drifter as Poet," 68.

149. Cook, "Frost's Asides on His Poetry," 35; Reginald L. Cook, "Frost on Frost: The Making of Poems," in *On Frost: The Best from* American Literature, eds. Edwin H. Cady and Louis J. Budd (Durham: Duke University Press, 1991), 49.

150. Malcolm Cowley, "The Case against Mr. Frost," in *Robert Frost: A Collection of Critical Essays*, 41–42.

151. Ibid., 42.

3. The Politics of the Visual Line (pp. 122–170)

1. Seymour Chatman's contention that "'Caesura, end-stoppage, and enjambment exist only in actual performance, since they are phonological, not orthographic phenomena'" severely underestimates the graphic dimension of these devices, and Hollander rightly has questioned Chatman's "insensitively performatory approach to the poetic line" (*Vision and Resonance* 98).

2. In her discussion of Byron's formalism in *Formal Charges: The Shaping of Poetry in British Romanticism* (Stanford: Stanford University Press, 1997), Susan J. Wolfson illuminates the ideological construction of enjambment in the eighteenth century, citing the conservative Lord Kames's contention in his much republished manual *Elements of Criticism* (1762) that enjambment, a French term, was linked to French "license" and neglect of rule (136). Enjambment had its defenders in the liberal political community of the day as well, where the prosodic practice was spun as an emblem of political liberty.

3. Cook, *Dimensions*, 63.

4. Cook, *A Living Voice*, 148.

5. Gibson, *Poems*, 327.

6. *Princeton Encyclopedia of Poetry and Poetics* 360.

7. Keats, *Endymion*, lines 89–100.

8. For an account of Williams's indebtedness to and early imitations of Keats's *Endymion*, see Cushman's *William Carlos Williams and the Meanings of Measure*, 19–20.

9. *The Golden Treasury of the Best Songs and Lyrics in the English Language*, ed. Francis Turner Palgrave, 6th ed. (1861; Oxford: Oxford University Press, 1994), 91–92.

10. Ibid., 275–76.

11. Quoted in Cook, *Dimensions,* 62.

12. Milton, "On Time," lines 1–3.

13. Ibid., lines 11–22.

14. Justus George Lawler, *Celestial Pantomime: Poetic Structures of Transcendence* (New Haven: Yale University Press, 1979), 79.

15. Shakespeare, *Twelfth Night,* 1.1.1–2.

16. See George T. Wright, *Shakespeare's Metrical Art* (Berkeley: University of California Press, 1988), especially his chapter entitled "The Play of Phrase and Line."

17. Lawler, *Celestial Pantomime,* 75–76.

18. Charles O. Hartman, "Verse and Voice," in *Conversant Essays: Contemporary Poets on Poetry,* ed. James McCorkle (Detroit: Wayne State University Press, 1990), 134.

19. Hollander, *Vision and Resonance,* 99.

20. Poirier, *The Work of Knowing,* 12.

21. Lawler, *Celestial Pantomime,* 42.

22. Ibid., 74.

23. Ibid., 74–75.

24. Christopher Ricks, *The Force of Poetry* (Oxford: Clarendon Press, 1984), 91.

25. Ibid., 94.

26. In my discussion of enjambment in this chapter, I rely on the descriptive terminology of John Hollander, who refers to a spectrum along which enjambments fall according to the relative "hardness" or "softness" of the cuts they make (*Vision and Resonance* 99).

27. Poirier, *The Work of Knowing,* 17–18.

28. Hollander, *Vision and Resonance,* 125.

29. Ibid., 124.

30. George S. Lipsitz, *Class and Culture in Cold War America: "A Rainbow at Midnight"* (New York: Praeger, 1981), 177.

31. Steven J. Diner, *A Very Different Age: Americans of the Progressive Era* (New York: Hill and Wang, 1998), 243–46.

32. For the handwritten version, see Newdick, *Season of Frost,* 416.

33. William Stott, *Documentary Expression and Thirties America* (Chicago: Chicago University Press, 1973), 251–52.

34. Ibid., 240.

35. W. E. B. Du Bois, *The Souls of Black Folk* (New York: Dover, 1994), 94.

36. Poirier, *The Work of Knowing,* 157–58.

37. Frost revealed that "A Lone Striker" was based on his own experience as a mill worker in Lawrence in the early 1890s, where, upon being locked out of the mill for being late, he "walked out of it all one day" (*CPPP* 760). He further explained its personal and political resonance at a public reading: "Now suppose I read you a few things. Suppose I begin with that very poem about me and the mills in Lawrence. This one is called, 'The Lone Striker.' It is all right to be a striker, but not a lone striker. You might think that I might get in right with my radical friends, but the trouble with me is that I was a lone striker; if I called it a "collectivist striker," that would be another matter. This was the way it was to me, not a very serious thing" (*CPPP* 763). It was perhaps "not a very serious thing" for Frost because he did not yet have to provide for a family. In "A Lone Striker" the privileged position that allows the young man to take so lightly his escape is telling in light of how one less carefree worker read that industrialized city: "'The mills are Lawrence and you cannot escape them'" (quoted in David J. Goldberg, *A Take of Three Cities: Labor Organization and Protest in Paterson, Passaic, and Lawrence, 1916–1921* [New Brunswick, New Jersey: Rutgers University Press, 1989], 85).

38. For the dating of the poem, see Thompson, *Years of Triumph,* 210.

39. These lines are published in Judith Oster, *Toward Robert Frost: The Reader and the Poet* (Athens: University of Georgia Press, 1991), 226.

40. Cook, *A Living Voice,* 235.

41. Quoted in Richard S. Kennedy, *Dreams in the Mirror: A Biography of E. E. Cummings* (New York: Liveright, 1980), 96. His parody of Amy Lowell's *vers libre* includes the following remarkable enjambment: "Rep- / lenishing." This break suggests Cummings's strong association of enjambment with nonmetrical verse as well.

4. Figures of Form, or Poetry and Power (pp. 171–220)

1. Cushman, *Fictions of Form,* 18.

2. Richardson, *The Ordeal of Robert Frost,* 169.

3. Ibid., 186–89.

4. *The Collected Writings of T. E. Hulme* 236.

5. Ibid., 235–36.

6. Eliot, "Reflections on 'Vers Libre,'" 185, 187.

7. Mertins, *Life and Talks-Walking,* 198.

8. Eliot, "Ezra Pound: His Metric and Poetry," in *To Criticize the Critic* (New York: Farrar, 1965), 167–68.

9. Ibid., 172.

10. *Poets at Work* 33.

11. Herbert Read, *The Meaning of Art* (London: Faber, 1931), 28.

12. Emerson, *Essays and Lectures,* 481–82.

13. Ibid., 953, 961.

14. Ibid., 957.

15. In "'Not Quite All, My Dear': Gender and Voice in Frost" (*Texas Studies in Literature and Language* 36, no. 4 [Winter 1994]), Donald G. Sheehy attests: "Such anxiety, as critics have noted, is evident in the 'male fear and rage' in modernist poetics, where a misogynistic 'masculinism' is not only promulgated at the level of Pound's diatribes against 'Aunt Hepsey' and a corruption of literature into a 'great passive vulva' but also encoded in such forms as Hulme's classicism, Eliot's impersonality, and Lawrence's cult of the phallus" (413).

16. Quoted in Thompson, *Years of Triumph,* 77.

17. These lecture notes are in Special Collections at Amherst College Library.

18. Quoted in *A Descriptive Catalogue of Books and Manuscripts in the Clifton Waller Barrett Library, University of Virginia,* comp. Joan St. C. Crane (Charlottesville: University Press of Virginia, 1974), 249–50.

19. Kilcup, *Robert Frost and Feminine Literary Tradition,* 185.

20. Ibid., 144.

21. Cook, *A Living Voice,* 189.

22. Faggen, *Robert Frost and the Challenge of Darwin,* 242.

23. Hollander, *Vision and Resonance,* 158.

24. Faggen, *Robert Frost and the Challenge of Darwin,* 243.

25. Ibid., 244.

26. For the dating of the poem, see Thompson, *Years of Triumph,* 541.

27. Kilcup, *Robert Frost and Feminine Literary Tradition,* 104.

28. Faggen, *Robert Frost and the Challenge of Darwin,* 174.

29. Donald G. Sheehy, "'Not Quite All, My Dear,'" 426.

30. *Ralph Waldo Emerson: Collected Poems and Translations,* eds. Harold Bloom and Paul Kane (New York: Library of America, 1994), 188–89.

31. Poirier, *The Work of Knowing,* 225.

32. Ibid., 225; quoted in Jay Parini, *Robert Frost: A Life,* 240.

33. For an account of Frost's relationship with Kay Morrison and the biographical impulses behind this poem, see Donald G. Sheehy, "(Re)Figuring Love: Robert Frost in Crisis, 1938–1942," *New England Quarterly* (June 1990): 179–231.

34. Tom Vander Ven, "Robert Frost's Dramatic Principle of 'Oversound,'" *American Literature* 45 (May 1973): 238–39.

35. Hollander, *Melodious Guile,* 57.

36. Ibid., 161.

37. Ibid., 148.

38. Ben Jonson, fourth poem of *Eupheme,* lines 37–40.

39. Hollander, *Vision and Resonance,* 42.

40. For discussion of the primitive strain in American arts, see Helen Carr's *Inventing the American Primitive: Politics, Gender, and the Representation of Native American Literary Traditions, 1789–1936* (New York: New York University Press, 1996).

41. See Mary Austin, *The American Rhythm: Studies and Reexpressions of Amerindian Songs* (New York: Cooper Square, 1970), 54. When Frost met Mary Austin, they talked at length about their theories of speech rhythm (Thompson, *Years of Triumph,* 377).

42. The handwritten transcript of this lecture is in Special Collections at Amherst College Library.

43. Emerson, *Essays and Lectures,* 569.

44. Ibid., 567.

45. Ibid., 567.

46. Ibid., 565–66.

47. Ibid., 566.

48. Quoted in Lawrance Thompson and R. H. Winnick, *Robert Frost: The Later Years: 1938–1963* (New York: Holt, 1976), 52–53.

49. Ibid., 53.

50. Quoted in Burnshaw, *Robert Frost Himself,* 258.

51. Newdick, *Season of Frost,* 363.

52. Poirier, *Poetry and Pragmatism,* 43.

53. Harold Whitehall, "Linguistic Patriot," in *Critical Essays on H. L. Mencken,* ed. Douglas C. Stenerson (Boston: G. K. Hall, 1987), 109. Frost's copy of the revised Fourth Edition of *The American Language* is in Special Collections at New York University Library.

54. H. L. Mencken, *The American Language: An Inquiry into the Development of English in the United States,* 4th ed. (New York: Knopf, 1980), vi, viii.

55. Ibid., 37.

56. Ibid., 34, 32–33.

57. John Erskine, "Do Americans Speak English?" *Nation* (April 15, 1925), 410–11.

58. Ibid., 410, 411.

59. Ibid., 411.

60. Coleridge, "Kubla Khan," lines 12, 14, 30.

61. Mertins, *Life and Talks-Walking,* 223.

62. Thompson and Winnick, *Later Years,* 225.

63. Ibid., 224.

64. Ibid., 223.

65. Ibid., 224.

66. Ibid., 225.

67. Cook, *A Living Voice,* 193. When the poem was published for the first time in

the *Virginia Quarterly Review* in 1942, Frost mentioned his reading of it in Williamsburg, Virginia, highlighting the connection between the poem and British colonialism (Thompson and Winnick, *Later Years*, 390).

68. Ibid., 194.

69. As Milton asserts, "The measure is *English* Heroic Verse without Rime, . . . an example set, the first in *English*, of ancient liberty recover'd to Heroic Poem from the troublesome and modern bondage of Riming."

70. *Family Letters* 267.

71. Ibid., 232–33.

72. Cook, *A Living Voice*, 193.

73. Ibid., 80, 194.

74. Quoted in Alan Trachtenberg, *The Incorporation of America: Culture and Society in the Gilded Age* (New York: Hill and Wang, 1982), 11.

75. Edward W. Said, "Yeats and Decolonization," in *Nationalism, Colonialism, and Literature / Terry Eagleton, Fredric Jameson, and Edward W. Said* (Minneapolis: University of Minnesota Press, 1990), 77, 74.

76. Tom Paulin, *Minotaur: Poetry and the Nation State* (Cambridge: Harvard University Press, 1992), 172.

77. Cook, *A Living Voice*, 80.

78. Paulin, *Minotaur*, 174.

79. Ibid., 178, 176. Like the political poems with ambivalent vocal contours discussed in Chapter 2, "The Vanishing Red" has been subject to radically different interpretations, because the tone of the speaker and, thus, Frost's personal politics are so hard to read. In *Robert Frost and Feminine Literary Tradition*, Karen Kilcup argues that the speaker evinces "unspoken but evident sympathy for the murdered man and horror at the Miller's deed" (57), while Robert Faggen, in *Robert Frost and the Challenge of Darwin*, contends that "The narrator coldly refrains from judging the Miller's actions" (121). I maintain that it is our inability to decide just what the narrator's attitude is—to what extent he is ironic—that provokes our intense political feelings.

80. Ibid., 177.

81. Tom Paulin, *Ireland and the English Crisis* (Glasgow: Bell and Bain, 1984), 174.

82. Paulin, *Minotaur*, 176.

83. Ibid., 177.

84. Ibid., 177.

85. Ibid., 178; Seamus Heaney, *Opened Ground: Selected Poems, 1966–1996* (New York: Farrar, 1998), 8.

86. Homi K. Bhabha, *The Location of Culture* (London: Routledge, 1994), 182–83.

87. Roland Barthes, *The Pleasure of the Text,* trans. Richard Miller (New York: Hill and Wang, 1975), 49.

88. Ibid., 49–50.

89. Ibid., 50.

90. Ibid., 50.

91. Ibid., 66.

92. *Homage to Robert Frost / Joseph Brodsky, Seamus Heaney, Derek Walcott* (New York: Farrar, 1996), 26. Subsequent references to this edition will appear in the text as HRF.

93. Solomon Volkov, *Conversations with Joseph Brodsky: A Poet's Journey through the Twentieth Century,* trans. Marian Schwartz (New York: The Free Press, 1998), 89.

94. Ibid., 93.

95. Joseph Brodsky, *Grief and Reason,* 32.

96. Ibid., 45.

97. Derek Walcott, *What the Twilight Says: Essays* (New York: Farrar, 1998), 138.

98. Seamus Heaney, *The Government of the Tongue: Selected Prose, 1978–1987* (New York: Farrar, 1989), xx.

99. Seamus Heaney, *Preoccupations: Selected Prose, 1968–1978* (New York: Farrar, 1980), 34.

100. Ibid., 34.

101. Heaney, *Government of the Tongue,* 106.

102. Ibid., 33.

103. "Poets' Round Table: 'A Common Language,'" *PN Review* 15 (1989): 3.

104. Heaney, *Preoccupations,* 37.

105. Dennis Lee, "Writing in Colonial Space," in *The Post-Colonial Studies Reader,* eds. Bill Ashcroft, Gareth Griffiths, and Helen Tiffin (London: Routledge, 1995), 200.

106. Heaney, *Opened Ground,* 58.

107. Ibid., 65.

108. *Conversations with Derek Walcott,* ed. William Baer (Jackson: University Press of Mississippi, 1996), 29. In his essay entitled "The Murmur of Malvern" in *The Government of the Tongue* Heaney remarks on Walcott's dual identity: "Africa and England are in him. The humanist voices of his education and the voices from his home ground keep insisting on their full claims, pulling him in two different directions" (24).

109. Walcott, *What the Twilight Says,* 69, 70.

110. Ibid., 70.

111. Heaney, *The Government of the Tongue,* 28.

112. *Conversations with Derek Walcott* 201.

113. Ibid., 163.

114. Bhabha, *The Location of Culture,* 85, 86. Walcott articulates the notion of the temporal limits of inimitability in his essay "The Caribbean: Culture or Mimicry?": "Here are three forms [Carnival, calypso, and the steel band], originating from the mass, which are original and temporarily inimitable as what they first attempted to copy" (*Journal of InterAmerican Studies and World Affairs* 16 [1974]: 9).

115. Bhabha, *The Location of Culture,* 112.

116. Ibid., 191.

117. Derek Walcott, *Collected Poems, 1948–1984* (New York: Farrar, 1986), 103.

118. Ibid., 307.

119. Walcott, *What the Twilight Says,* 37.

120. Ibid., 9, 39.

Conclusion (pp. 221–232)

1. Poirier, *The Work of Knowing,* 230–33.

2. Quoted in Parini, *Robert Frost: A Life,* 337.

3. Ibid., 310.

4. Ibid., 373.

5. Parini, *Robert Frost: A Life,* 280.

6. Kilcup, *Robert Frost and Feminine Literary Tradition,* 144.

7. Richard Hofstadter, *The Age of Reform: From Bryan to F.D.R.* (New York: Vintage, 1955), 241.

8. Ibid., 261, 234.

9. Newdick, *Season of Frost,* 268.

10. Quoted in Parini, *Robert Frost: A Life,* 299.

11. Hofstadter, *The Age of Reform,* 11.

12. Ibid., 308.

13. Ibid., 134, 217.

14. Irving Bernstein, *Turbulent Years: A History of the American Worker, 1933–1941* (Boston: Houghton, 1970), 142.

15. Quoted in Thompson, *Years of Triumph,* 457.

16. Ibid., 460.

17. Hofstadter, *The Age of Reform,* 239.

18. Ibid., 20–21.

Index

King When It's in You and in the Situation," 101, 201–4

"How to Read" (Pound), 240n

Howells, William Dean, 58, 153

Hugh Selwyn Mauberley (Life and Contacts) (Pound), 176

Hulme, T. E., 7, 14–15, 16, 29, 37, 43–44, 45, 46, 54–56, 61, 63, 64, 174–75, 234n, 238n, 240n, 247n

"Hyla Brook," 130–31

hypotaxis, 80, 158, 160

"I Stood Tip-Toe," 73–74

"If by Dull Rhymes" (Keats), 73

imagism, 7–8, 16, 32–33, 45–63, 238n, 241n

immigration and immigrants, 27, 132, 194–95

imperialism, 11, 20, 212, 217. *See also* anti-imperialism

impressionism (literary), 7, 45, 50

"In a Poem," 130

"In Divés' Dive," 149–50

"In Hardwood Groves," 98

"In Neglect," 98

In the Clearing, 152–53

Independent, 16–17, 25

individualism, 9, 27, 31, 37, 41, 44, 63, 135, 161, 175, 186–87, 191, 222, 226–27

industrialism, 9, 21–23, 24–27, 117, 119–20, 132, 153, 160–62, 223–30, 246n

International Workers of the World (I.W.W.), 119–20

intonation. *See* "sound of sense, the"

"Introduction" to E. A. Robinson's *King Jasper,* 124, 178, 221

Irish Home Rule, 6, 20

isolationism, 11, 132, 153–54, 162–63, 194–200, 222, 231

"It Bids Pretty Fair," 164

"It Is Almost the Year 2000," 163, 167

italicization, 8, 79–80, 92, 97–101

Jakobson, Roman, 69, 92

James, Henry, 57

James, William, 6–7, 16, 29–44, 48, 236–37n

Jarrell, Randall, 3, 118–19, 234n

Jefferson, Thomas, 191, 205–6

Jonson, Ben, 188

Journey from This World to the Next, A (Fielding), 87

Kandinsky, Wassily, 56

Kant, Immanuel, 202

Karki, Mohan Singh, 66

Kayman, Martin A., 240n

Kearns, Katharine, 5, 45, 75, 105, 106

Keats, John, 73, 126–27, 245n

Kennedy, John F., 2, 200, 206, 216–17

Kenner, Hugh, 240n

Kern, Robert, 33, 45, 47, 241n

Keynes, Maynard, 28

Kilcup, Karen, 5, 23, 75, 104, 178–79, 182, 222, 234n, 235n, 238n, 249n

Kinsella, Thomas, 215

Kipling, Rudyard, 20, 205

"Kitty Hawk," 101

"Kubla Khan" (Coleridge), 196–97

labor issues, 21–22, 24–27, 81, 119–20, 132, 153, 161, 162, 222, 223–27. *See also* unionism

Lanier, Sidney, 95–96

Lassere, Pierre, 55, 174–75

Lathem, Edward Connery, 90, 94–95, 96, 97, 236n

Lawler, Justus, 9, 128–30, 131, 144

Lawrence, D. H., 247n

"Leaf Treader, A" 68, 156–57

Lee, Dennis, 215

Lentricchia, Frank, 3–4, 29, 44, 63, 65, 70, 83

"Lesson for Today, The," 147–48

"'Letter' to *The Amherst Student*," 147–48, 172

Levenson, Michael, 46, 49, 50, 54, 55, 58

Levin, Samuel, 91–92

Lewis, Wyndham, 57

liberalism: Frost's politics of, 1, 5, 9, 22–28, 131–32, 151, 162, 171–72, 231, 234n; Frost's rejection of the politics of, 110, 147–48, 163, 166–67, 194, 205, 222–23, 226, 229

libertarianism, 222

Lincoln, Abraham, 191, 195

Lindsay, Vachel, 86, 95

lineation. *See* endstopped lines; enjambment

line-sentence counterpointing. *See* enjambment

Ricks, Christopher, 131, 132
Riding, Laura, 92
Riley, James Whitcomb, 3
"Road Not Taken, The," 112–13, 117, 166
"Road Taken, The" (Walcott), 171, 216–20
"Roadside Stand, A," 152
Robinson, Edwin Arlington, 16, 58, 97–98, 124, 178, 221
"Romantic Chasm, A," 20, 196–97
Roosevelt, Franklin Delano, 146, 229
Roosevelt, Theodore, 229
"Rose Pogonias," 75
Rossetti, Christina, 47
Rural America, 230

Sabin, Margery, 214
Said, Edward, 206–7
Sandburg, Carl, 78, 189, 203
Sarah Lawrence College, 172
Sarduy, Severo, 209–10
Schneidau, Herbert, 54–55, 58
Science of English Verse, The (Lanier), 95–96
Scribner's, 2
Sears, John, 45, 238n, 241n
Sedgwick, Ellery, 58–59, 177
"Self-Seeker, The," 26
sentimentalism, 21, 22–23, 49–50, 119, 120, 178–79, 182, 235n
Sergeant, Elizabeth, 82
Sergeyev, Nicholas Grigorievich, 211
"Serious Artist, The" (Pound), 48, 49, 50
sexuality: Frost and, 9, 75–80, 131, 144–46, 177–78, 179, 188; Shakespeare and, 129–30
Shakespeare, William, 26–27, 59–60, 77–78, 86–87, 92, 116, 129–30, 177, 187, 189
Shapiro, Karl, 150
Shaw, George Bernard, 6, 19, 20–21, 235n
Sheehy, Donald G., 185, 247n
Shelley, Percy Bysshe, 59, 146–47, 208
Shenandoah (song), 115
Shetley, Vernon, 2
"Silken Tent, The," 72–74
Sinclair, May, 16
"Slag, The" (Gibson), 22–23
Smart Set, The, 27–28
Smith, John, 207
socialism: Frost and, 9, 19–20, 131–32,

146–48, 153, 163, 187, 190, 202, 226, 227, 228, 229; Untermeyer and, 223
Socrates, 88–89
"Solway Ford" (Gibson), 125–26
Some Imagist Poets, 57
Sonnet 151 (Shakespeare), 129–30
"Soul and the Body, The" (Bergson), 38–39
Souls of Black Folk, The (Du Bois), 159
"sound of sense, the": ambiguity of, 8, 84–121, 249n; anti-imperialist politics of, 19, 29; Bloomsbury formalism and, 27–29; capitalization and, 101; figures of, 171–220; imagism and, 45–63, 238n; industrial capitalism and, 21–29; italicization and, 8, 92, 97–101; *vs.* meter, 10, 11, 12, 66, 122, 171–88; modernist literary politics and Frost's theory of, 1–4, 12–18; modernist philosophy and, 29–44; modernist poetic manifesto and Frost's theory of, 1–2, 4, 64–66, 241n; nationalism and, 188–204; postcolonialism and, 204–20; punctuation and, 8, 90–97; *vs.* segmental prosody, 7–8, 64–84; *vs.* syntactic schemes and tropes, 74–84; vorticism and, 56–63
Speculations (Hulme), 238n
speech *vs.* writing, 8, 84–87
speech rhythm. *See* "sound of sense, the"
Spencer, Herbert, 7, 42–43, 61, 96, 238n
Spenser, Edmund, 179, 187–88
"Spring Pools," 82, 136–37
Sputnik, 213
Stalin, Joseph, 153
stanzaic patterning, 124–25, 127–28, 135, 139, 143, 144
Steeple Bush, 10, 168, 198; critical reception of, 222
Steffens, Lincoln, 27
Stein, Gertrude, 57, 93
Stevens, Wallace, 43–44
"Stopping by Woods on a Snowy Evening," 90, 96–97
Stott, William, 157–58
"Subverted Flower, The," 145–46
suffrage movement (Great Britain), 6, 19, 20
Survey of Modernist American Poetry, A, 92
Swinburne, Algernon Charles, 67, 89

"Wood-Pile, The," 208
Woolf, Virginia, 6, 28–29, 236n
Words and Ways of American English, 195–96
Wordsworth, Dorothy, 24
Wordsworth, William, 24, 49, 50, 51–52, 59–60, 61, 127–28, 146–47
World War I, 6, 10, 11, 28, 71, 152, 162, 165–66, 188, 189, 194, 195, 203–4, 222

World War II, 6, 11, 76, 148, 152, 163, 168, 188, 189, 192–93, 197, 205
Worringer, Wilhelm, 55, 61
Wright, George, 129
Wright, Orville, 101
Wright, Wilbur, 101
writing *vs.* speech. *See* speech *vs.* writing

Yeats, William Butler, 16, 239n